Resources for Teaching

OURSELVES AMONG OTHERS

CROSS-CULTURAL READINGS FOR WRITERS

Third Edition

PREPARED BY

Alice Adams

Miami University of Ohio

and

David Londow

Miami - Dade Community College

BEDFORD BOOKS *of* ST. MARTIN'S PRESS • BOSTON

5 4 3 2 1 0
f e d c b a

For information, write: St. Martin's Press, Inc.
175 Fifth Avenue, New York, NY 10010

Editorial Offices: Bedford Books *of* St. Martin's Press
29 Winchester Street, Boston, MA 02116

ISBN 0–312–08679–2

PREFACE

We are often told that today's students are less interested in other cultures and contemporary history than past students, but the experience of instructors using previous editions of *Ourselves Among Others*, suggests otherwise. First of all, many of our students come from multicultural backgrounds within the United States or from foreign homelands. The selections in this reader provide a chance for such students to find themselves recognized for their unique contributions and the alternative points of view they can provide. Second, instructors report that students browse through this reader, finding writings of particular interest to them, and request that they be included in class assignments. Students are motivated enough by the subject matter to want to share in the shaping of class discussion and assignments. Doubtless the primary purpose of this text is to help students develop as writers, and students who are interested and involved will engage more readily both with the selections in hand and with their responses to them. Yet a further benefit of this work will become apparent as students become more aware of and better informed about other peoples and cultures. They will unconsciously absorb a great deal of geography, history, and political knowledge that should help them prepare for life in the twenty-first century.

However, many of the instructors using *Ourselves Among Others* think of themselves primarily as teachers of writing and literature. They do not necessarily have real expertise in other disciplines. Some might question whether the lack of a specialized background makes it difficult for an instructor to approach these texts. Our answer is that these essays and short stories, which have headnotes and background information provided, are very accessible. Students and instructors encounter these texts together, and they can focus on the ideas under discussion without needing to rely on additional facts. The discussions generated by these texts do not focus on "right" or "wrong" answers: Rather, the texts and the questions following then encourage readers to explore the relationships between ideas.

This manual is designed to guide instructors through the maze of new material presented in the text, providing necessary assistance in both planning and implementing the course. Used in conjunction with the text, the manual should temper the apprehension accompanying any new venture for instructors new to this reader, and it also should provide instructors, even those familiar with the earlier editions, with suggestions for ways of approaching and teaching the selections. In particular, the manual includes

An introduction, exploring teaching possibilities and providing suggestions for getting the course off the ground

Brief introductions to each unit, suggesting various combinations and subthemes and listing corresponding readings from more familiar American and European authors

Biographical notes for the authors of passages in "Looking at Ourselves"

Preface

Discussion of all Explorations and Connections questions, paying particular attention to possible student reaction to more controversial pieces

Carefully structured additional questions following the same pattern for each unit, including journal suggestions, imitation of forms, short essay assignments, research of current related topics, and further research into cultures represented in selections

Suggested syllabi, adapting the text to different types of courses

A rhetorical index, pointing out those selections that make use of particular organizing strategies

A chart of rhetorical writing assignments in the text

Additional Resources, including an index to headnote information and a concise list of reference materials to facilitate research into other cultures

A list of film, video, and audio cassette resources

Working with *Ourselves Among Others* will provide a challenge: There are always pitfalls involved when we leave familiar territory behind. But using this manual as a road map, both students and instructors should discover that, when we explore it thoroughly, the foreign territory isn't all that unfamiliar. And the people — well, now and then we see glimpses of ourselves among others.

We gratefully acknowledge the work of our predecessors, Kathleen Shine Cain (who prepared the manual for the first edition of *Ourselves Among Others*) and Marilyn Rye (who prepared the second edition manual).

CONTENTS

Contents

INTRODUCTION

Ourselves Among Others can be adapted to courses employing a number of approaches. As a thematic reader, it's well suited to an introductory writing course or a standard, reading and research oriented second-semester composition course. But its flexibility allows for use in several other types of courses as well: Instructors who focus on rhetorical analysis will find a variety of personae, tones, organizational strategies, and stylistic techniques represented in these selections. The manual includes a rhetorical index designed to assist instructors in choosing examples of various forms. The Chart of Rhetorical Assignments (p. 193) lists "Elaborations," the text's writing assignments, according to the particular rhetorical strategy the students are encouraged to use in their essays. In addition, a number of questions in the text focus precisely on style, emphasizing the profound effects realized by seemingly inconsequential choices. Several questions on Paz's "Hygiene and Repression," for example, focus on diction and imagery; a question on Carroll's essay, "Money and Seduction," focuses on tone. After answering the questions on Sophronia Liu's "So Tsi-fai," students will become aware of the use of varied sentence construction to suggest changes in the narrator's point of view. A question on Susan Orlean's "Quinceañera" will help students realize the uses of interview as a method of research. These represent only a few of the stylistic questions to be found in the text.

Those who focus on writing across the disciplines will find selections by journalists (Binur, Reynolds), anthropologists (Shostak, Minai, Carroll), political figures (Shevardnadze, Havel), and literary figures (Tan, Vargas Llosa, Rushdie), among others. For those who focus primarily on personal writing, numerous models are available (for example, Soyinka's "Nigerian Childhood," the selection from Angelou's autobiography, and Erdrich's "Adam"). The writing suggestions accompanying these and other selections offer a variety of personal essay assignments. Instructors who want to integrate "creative" literature with nonfiction will find a number of short stories (identified in the table of contents) to compare with the essays in the book.

Finally, these readings work well when used in conjunction with a longer text. For example, instructors could ask students to consider the topic of coming of age in selections by Vargas Llosa, Shostak, and the novel *Upon This Mountain* by Timothy Wangusa. Students can see how the role of women is defined in different societies according to Cooke, Beauvoir, and Duras and then examine the role of women in longer works such as *Things Fall Apart* by Chinua Achebe or *The Joys of Motherhood* by Buchi Emecheta. Other possibilities for longer texts are *Hunger of Memory* by Richard Rodriguez, *Chronicle of a Death Foretold* by Gabriel García Márquez, *I Shall Not Be Moved* by Maya Angelou, *In Good Faith* by Salman Rushdie, *Tracks* by Louise Erdrich, and *The Bluest Eye* by Toni Morrison.

Ourselves Among Others is also adaptable to various teaching techniques. The book suits the standard lecture-discussion quite well, especially in the discussion questions following each selection. The questions will also prove useful for instructors who opt for a collaborative classroom. Comparisons between various groups' responses, especially to "Connections" questions, should make for enlightening discussion when the class convenes as a whole.

Introduction

Regardless of the focus or teaching approach, however, it is probably best to acknowledge the "foreignness" of this material immediately. Traditional college-age students are still at a stage when differences are perceived as threatening, and in recent years a tendency toward chauvinism has emerged in the United States. Perhaps one of the best ways to begin to chip away at prejudices and provincialism is to discuss different cultures and values represented by the class. A logical next step would be to look at other cultures' views of the United States, reexamining a familiar subject from unfamiliar viewpoints. The opening section, "The West and the World," should jolt students out of complacent views of their own society and result in some lively and emphatic responses. Also, it should allow students to broaden their horizons and become more tolerant of difference, so when they move on to subjects in the following sections they will be less judgmental and more open-minded.

Instructors can follow the introductory unit with any unit, but since students usually respond well when moving from familiar to less familiar ground, most instructors will probably choose to begin with "The Family" or "Landmarks and Turning Points." These units provide ample opportunities for students to draw on their own experience and to consider the experiences of others by comparing them with their own.

If students explore the idea of "the family" early in the course, they can use different types of writing to help them think about a familiar concept in unfamiliar cultures. Depending on the approach adopted, students may be asked to write in their journals, compose a paper, or discuss in small groups their family values and traditions. Possible topics include "Rules and Regulations for Living in the Family," "Ethnic (or Religious) Influences in the Family," "Relationships Between Members of the Family," and "Expectations Within the Family." Each of these topics is broad enough for the instructor to adapt to a particular class or for students to narrow themselves. The purpose of the assignment is threefold: One, in discussing their responses, students should discover some unusual customs among people they consider to be just like them; two, they should discover familiar customs among people they consider different; and three, after examining these customs, they should come to the conclusion that neither the similarities nor the differences mean much in the larger world. These revelations will become useful to students as they attempt to understand a wide range of customs during the semester. As they discuss the origins of family patterns, values, and relationships, as well as their benefits and liabilities, students should lose some of their suspicion of things different. After discussing their own differences, students might enjoy reading Gyanranjan's "Our Side of the Fence and Theirs" (p. 134), solely for the purpose of recognizing that we all look askance at customs that differ from our own. It's not necessary to go into a detailed analysis of the story at this point; a mere surface reading should accomplish the goal.

Once students have been introduced to the idea of differences, the course should be able to continue as the instructor wishes. Several possible syllabi, designed to adapt the text to a variety of approaches, are included at the end of the instructor's manual (p. 166).

Part One

THE WEST AND THE WORLD

INTRODUCTION

Before looking into other cultures through the eyes of others, students first have the opportunity to look at their own culture through the eyes of others. The selections in this section do not focus on any common issue, such as family, sex roles, or work; the subject is foreignness itself. Here students will be introduced to a few of the reasons we sometimes have trouble understanding each other, as well as the reasons Western culture has become dominant in the world.

To begin working on the section, instructors may want to ask students to consider and list the views they've developed of these other cultures. These lists can then be compared with the views of the West provided in the selections. Students might also try to articulate how some of their prior prejudices or misunderstandings have been mitigated by their exposure to different cultures. These statements can be compared with the explanation of cultural differences found in the section. As they explore the selections, students will encounter some intriguing revelations about our own perceptions of others and about others' perceptions of us.

A few subthemes in the section include Western influence on other cultures (Mphahlele, Harrison, Naipaul, Smith), other cultures' perceptions of the West (Paz, Carroll, Jen, Smith, and Naipaul), and the West and the Third World (Mphahlele, Naipaul). Another important theme is the need to perceive the United States in a new light and to reconceive its cross-cultural relationships (Reed, Atwood).

Instructors may wish to consult the following familiar works in preparing related selections from *Ourselves Among Others*:

Essays

James Baldwin, "Stranger in the Village" (*Notes of a Native Son*, Dial Press, 1955).
Alex Haley, "My Furthest-Back-Person — 'The African'" (*New York Times*, July 16, 1972).
Maxine Hong Kingston, "No Name Woman" (*The Woman Warrior*, Knopf, 1976).
George Orwell, "Shooting an Elephant" (*Shooting an Elephant and Other Essays*, Harcourt, 1950).
Richard Rodriguez, "Aria" (*American Scholar*, Winter 1981; *Hunger of Memory*, David R. Godine, 1982).

Short Stories

Toni Cade Bambara, "The Lesson" (*Gorilla, My Love*, Random House, 1972).
Ralph Ellison, "Flying Home" (*Cross-Section*, ed. Edwin Seaver, Fischer Pub. Co., 1944).
Louise Erdrich, "American Horse" (1983; in *Imagining America*, ed. Wesley Brown and Amy Ling, Persea, 1991).

1–59 (Text pages)

Franz Kafka, "The Metamorphosis" (*The Penal Colony*, Schocken, 1948).
D. H. Lawrence, "The Blind Man" (*The Complete Short Stories*, Vol. 2, Penguin, 1976).
Flannery O'Connor, "The Displaced Person" (*Complete Stories*, Farrar, Straus, 1971).
Frank O'Connor, "Guests of the Nation" (*Collected Stories*, Knopf, 1981).
Philip Roth, "Conversion of the Jews" (*Goodbye, Columbus*, Houghton Mifflin, 1959).

ISHMAEL REED, What's American About America? (p. 3)

Explorations

1. This essay demands that many students readjust their image of how American culture has evolved. Many of the ethnic foods they eat, like pizza, have become "as American as apple pie." The idea of a melting pot, which students are familiar with, implies that ethnic groups are assimilated into the dominant culture the way pizza has been assimilated into American cuisine. Americans assume that foreign traditions will contribute to and become part of the mainstream culture. However, most students have probably never eaten bouillabaisse and will need to know that it is a highly seasoned fish stew from the French Mediterranean. Several kinds of fish and shellfish are cooked so that their flavors remain distinct when they are served together. This culinary metaphor suggests that the United States consists of many colorful traditions and ethnic groups that do not become assimiliated into a homogeneous and bland culture, as the term melting pot suggests. In a "cultural bouillabaisse," cultural traditions remain distinct. Also, the use of an untranslated term demands that readers respect the distinctive cultural identity of the dish, which, unlike pizza, has not become assimilated into American cuisine. Students may end by discussing the extent to which a food like pizza does retain its ethnic identity.

2. Reed's main purpose is not to prove the existence of the bias in favor of "Western civilization," but to attack the assumption on which it is based. "Western civilization," Reed argues, is not a monolith, but is the result of the meeting of many cultures. Reed offers five examples from various media to support his assumption that U.S. educators, art critics, and writers favor the monolithic model of Western civilization, but he does not cite sources. He does not name the famous novelist who says "Western civilization was the greatest achievement of mankind" (9). He does not cite the schoolbooks that idealize the Puritans (10), nor does he name the "the president of a distinguished university," the television network, or the schoolteacher who promote the idea that Western civilization is superior (13, 14). When students realize that Reed has not cited concrete sources in support of one of his major claims, they are likely to feel that his argument loses some of its credibility. Reed's strategy, however, is to convince the reader that the notion that Western culture is superior is ubiquitous among the "nation's present educational and cultural elect." He implies that anyone who watches television or reads the newspaper has encountered the bias in favor of Western civilization. However, he is more careful to cite sources to support his main point, that Western civilization is a "cultural bouillabaisse." He begins his essay with a dated quote from the *New York Times*, and although he doesn't name all his sources thereafter, he uses dates and place names to give concreteness to his argument.

2

3.   Reed emphasizes that the term "Western civilization" has been used in a misleading way
     to suggest the European roots of our culture. He uses numerous examples (6–8) to show
     the many non-Western cultures that have helped to shape "Western" traditions. His thesis
     is that Americans need to abandon the idea that American society is heir only to the
     traditions of a white European cultural elite (the Puritans, 10) because it denies the
     multicultural nature of contemporary society and the influence of other ethnic traditions
     in shaping American culture. The habit of elevating one cultural tradition above the
     others leads to a devaluation of other cultural traditions and to cultural imperialism. Reed
     directs his criticism to "the nation's present educational and cultural elect" (6), formed
     by those like the schoolteacher (14) and the university president and the television
     producer (13) who see America as the product of European culture. He recommends that
     they learn to see America as a place where the world's cultures meet, thrive, and
     contribute richly to contemporary society (15).

Connections

1.   To begin a discussion of this question, you might ask students to add to Harrison's
     examples illustrating the spread of Western culture. The worldwide craze for blue jeans
     and rock 'n' roll music and the spread of McDonald's to Moscow are some obvious
     additions. As Harrison contends, the technological advances promised by Westernization
     are almost impossible for developing countries to resist (in spite of the environmental
     and political hazards that accompany them). Survival as a country is at stake. And a
     country cannot adopt Western technology without adopting other Western institutions
     and ideas, which replace their traditional counterparts. Whereas Harrison argues that the
     Westernization of the world promotes global cultural uniformity, Reed seems to describe
     a future in which diverse cultures can coexist without threatening or transforming one
     another. Although Harrison and Reed might disagree about how cultures interact, they
     would probably agree that it is not possible for cultures to exist in isolation. The idea of
     a "pure" culture, unaffected by outside influences, is foreign to both Harrison and Reed.

2.   For many students, Morrison's piece will offer a perspective on American literature and
     culture they have never considered before. Morrison contends that American literature
     (and, by analogy, mainstream American culture) was essentially formed by the
     philosophies, institutions, and ideologies that made slavery possible in the United States.
     Although Africans and African-Americans do not receive much attention in the literature
     that constitutes the American canon, according to Morrison, without the influence of
     people of African heritage, American literature and culture would be entirely different.
     On the issue of Euro-American culture, Reed cites the example of a Yale professor who
     was condemned for his view that African cultures had influenced the development of
     American cultures. This example suggests that he would agree with Morrison that
     Americans are unwilling to confront the fact that American culture has always been based
     on multicultural interaction. However, Reed and Morrison differ in that Morrison's
     strategy is to point out the influence of Africans and African-Americans on canonical
     Euro-American literature, while Reed is more concerned with deconstructing the basic
     idea that there is such a thing as "monolithic" Euro-American culture (6).

RAYMONDE CARROLL, Money and Seduction (p. 8)

Explorations

1. Carroll's thesis is that the American attitude toward money and the French attitude toward sexual conquest function in similar fashions, since each suggests the measure of an individual's success in the respective society. Both are metaphors for success, and they allow for the crossing of class boundaries. While Carroll includes references to books, the main source of information cited appears to be conversations with French and American friends or acquaintances (para. 1). Sometimes she refers to specific individuals, such as the French woman with the American brother-in-law. More often, Carroll refers to a larger group of respondents, as if to emphasize the uniformity of the response. Thus she writes of "many French informants" (2) or "many Americans" (3). Some students will recognize that, since Carroll is using evidence that is not verifiable, any observer similarly positioned between the cultures could readily refute or support her thesis using Carroll's own rules of evidence. However, her thesis depends on logic, as well as evidence. The specific ways in which French and American cultures measure personal success may be less important to Carroll's thesis than the general idea that cultures use metaphors (such as money or seduction) to express and measure movement up or down the class hierarchy.

2. In her last paragraph, Carroll writes that "the greatest attraction of cultural analysis . . . is the possibility of replacing a dull exchange of invectives with an exploration that is . . . fascinating" (20). In her essay she shows that the French and the Americans have misunderstood each other's behavior, a misunderstanding that has led to derogatory remarks about foreign cultural practices. Carroll believes that instead of rejecting cultures on the grounds of difference, people should explore foreign cultures to find resemblances to their own. By "inviting" people to proceed in this fashion, Carroll encourages them to take a positive attitude toward foreign cultures and pays them the compliment of assuming they can arrive at analyses similar to her own. Her noncritical approach prevents readers from defending their own prejudices and identifying with only one of the cultural attitudes under discussion.

3. Students may bring their own concept of American Playboys to this question, yielding a definition more sexually oriented than Carroll's and thus closer to her definition of French playboys. The essay contrasts not only American and French playboys' behavior, but attitudes toward them in the societies they live in. The American playboy is described as one who "squanders an inherited fortune" (8). The author makes no comment about the American playboy's sexual habits but implies that his spending habits do not help him realize his potential (8). He has "wasted the 'opportunities' offered by . . . parents or by society" (8). In contrast, being a French playboy involves hard work, for "Seduction is an art which is learned and perfected" (16). Like all art, it requires "intelligence," "expertise," and "talent" (18). Thus the French playboy is admired for his achievement, not censored for immoral behavior. An American playboy might underestimate or not appreciate how hard the French playboy must work. The French playboy might think the American playboy buys his successes, obtaining only easy victories.

Connections

1. Carroll's focus is not on "social realities" but on "cultural premises." (para. 9). She uses qualifiers to hint that, in reality, class mobility in the United States is more restricted than the "cultural premise" would suggest: "[money] is *supposed* to be accessible to all"; "The highest social class is, in principle, open to everyone" (9). However, since she wishes to generalize about American culture, she does not go further in discussing the ways in which race and cultural diversity in the United States affect the social reality of class. As a result, she seems to side with the melting-pot view of American society rather than with the "cultural bouillabaisse" view Ishmael Reed proposed. Although she gives a diverse list of the many symbolic meanings of money in the United States (7), she refers to "Americans" as though every American was in a position to consider money as an abstract concept. She claims that "money has become a common denominator" (9) and refers to "the essentially idealistic significance of money in American culture" (10).

2. According to Ishmael Reed, racial and ethnic differences provide the context for the formation of cultural subgroups in the United States. Students may need help to understand how class differences intersect with racial and ethnic differences. Because many middle-class students hold the view, expressed by Carroll, that monetary success depends solely on individual effort (9), it may be hard for them initially to recognize the confluence of race and class inequalities in our society. Once they do, the notion that money is "the only true class equalizer" in the United States will be called into doubt. Reed's essay contains a historical example of Western European culture in the United States that suggests why money, rather than seduction, would become the primary measure of success here. He recalls that the Puritans are idealized as "industrious, responsible" creators of the work ethic, but that they were also repressive and intolerant. The art of seduction, in a Puritan society, would be considered at best a waste of time and at worst a sign of immorality.

OCTAVIO PAZ (Ok-TAH-vee-oh PAHS), Hygiene and Repression (p. 15)

Explorations

1. Most students have probably encountered the word hygiene in contexts suggesting that good hygiene is a positive goal. Therefore, Paz's use of the word in a negative sense may be unexpected and confusing. Paz defines hygiene as an American obsession with cleanliness stemming from a desire to remain morally separate, untouched, and pure. He terms the American concern with the purity of food a "maniacal preoccupation" that also expresses itself as a desire for racial and cultural purity (para. 1). In paragraph 6, Paz uses the example of the fear of contagion and germs experienced by Americans traveling abroad. He compares the American fear of physical contagion with the Brahman fear of moral contamination, showing that scientific and religious conditioning can result in similar behavior and that scientific values can mask moral values. Students who have traveled abroad might consider whether they were concerned with the cleanliness of conditions. Nearer to home, they might consider the advertisements promoting cleaning agents from toothpaste to detergents that suggest that cleanliness is the basis of a healthful and moral life.

2. By his constant references to "Americans," as if all Americans belong in one category, Paz suggests that American culture is uniform and America is a melting pot. Yet since he compares the culture to the cuisine, he obviously believes that this melting pot produces a homogeneous mixture not by combining distinct flavors but by excluding any different flavors or cultures. He first characterizes American cuisine as "simple" and "nourishing" (1), but his later comparison of it with other cuisines suggests that it is without interesting nuances (3), indulges infantile longings in preferences for milk and milkshakes (2), and lacks spice or passion (4). Americans eat to be healthy and able to work, not to find pleasure in their food (5). American cuisine is compared to the "virtuous discourse" of the "Founding Fathers," a watercolor painting, and a pastel drawing of delicate shades (1).

3. Paz uses religious terms throughout his essay, and it may be difficult for students unfamiliar with these terms to grasp the analogies he sets up. For example, some of the terms used are "transubstantiation" (1), "communion" (1), "devil" (2), "apostolic" (2), and "Eucharist" (3). By drawing an analogy between eating and religious experiences, he suggests that eating has important symbolic, as well as practical functions, such as the experience of communion between elements on the plate and persons at the table. Paz is preparing the reader for his comparison of the American dread of physical contagion with the Brahman fear of moral contamination, stressing their similar origins. Because most students consider science and religion as separate categories, they will need to discuss and understand the idea of taboo before understanding the relationship between purity and isolation in both scientific and religious contexts.

4. Students might approach this essay by considering their dinner of the night before or the types of meals usually served in their homes. They should be encouraged to discuss whether Paz's descriptions of American eating habits are accurate or speak to a conceptualization of American cuisine. Some students may resent his overly simplified description of American eating habits, especially if they are familiar with the diversity of American cuisines. They might discuss Paz's distinction between "ideas and social values" and "more or less secret realities" (5) in order to understand why he does not discuss other ethnic groups. Paz himself seems to enjoy suggesting that the puritanical repressiveness of American eating habits condemns Americans to bland cuisine and a diminished sense of sin. His humor, like the Mexican cuisine he describes (3), makes contradictory and unexpected associations. For example, if a milkshake is a sign of "pregenital pleasures" (2) and can be associated with milk, home, and mother, it also can be associated with "orgies" of sugar (2). Paz implies that Americans unknowingly express moral attitudes through their food habits, but he quite consciously describes food choices in moral and religious terms. The humor here derives from his playfulness in using language, for he is not amused by his discoveries. Using a Freudian framework, Paz traces the evolution of the rationalism and plain cuisine of the Founding Fathers into a "maniacal preoccupation" with purity (1). Paz shows that Americans are not following the principles of "temperance, moderation, [and] reserve" (6); their actions are governed by "obsession" and "dread." The conclusions he reaches after comparing the attitudes of several cultures toward food lead to labels many Americans may resent hearing applied to themselves: uncommunicative, unsocial, superstitious, and, by implication, racist (7). Thus, the tactic of drawing unfavorable comparisons should generate an emotional response from readers.

Connections

1. Raymonde Carroll says that Americans display "disgust" for French people who boast about their sexual achievements, and she contends that Americans consider sex a subject suitable only to "uncivilized" settings such as locker rooms (para. 14). The French, according to Carroll, consider this evidence of a sexual puritanism among Americans. Paz describes a similar view of American attitudes toward food. He says that "Yankee food, impregnated with Puritanism, is based on exclusions." American food, Paz argues, reflects a culture-wide concern for racial, religious, and sexual purity (1). Food, like work and sports in the United States, is supposed to be turned to productive ends (5), not enjoyed simply for the pleasure of it.

2. Reed's essay is full of descriptions that suggest the need to replace the idea of a traditional American cuisine and culture with the idea of a variety of ethnic cuisines and cultural traditions. Instead of roasts, carrots, and potatoes, Reed mentions pizza, Italian ices, and knishes. He sees Vietnamese grocery stores, Islamic mosques, and paintings with African mythological imagery in fast-food restaurants. He discusses the influence of the Puritans, yet he also mentions the contributions of Native Americans to American culture. Reed rejects the idea of a monolithic, Eurocentric American culture and encourages others to do the same.

3. Both Reed and Paz refer to the historic influence of the Puritans in the development of American culture and attitudes. Reed suggests that the Puritans' inhuman treatment of those not part of the ruling elite, such as children, Indians, and servants from Barbados, reflected their distrust of difference (11). Paz sees the same attitude of the Puritans in "Yankee food, impregnated with Puritanism" (1). Reed writes that the other side of the Puritan legacy of hard work is "the strange and paranoid attitudes of that society toward those different from the elect" (12). Paz states that "the maniacal preoccupation with the purity and origin of food products has its counterpart in racism and exclusivism" (1).

GISH JEN, Helen in America (p. 22)

Explorations

1. Helen considers her life in China perfect for several reasons. Students may have trouble understanding why the fact that Helen had a twin sister who died was a lucky beginning, or why her "touch-and-go start" on life turned out to be a blessing (para. 1). Girls are usually considered of less value than boys in China, but Helen became precious in part because her parents had suffered the loss of her sister and because they came close to losing Helen herself. However, many students will remember receiving special attention when they were sick during childhood, and those memories will make it easier to understand why Helen would consider her childhood illnesses a boon. Once in the United States, Helen tries to recreate her life in China by maintaining the same stillness she enjoyed there and by refusing to become involved in American cultures (2, 3). She refuses to eat American food and often goes hungry, which she hopes will make her sick again (3). She remains healthy, however, and eventually finds herself becoming interested in her new home. She gives up her isolation, even agreeing to marry, an idea that had horrified her in China.

7

2. The story about the man who took his house apart and rebuilt it elsewhere suggests the Changs' efforts to reproduce certain aspects of their life in China in their new life in the United States, including Ralph's marriage to Helen, who resembles the Changs' younger sister. In the story Ralph tells, the house the man rebuilds has the same leak as the first and is still too small — flaws that, when applied to the Changs, may mean that their efforts to live as they did in China may not be the best solution to the challenges of living in a new culture. However, Theresa speculates that maybe the man rebuilt his house because he was used to it, even with all its flaws (13). The Changs have done their best to bring over the values of their own culture, but even so they are not always comfortable in their new country (especially when they have to move into an apartment that has many more flaws than their house in China).

3. This should be an easy question for students to think through once they understand that sometimes the Changs are seeing their own characteristics reflected in the Americans around them. Helen complains of "'typical American just-want-to-be-the-center-of-things,'" a desire she has always felt herself (39). Some of their derogatory remarks ("'typical American don't-know-how-to-get-along'" and "'typical American just-dumb'") reflect their own anxieties about getting along in the United States and mastering the English language.

4. The main sources of the Changs' information about American life are the newspaper, popular magazines, the radio, and their neighbors. These are all rich sources of information, but much of what they see and read is incomprehensible to them until they read a newspaper article about how Americans have degenerated since World War II (41). After reading the article the Changs are pleased to find that Americans agree with their perceptions of the degeneracy of American life. They think they have found rational support for their need to maintain some distance from American culture, because too much contact would cause them to become "wild" (39) and deteriorate like the Americans. The evidence they gather for their hypothesis is drawn from contact with their super, neighbors, and shopkeepers, as well as from tabloid articles about bizarre occurrences, such as the animal trainer biting off his wife's ear (41). Therefore, their sources are either unreliable or merely anecdotal, feeding their tendency to generalize about "typical American" defects.

Connections

1. Examining Octavio Paz's essay in conjunction with "Helen in America" will illuminate some of the ironies involved in trying to identify traits that are "typical" of any nationality or race. Paz's critique of Americans focusses on what he views as their characteristic lack of tolerance. He writes that Americans demand the "extirpation or separation of what is alien, different, ambiguous, impure" (para 8). Paz is primarily interested in any behavior that tends to support this view of the typical American; therefore, he discusses primarily "traditional" American cuisine, which he contends "is like watercolor painting or pastels" (1) and the behaviors of American travelers abroad, where they evince a boundless "dread of contagion"(6). This "dread" of moral and physical infection leads to the characteristic American intolerance of whatever is foreign. The Changs, by contrast, are most interested in American behaviors when they seem to provide evidence that Americans are foolish, immoral, or incomprehensible. They discover "typical" American characteristics such as an overblown sense of self-importance, the tendency to use brute

force, and an inability to cooperate. Denigrating Americans helps them to diffuse the tensions of being foreigners in a sometimes hostile environment, but it also demonstrates the tendency Paz claimed was typically American: the tendency to condemn things and people who are foreign.

2. Most students will realize that the Changs' value economy, as their choice to live in a run-down apartment as a money-saving measure shows (26). They also value hard work, exemplified in Ralph's assertion that Pete is "fooling himself" in thinking he could become a doctor or engineer without putting in years of hard work and sacrifice (31–33). Carroll says that for Americans, "to earn money, a lot of money, and to spend it, is to give the most concrete, the most visible sign that one has not wasted the 'opportunities' offered by one's parents or by society . . ." (8). Reviewing this statement may help students consider differences between the Changs' view of money and the "American" view. The Changs share with Americans a commitment to the work ethic, but they would not agree that using money as a "visible sign" of success is a virtue. Similarly, according to Carroll, seduction is a visible measure of success for the French, and it is likely the Changs would consider bragging about sexual exploits to be just as offensive as flaunting wealth.

3. The Changs enjoy certain aspects of American culture, including American print media and radio (5), but when Helen first arrives, she depends on trips to New York's Chinatown to give her a feeling of being at home. There, also, she can buy Chinese food. Other influences, such as the presence of black people in the poor apartment building the Changs move to, are harder for them to accept. But the cultural eclecticism the Changs' encounter helps them to feel that "everything . . . was going to be okay" (45).

MARGARET ATWOOD, A View from Canada (p. 29)

Explorations

1. Margaret Atwood sums up her youthful view of Americans when she recalls her shock at realizing her country "was owned by the kind of people who carried tin boats across portages and didn't burn their garbage" (para. 4). Earlier still, she sums up her attitude this way: "Americans were wimps who had a lot of money but did not know what they were doing" (1). Students may come up with a variety of examples from the text that reveal Atwood's current view of the "typical American." Atwood describes the United States as an isolationist nation (10, 11) and points out that Americans always try to take their American lifestyle with them when they travel internationally (12). Perhaps the most telling statement Atwood makes is that "Americans experience themselves, individually, as small toads in the biggest and most powerful puddle in the world" (13). She recognizes that Americans experience "a sense of power [that] comes from identifying with the puddle." At the same time, her image suggests that the size and power of their own country make Americans feel small and swallowed up by it.

2. Students will need help identifying the subtle indications that "A View from Canada" was written as a speech: the conversational and often jocular tone, frequent use of short phrases, and departures from formal diction ("hamburgers, cokes, and rock music surrounded you" (12)), are not obtrusive. However, it is obvious in paragraph 14 that

Atwood is giving a speech, and that her audience is American, when she says, "south of you you have Mexico and south of us we have you" (15).

3. Atwood begins to indicate a problem with Canadian self-image when she comments on the lingering effects of British colonialism, for instance the fact that British history was taught in schools in preference to Canadian history (2-3). After the war, Americans bought into the place left vacant by the British, leaving the Canadians feeling that "they'd sold their birthright for a mess" (4). However, Atwood points out the positive aspects of the Canadian outlook (although with some irony) when she writes that "Canada, having somehow become an expert at compromise, was the mediator" between Britain and the United States. Canadians are far more interested in international relations than are Americans (10). According to Atwood, unlike Americans, Canadians realize they are not isolated from the world at large (11, 12). But they also think of their country as "a small sinking Titanic squashed between two icebergs" (11), a comment Atwood supports with the example of the Canadian politician who said that Canada walks in the footstep of the United States (13).

4. Students will be able to locate many places where Atwood uses humor, but it is important to point out that Atwood's humor can be ironic, with a serious and often barbed comment buried in it. The vision, in the first paragraph, of American ineptitude exemplified in Atwood's portrait of Americans portaging a metal boat ("Typically American, we thought, as they ricocheted off another tree") offers not only a view of Americans as slapstick incompetents, but also suggests that Canadians underestimated the ability of Americans to colonize Canada with money and cultural influence. Atwood recalls the sharp-edged humor of her first example in paragraph 4, when she says Canadians woke up in the sixties to realize their country was owned by incompetents. Lighter uses of humor include Atwood's wry comments on her own history: "I know it's hard to believe in view of my youthful appearance, but when I was child there was no television" (5); "By this time I wanted to be a writer, and you can see it would be a dilemma . . . how could one be a writer and somehow manage to avoid having to become British and dead?" (7).

Connections

1. In Gish Jen's "Helen in America," Theresa contemplates the run-down apartment the Changs share and comments, "We're not the kind of people who live like this" (para. 26). The soft, crumbling plaster and the crack in the wall indicate the Changs' lack of protection against the world outside. Unlike the Americans, who in Atwood's view "enter the outside world the way they landed on the moon, with their . . . protective spacesuits firmly in place" (12) the Changs must deal with the world directly. Nevertheless, as the story Ralph tells about the man who moves his house suggests (10), the Changs have brought their own culture and attitudes with them. When they, like Atwood, make fun of the "typical American," they are setting up walls between themselves and American cultural influences.

2. Octavio Paz writes that when he was in India, he "witnessed the obsession of Americans with hygiene" (6). They feared germs from food, water, people, and the air. Similarly, Atwood writes that Americans in New Delhi lived behind walls, insisted on eating American food, and seemed to have "their own oxygen tanks of American air strapped to their backs" (12). Paz points out that American isolationism abroad indicates a preoccupation with purity (6) that is not shared with people from other nations.

3. Because they are more used to considering themselves "Americans" than as "United States citizens," students may not realize the implications of Ishmael Reed's use of the term "North American" when he is discussing the United States (as when he says that the surrealists, "in their map of North America" made "Alaska dwarf . . . the lower forty-eight states in size" (7). Reed makes no mention of the Canadian provinces that also compose North America. All of Reed's examples of American prejudices come from the United States. In his conclusion, Reed blatantly subsumes Canada into the United States, saying the nations are "unique in the world" in that many world cultures converge in them. Atwood would disagree with Reed's tendency to assume Canada and the United States are the same, but she generalizes about Americans in such a way that the multicultural composition of the United States is suppressed.

ES'KIA MPHAHLELE (Em-fa-LAY-lay), Tradition and the African Writer (p. 35)

Explorations

1. Belonging to both the Western and the African worlds forces Mphahlele and his fellow artists to choose between their present, represented by Westernization, and the past, represented by African tradition. In attempting to reconcile the two, the artists must balance several opposing influences: Christianity versus traditional African religions; fact-oriented Western education versus the more spiritual knowledge of family and tribe; traditional tribal philosophy versus the European language used to articulate it; reverence for the artifact versus the creative process; and the local African community versus the larger, predominantly Western, surrounding world. Specifically, the artists choose whether to adopt Western ways, gaining power in the larger world at the risk of losing African understanding, friends, and kinship ties.

2. African writers will need education to succeed in the world beyond the community, and that education will in turn open up still newer worlds to them. But it also opens up a gulf between writers and African tradition. Writers must attempt to reconcile the education with the traditions or risk losing their moorings. Education provides new viewpoints, new subject matter, and many other sources of enrichment for writers. However, it may alienate them from the viewpoints and subject matter to which they feel closest and about which they can write most successfully. To reject education is to cut themselves off from the larger world in an attempt (not necessarily successful) to preserve the smaller one.

3. Mphahlele's first indication of his Western heritage is found in the first paragraph, when he refers to "Hegelian historical determinism." Among other illustrations of Western influence are his ability to understand the influence of his European education (para. 2), his discussion of parent-child relationships (4), and his essay's diction throughout. His African heritage is more evident, illustrated by his understanding of the value of the creative process (6) and his acknowledgment of the spirit of his ancestors (8).

4. In his essay, Mphahlele uses the word *tradition* in two ways. He says his education has taught him to use the tradition of the West as a point of reference for himself (2), yet he notes that this tradition has been superimposed upon a stronger indigenous African

11

religion and civilization (3). His thesis is that the education of the African writer places him between these two traditions and alienates him from the majority of Africans, who remain closer to the traditions of their ancestors (4). African parents desire the benefits that an education can confer, but they despair over their children's shift in allegiance. Mphahlele takes a more positive attitude toward the dual allegiances and feels that African writers can successfully reconcile, or "harmonize," the two traditions (4). Since Mphahlele doesn't quote any outside sources, he seems to generalize from his own experience (2). He includes himself in his observations by using the pronouns we (3) and you (6) when explaining the situation of African writers.

Connections

1. Like Margaret Atwood, Es'kia Mphahlele received an education that disparaged the history and religions of his continent. Mphahlele writes, "I was brought up on European history and literature and religion and made to identify with European heroes . . ." (para. 2). Atwood recalls that in school she was introduced primarily to British literature (7) and European and American history (8). It will be a challenge for students to deduce what changes in education Mphahlele and Atwood might recommend. Atwood might recommend developing a curriculum that emphasizes Canada's role as an international mediator (11, 12) as a way of inducing Canadians to feel less powerless (13). Mphahlele might recommend different tactics. He writes that most parents recognize that "the benefits of a modern education are tangible, real" (5), but he seems to regret the "ever widening gulf between one and one's parents and one's community" that a modern, or western, education produces (6). Some students will say that the educational system would be improved, and the gulf between generations could be reduced, if schools could incorporate more African history and literature into the curriculum. But Mphahlele has a different way of approaching the problem of what to do with the "ambivalent character" he has become as a result of his western education (2). In his conclusion, Mphahlele writes that "we need to appreciate these distances" between African traditions and the westernized modern world. This strategy, of appreciating cultural and historical differences rather than ignoring them or trying to obliterate them, would create an educational system that would better prepare the African writer to take part in "the whole pattern" (9).

2. Both Atwood and Mphahlele grew up far from the European culture that defined *writer* in their countries. The obstacles Atwood faced included the general sense among Canadians that their history and cultures are uninteresting (9) and the fact that her education taught her to regard British literature as the only literature of merit (7). She also had to contend with the complications of gender, as suggested in her comment that she finds it hard to accept it as a compliment when men tell her she thinks like a man (1). Fortunately, her education allowed her to read British women writers, helping her to realize she did not have to identify herself with men in order to write (7). Mphahlele's main obstacle may have been the "humiliating" sense of having to continually reassess himself "with reference to . . . the tradition of the West" (2). The effort to reconcile Western influences and African traditions is "agonizing" (2). His reference only to male figures of cultural authority (3, 8) suggest that his most obvious advantage over Atwood is his gender, while her most obvious advantage over him is her European descent, which exempts her from the racial bias Mphahlele describes (3). On the other hand, Mphahlele is backed up by a long African tradition of cultural expression that he feels is as important

to his writing as the Western influences. Atwood, as a citizen of a nation with a relatively short history, has no long tradition of Canadian writing to draw on. Unlike Africans, Canadians cannot look back to a point in history when their ancestors were not a part of western culture. But Atwood makes this lack of an established tradition a strength; she is forging the literary traditions future Canadian writers will build on.

3. Respect for tradition and an appreciation of metaphor are as important to Gish Jen's "Helen in America" as they are to Mphahlele's "Tradition and the African Writer." In Jen's story, the Changs' household, especially the marriage between Ralph and his sister Theresa's best friend Helen, is arranged according to a pattern their parents would approve (10). The Changs express the appropriateness of their arrangements by evoking two metaphors. Ralph implies a comparison between their household and that of a man who "took his house apart, and moved it, and then rebuilt it, just the way it was" (10), and Helen reminds Ralph and Theresa of the saying that a wife's ankle is tied to her husband's from the time she is born (20, 21). Each of these metaphors is a way of affirming their solidarity and showing respect for Chinese tradition.

4. Both Africa and Latin America were colonized by Western Europeans who imposed their own religious and educational traditions upon the indigenous culture, although the colonizations occurred during different historic periods. Yet the resultant culture described by Paz seems able to reconcile disparate elements or opposites. Paz enjoys the sensuous nature of Mexican food, which denies the Puritan heritage of separation and subordination of foreign elements. Unlike the American cuisine, which is "based on . . . exclusions," the Mexican cuisine reflects a "fondness for dark, passionate stews . . . , for thick and sumptuous red, green, and yellow sauces (1). Mphahlele finds a similar sensuousness in language. The indigenous African languages (unlike the "unaffected sentences of virtuous discourse" described by Paz (1) influence modern witnesses to "operate in metaphor and glory in the sensuousness of the spoken word" (8).

PAUL HARRISON, The Westernization of the World (p. 41)

Explorations

1. The "European road" Harrison mentions is characterized by a worship of technology (especially military), a preoccupation with highways and large buildings, an infatuation with Western dress, and a rejection of traditional culture (note the opening anecdote). His examples, ranging from the bank manager's television (para. 4) to the Ivory Coast's four-lane highway going nowhere and Jakarta's "neo-fascist monuments" (12), are all traceable to a desire to impress others in the Third World with one's own successful adoption of Western ways.

2. That the general cause of the Third World's Westernization is European colonization should be readily apparent to all students. But recognizing the three specific channels through which Westernization was realized will take careful reading. Some students may point immediately to the political, economic, and cultural imperialism mentioned in paragraph 6, failing to realize that the article doesn't discuss political and economic

factors. Cultural imperialism itself is the subject of the selection, and the channels are identified in paragraphs 9, 10, and 11 as the "indoctrination [by the colonial powers] of an elite of local collaborators"; the existence in the native population of "reference-group behavior," or imitation of the behavior of the elite group; and the practice of racial humiliation "deriving from the arrogance and haughtiness of the colonialists." Harrison cites self-righteous Pauline Christianity, cultural arrogance, racial prejudice, and the possession of power as the critical factors in the colonialist attitude and a total lack of the same among the natives as the reasons for the success of Westernization. The natives had no sense of their own value with which to fend off the assault of European influence.

3. Harrison cites "consciousness of Western military superiority" (14) as the primary force behind Westernization of noncolonial nations. The overwhelming desire to compete militarily with the European powers resulted in far-reaching social, economic, and political changes in these societies. Also important, according to Harrison, is the pervading racial prejudice of the West, leading some of the "Young Turks" who gained power in the noncolonial societies to further emulate European culture. Now that they've cast their lot with the West, a return to their own traditions would be extremely difficult. His observation that "contact with Europe shook nations to the foundations, calling into question the roots of their civilizations and all the assumptions and institutions on which their lives were based" (14) makes it quite clear that there is no turning back once Western culture has been embraced. Students may also point out his observation on the cultural price Japan has paid to become one of the leading industrial nations (16).

4. Harrison supports his ideas with diverse and substantial evidence, including his own direct observations and also those of a range of other writers. For instance, he cites such Third World intellectuals as Fanon on racial humiliation and Chiang on the influence of military technology on society as a whole. Students can identify the types of information Harrison relies on by looking at the similarities he cites among British, French, Dutch, Iberian, and Portuguese colonies. The native "aristocracy" in all the colonies, he contends, exhibit similar proclivities, among them styles of Western dress, designs of cities and buildings, construction of highways, and mimicry of behavior. Although much of his evidence is superficial (dress, architecture, social behavior), these aspects reflect cultural values. In this sense then his evidence is sound.

Connections

1. In calling Africa "mission-ridden" (para. 3), Mphahlele indicates his opinion of Christianity's role in his culture. The missions set up a power structure in which a native was unable to get a job without a testimonial from a white minister. Even the black ministers were unable to rely on one another for testimonials; references had to be from a white person. Christianity also "smoked out" all the ancient African gods (2). Mphahlele describes the steps Africans follow when being drawn into this new power structure. First the African is baptized, a process that may turn him into a Christian in little more than name but that qualifies him for attending a mission school (3). At school the young African learns to elevate the tradition of the West and to downplay his own. Parents may fear that a separation between themselves and their children will result from education, but their fundamental attitude encourages their children to acquire and benefit from a modern education. The attitude helps young Africans take the important step of "harmonization," of reconciling the difficulty of communicating with their parents with the exhilaration of

assimilating foreign patterns of thought (4). At this point the Africans are not completely assimilated into Western culture but are somewhat distanced from their own. For example, they may still feel "reverence" for an indigenous religion, but they no longer practice its ritual (2).

2. The Spanish are included among the Iberian conquerors discussed by Harrison in paragraph 7. He contrasts them with the British, noting that the Iberians were free from racial prejudice, which meant that, unlike the British, they intermingled with the native population, living with native women and fathering interracial children. Paz establishes that the same attitude toward "mingling" dominates Latin American cuisine and culture when he draws an analogy between gastronomy and the erotic, where "it's desire that sets substances, bodies, and sensations in motion . . . that rules their conjunction, commingling, and transmutation" (3). According to Paz, Mexican cuisine, composed of opposites which shock the taste (3), is "dark, passionate, . . . thick, . . . sumptuous," colorful, and not based on the principles of separation and exclusion (1).

3. In paragraph 10 Harrison discusses reference-group behavior when he explains that the Africans copied the customs and habits of their conquerors. The desire to mimic created a subaltern ruling class of a native elite that adopted Western ways in place of their own traditions. Carroll's essay also gives several examples of individuals conforming to the values of a more dominant group, although the groups in her essay are formed from the indigenous culture. Thus, American men may conform to the atmosphere of the locker room, behaving quite differently than they would elsewhere, where frank discussion of their sexual exploits would be unacceptable (14). More important, Carroll notes that the symbolism of money changes quite radically depending on the group discussing it. The self-made person who discusses his wealth is encouraging others to follow his example. Since he represents a different life-style and economic status, which encourage others to emulate him, he functions very much like the reference groups in Africa or India that encourage the formation of an elite (10).

V. S. NAIPAUL (NYE-paul), Entering the New World (p. 48)

Explorations

1. The attitude of the waiters, the poor service, and the inaccurate bill all indicate to Naipaul that the problem is "more than a matter of an off day" (para. 20). He assumes that the French or European owner or manager is no longer with the restaurant. How does he reach this conclusion? He has determined, after listening to Ebony's imitation of the French intellectual, that Westernization is merely an idea. Ebony is unable to support any of his pronouncements, leading Naipaul to the belief that they are all borrowed. Thus when he sees what's happening in the restaurant, he imagines that the place itself was just an idea. He sees in the waiters' faces "various degrees of tribal authority" and concludes that "the true life was there, in the mysteries of the village." Now that the people who conceived the idea of the restaurant are gone, the place itself, "with its false, arbitrary ritual, was [a] charade" (20).

15

2. Naipaul's observation that Ebony is concerned with "antithesis, balance" will need some attention before students go on to interpret Ebony's comparisons between Africans, the French, and the British. Naipaul's observation suggests that Ebony has an aesthetic appreciation for an argument that balances itself by evoking antitheses. Thus Ebony argues that the French create the bourgeois (who want peace), but the English create entrepreneurs (who want change) (9). He produces a similarly symmetrical argument when he says that "Africans live at peace with nature. Europeans want to conquer or dominate nature" (11). Throughout his conversation with Ebony, Naipaul seems skeptical of Ebony's seriousness as a thinker. Naipaul says that Ebony's ideas are "scattered" and that he is not as anxious about the fate of Africa as he should be (18). Under the influence of Naipaul's skepticism, many students will agree that Ebony is more interested in the beauty than the validity of an idea. But some may realize that Ebony may evoke "antitheses" as a way of establishing distance between himself and western influences. Ebony's story about his French education, when he considers the differences in nonverbal communication that led the French to consider the Africans hypocritical (13), provides him with a way to distance himself from the French colonial influence. The point of the story, Ebony maintains, is that he considered his French teachers "inferior" (15). By opposing the European to the African cultures, Ebony can draw whatever he can use from the Western tradition while still remaining allied with African perspectives.

3. In the first half of the essay Naipaul almost seems to be poking fun at Ebony. He characterizes the man as a child trying to impress an adult. A number of Naipaul's comments create this impression, among them "I felt it had been said before" (9), "Antithesis, balance: the beauty rather than the validity of a thought" (10), and "I felt this racial story, with its triumphant twist, had previously had a sympathetic foreign listener" (16). But after Ebony leaves and Naipaul visits the restaurant, he seems to realize that the fault isn't Ebony's. He, along with all his fellow citizens, has been sold a bill of goods; there is no substance to the "idea" of the new world. When the French departed, the Africans were left to create their own "new world" out of the changes that colonialism had brought about in their nation.

4. Ebony's view of the French influence on the Ivory Coast can be gleaned from three comments. In paragraph 8, Ebony points out that "Charlemagne wasn't my ancestor," suggesting that the French had no business imposing their history and culture on the Ivory Coast. In the next paragraph, Ebony goes on to talk about how badly the French governed their colonies. Somewhat later, commenting on his education under the French, Ebony implies that the French failed to understand African culture and that this failure lost them the respect of the Africans. Naipaul's view of the French is filtered partly through his observations of Ebony. His perception of the effects of Ebony's French educaton does not reflect well either on the French or on Ebony, who according to Naipaul appreciates "the beauty rather than the validity of a thought (10)." Later Naipaul comments that Ebony's ideas are merely "part of his relishing of life, part of his French-inspired role as intellectual. . . ." (18). However, Naipaul also credits the French with creating and maintaining order in the restaurant: "Someone was missing, perhaps the French or European manager. And with him more than good service had gone: The whole restaurant idea had vanished" (20). Students may infer that Naipaul is implying the French have played a similar organizing role in the Ivory Coast as a whole.

Connections

1. Harrison says that the French colonialists had aimed for "'assimilation' of gifted natives" through "indoctrination of an elite of local collaborators" (para. 9). Both Naipaul and Ebony acknowledge this — Naipaul by observing the French influence in Ebony's expressions and Ebony himself (albeit unwittingly) by deciding, "as a poet and intellectual . . . to try out his ideas" (5). But Naipaul's assessment of European influence does not seem quite as harsh as Harrison's: The latter chronicles over a century of economic, social, and political undermining of African traditions, whereas the former focuses almost exclusively on the intellectual influence. In acknowledging the vacuousness of the French contribution to African culture, Naipaul's tone at the end seems wistful; Harrison's, in an outright condemnation of colonialism, is biting.

2. While Ebony distinguishes between the French and the British, he ends by placing them in the same category of "European" in opposition to the category of "African." According to him, the French create a "bourgeois people" content to live life routinely, uncommitted to change, desirous of peace and stability. Ebony sees a striking difference in the British, whom he terms "entrepreneurs . . . dedicated to radical change" (9). This attitude most closely reflects his own, which embraces the opportunity to enter a "new" or changed world and makes it appear that he has more respect for the British. Furthermore, his conscious attitude toward the French is one of contempt, so one could assume that he values any differences from the French. His conclusion about the inferiority of the French teachers is meant to sum up his various condemnations of French influence. Yet, of course, in many ways he displays the influence of these teachers in his attempts to assume the "French-inspired role as intellectual" (18). Harrison's view would provide a means for evaluating Ebony's experience. Although Harrison does not specifically discuss the French, he does see two experiences of colonization. The British held themselves apart from the natives, with the result that the natives who imitated the British, like the Indians, rejected their own culture. The French appear to be more like the Iberians, who interacted with the native culture. Harrison and Ebony would agree that the French were less separated from native cultures, but they would disagree about the extent of French influence upon Ebony. Harrison would see Ebony as assuming European values, not able to sustain his categorization of European versus African. Ebony would not admit to the extent of French culture's influence upon him, but Harrison would argue that, although Ebony does not abandon or denigrate his own culture, he has become Westernized.

3. Ebony's Volta costume and his habit of chewing a cola nut (and offering one as a sign of friendship) indicate African influences. But his compulsion to engage in "intellectual" sparring with another writer, as well as his conviction that he is living in the "new world" (even if that world involves a salary that's less than his monthly rent), reflects his fascination with Western influences. His refusal to offer any support for his convictions suggests that the cultural conflicts remain unresolved, but he does not see this as a problem. Instead, his lack of "true anxiety behind his scattered ideas," his "relishing of life," and his sense of being "relaxed, a whole man" (18) all point toward a contentedness alien to Mphahlele's artists.

PATRICK SMITH, Nippon Challenge (p. 53)

Explorations

1. Smith cites three reasons for the failure of Japan to enter a sailing team in the America's Cup competition. The first is historical: The isolationist policies of the Tokugawa shogunate in the seventeenth century prevented sea trade (para. 3). The second reason is economics. Until 1989, sailboats were considered a luxury and were so heavily taxed that few could own them (4). The last reason has to do with what Smith implies is the national personality of the Japanese. He says they lack the flexibility and swift responses necessary to be competitive sailors (5).

2. Smith quotes Japanese sailor Taro Kimura, who said that the Japanese "had wealth, but we wanted to find some other value in life besides working and producing" (10). This is the motive that finally won support for the Nippon Challenge. In his mock editorial, Kimura appealed to the desire of the Japanese to prove to the West that they are more than "economic animals" by investing "in the world's greatest meaningless event" (14–17). In his opening sentence, Smith prepares us to appreciate Kimura's comments by suggesting that Westerners rarely have a chance to see the Japanese as they really are — not, in other words, as merely "economic animals," but as people.

3. Before talking about the differences Smith identifies between Japanese and Western attitudes, it may be a good idea to have students talk about their own impressions of Japanese business and culture. This will help them recognize the stereotypes they have been exposed to. Smith identifies a difference in how the Japanese and Westerners approach competition. Westerners, Smith says, value the ability to adapt quickly, and they always aim for the top: the America's Cup "requires a dedication . . . to winning which allows nothing else to matter" (5). The Japanese, on the other hand, disdain the philosophy of individualism that permeates Western society, aiming instead to prepare well ahead of time, perfect a process, and honor tradition. Their philosophy of *wakon yosai*, meaning "Japanese spirit, Western things, . . . has not... produced the kind of inner-driven individuals needed to steer a yacht to victory" (6). Smith says the Japanese tend to copy, and improve on, Western technology rather than invent their own (7). Their philosophy of sports is not individualistic either; they value "play, participation, doing one's best as a Japanese" over winning. Smith's source for the Japanese philosophy of progress and competition comes from Japanese history books (6). He gives examples of these philosophies in action from sumo wrestling (8) and corporate life (9). His sources for information on Western attitudes come primarily from the America's Cup competition itself and personal experience as a Westerner. He says that since 1851, when the competition began, its slogan has been "There is no second" (9). The America's Cup demands individuals who are "willing to drop everything and start anew in response to technical discoveries, altered weather conditions, or a surprise development on the part of an opponent" (5); these are, according to Smith, preeminently a Western ability.

Connections

1. Students may be divided on the question of whether the Japanese decision to enter the America's Cup competition represents a desire to become more like Westerners or just to "enter the new world." The essay supports both positions. The philosophy of

modernization that brought the Japanese into the industrial age, according to Smith, is one of "Japanese spirit, Western things" (5), suggesting that the Japanese sought to master Western technologies without absorbing the Western philosophy of individualism. They would enter the new world, in that they would join in international trade and bring home certain kinds of technological knowledge, but they would not become like the "white man." However, Kimura's editorial, quoted near the end of the essay, suggests that, with their entry into the competition, the Japanese were seeking to prove that they, like Westerners, are able to invest themselves in an enterprise that emphasizes competition over cooperation and pure sport over productive work.

2. Paul Harrison's comments in "The Westernization of the World" about Japan's loss of cultural autonomy suggest that Japan was transformed by haircuts, ballroom dancing, and Western clothes (16). Harrison and Smith would agree that Japan successfully integrated Western technology into its culture, and that this transformation helped Japan achieve economic independence. However, Smith's view of Japanese culture takes into account more than the superficial signs of Western influence. He examines Japanese philosophies of life and work to reveal how they have managed to retain significant aspects of their traditional culture while enjoying the economic benefits of Westerniza- tion. However, the efforts of the Japanese to compete for the America's Cup is a sign that they are changing in more significant ways (2). The sailing competition "requires them to do so many things they have never even attempted before," including overcoming geographical and cultural isolation and adopting a Western sense of individualism and innovation.

3. In responding to this question, students may want to rely on Smith's commentary about the differences between Japanese and American perspectives on culture and competi- tion, but they will be able to learn more about what qualities a Japanese person would consider "typical American" by rereading Kimura's mock *New York Times* editorial. Kimura describes the America's Cup as "the world's greatest meaningless event," suggesting that Americans like to show off their wealth by sinking millions of dollars into an enterprise that produces nothing but an "old vase" (15). Westerners, unlike the Japanese, are not only wasteful but self-centered, in that they consider themselves to be fully human, while the Japanese are just "economic animals" (14).

ADDITIONAL QUESTIONS AND ASSIGNMENTS

1. In a journal entry or a collection of informal notes, discuss the perceptions that people in other cultures have of the West, particularly the United States. Consider such issues as materialism, views of government, the concept of freedom, and any other issues you find relevant. As you look over your notes, try to discover similarities and differences among others' perceptions and our own. Can you identify any reasons for the differences?

2. Interview someone who has come to the United States from another country, preferably a non-Western one. As you gather information, focus on the individual's response to our concepts of government, individual freedom, and rights and responsibilities, as well as the individual's perception of our culture as compared with his or her own. As you write an account of the interview, try to intersperse your own observations on the cultural differences with those of your subject.

19

3. Write a newspaper column in which you describe your reaction on finding yourself in the midst of a different culture. Even if you've never visited another country, you may recall different customs in other parts of the United States, in the city or the country, in a large university or a small college, or even in the home of a different family. Try to find one image to use as a focal point, then analyze the reasons you had trouble adjusting to the different environment.

4. Several writers in this section attempt to generalize about American culture by focusing on a particular aspect of it. Raymonde Carroll zeroes in on the significance of money in order to generalize about the American psyche. Octavio Paz analyzes the American mind by examining conventional American cuisine. Patrick Smith focuses on American sports competitiveness as a way of defining what differentiates Americans from the Japanese. Ishmael Reed's essay, by contrast, uses personal anecdotes and examples from television and other media to demonstrate that American culture is too diverse to allow for generalizations about a collective American mind. Research a single aspect of contemporary American culture (fashion, movies, art, television, architecture, cuisine, dance) in popular magazines and newspapers, searching for evidence of the diversity of American cultures. Using Reed's strategy as a model, write an analytical essay about a certain aspect of culture in which you discuss the difficulties of generalizing about American culture and the American mind.

5. Conduct further research into one of the cultures represented in this section, focusing specifically on its perception of Western culture. It would be wise to choose a culture about which information is readily available — the "Arab World," Mexico, the Soviet Union, Japan, and Africa are likely candidates. If the selection is an excerpt from a larger work, look first at that work. You can find other sources by consulting the headnotes for other selections from that culture (if there are any) and a general encyclopedia, as well as journals devoted to the study of that culture. Narrow your topic to something manageable — such as Western influence on industry, architecture, government, or sex roles; views of Western philosophy; or rejection of Western influence — and write an expository paper in which you objectively describe the culture's encounters with and reactions to Western influences.

Part Two

THE FAMILY:
CORNERSTONE OF CULTURE

INTRODUCTION

A problem that may arise in discussing any of the selections in this book is a propensity to revert to stereotyping, especially when it comes to Communist or Middle Eastern cultures. In this section, the most difficult piece to deal with objectively will be Sa'edi's "The Game Is Over": Students may need to be reminded of the overwhelming poverty and isolation of Hasani's village. But if class discussion can emphasize the profound effect of economic and geographic forces on a given society, not only will students understand Sa'edi more fully, they will be more likely to appreciate the problems faced by Adam in Erdrich's piece and others in this section as well.

A number of possible approaches to teaching this section present themselves. Among the topics explored are methods of child rearing (Soyinka, Menchú, Erdrich, Duras, and Sa'edi), the role of the family in promoting cultural values (Heng and Shapiro, Morley, Duras, Gyanranjan, and Menchú), the concept of extended family (Menchú, Gyanranjan, Morley, and Soyinka), and the various relationships among family members (all selections). The glimpses of familiar family situations provided in *Looking at Ourselves* should ease students into the section. Many will recognize the issues raised by Novak, Schroeder, Fomby, and Davis. Students' writing about their own family experiences can be used as the foundation for discussion of selections within the unit. If the students highlight first the differences and then the similarities among their own accounts, they'll be better prepared to deal with the various images of family life awaiting them in their reading. This method might be extended to the readings themselves. Students will be confident in their ability to locate differences in family life between these cultures and their own, but they may be surprised at how quickly they compile a list of similarities. From Liang Heng's feeling caught in the middle of a conflict between his parents, through Wild Christian's use of religion to keep the children in line, to Hasani's desire to make his parents suffer, students will find many points of convergence.

Instructors may wish to consult the following familiar works in preparing related selections from *Ourselves Among Others*:

Essays

Laura Cunningham, "The Girls' Room" (*New York Times*, September 10, 1981; *Sleeping Arrangements*, Knopf, 1989).
Joan Didion, "On Going Home" (*Slouching Towards Bethlehem*, Farrar, Straus, 1968).
Jane Howard, "Families" (*Families*, Simon and Schuster, 1978).
Maxine Hong Kingston, "No Name Woman" (*The Woman Warrior*, Knopf, 1976).
Adrienne Rich, "The Anger of a Child" (*Of Woman Born*, Norton, 1976).

61–184 (Text pages)

Richard Rodriguez, "Aria" (*American Scholar*, Winter 1981; *Hunger of Memory*, David R. Godine, 1982).
Arlene Skolnick, "The Paradox of Perfection" (*Wilson Quarterly*, Summer 1980).
Alice Walker, "In Search of Our Mothers' Gardens" (*In Search of Our Mothers' Gardens*, Harcourt, 1983).
E. B. White, "Once More to the Lake" (1941; *Essays of E. B. White*, Harpers, 1977).
John Edgar Wideman, "Our Time" (*Brothers and Keepers*, Henry Holt, 1984).

Short Stories

Rick De Marinis, "Gent" (*Best American Short Stories 1984*, ed. John Updike, Houghton Mifflin, 1984).
Andre Dubus, "A Father's Story" (*Selected Stories of Andre Dubus*, David R. Godine, 1988).
William Faulkner, "The Bear" (*Go Down, Moses*, Random House, 1942).
D. H. Lawrence, "A Rocking Horse Winner" (*Complete Short Stories*, Vol. 3, Penguin, 1962).
Flannery O'Connor, "Everything That Rises Must Converge" (*Complete Stories*, Farrar, Straus, 1971).
Frank O'Connor, "My Oedipus Complex" (*Collected Stories*, Knopf, 1981).
Tillie Olsen, "I Stand Here Ironing" (*Tell Me A Riddle*, Delacorte, 1961).
John Updike, "Still of Some Use" (*Trust Me*, Knopf, 1987).

BIOGRAPHICAL NOTES ON LOOKING AT OURSELVES

1. A conservative Roman Catholic educator, columnist, and political activist, Michael Novak is the author of *A Theology for Radical Politics* (1969), *The Joy of Sports: End Zones, Bases, Baskets, Balls, and the Consecration of the American Spirit* (1976), *Free Persons and the Common Good* (1988), *This Hemisphere of Liberty: A Philosophy for the Americas (1990)*, and *The Spirit of Democratic Capitalism* (1991).

2. Born in 1951 in Nashua, New Hampshire, Norman Boucher has held jobs as a factory worker, groundskeeper, teacher, and editor. For the past 15 years, he has been primarily a writer whose journalism, essays, and reviews have appeared in many newspapers and magazines, including the *Boston Globe Magazine* and *SELF* magazine.

3. William R. Mattox, Jr. is a policy analyst who focuses on work and family issues for the Family Research Council in Washington, D.C.

4. Marilyn Berlin Snell is the Managing Editor of *New Perspectives Quarterly.*

5. Patricia Schroeder, an attorney, has been a member of the House of Representatives for Colorado since 1972 and serves as the Chairman of the Select Committee on Children, Youth, and Families.

6. Angela Davis, a professor at San Francisco State University, has long been an activist on behalf of the African-American community. She is the author of *If They Come in the Morning: Voices of Resistance* (1971), *Women, Race, and Class* (1983), *Violence Against Women and the Ongoing Challenge to Racism* (1987), *Angela Davis: An Autobiography* (1988), and *Women, Culture, and Politics* (1989).

7. Paula Fomby writes for *Mother Jones*, among other publications.

8. Richard Rodriguez, a well-known opponent of bilingual education and affirmative action and a former college teacher, is the author of *Hunger of Memory* (1982) and *Days of Obligation: An Argument with My Mexican Father* (1992).

9. A Pulitzer Prize-winning columnist for the *Boston Globe*, Ellen Goodman has had several collections of her columns published, including *Close to Home* (1979), *At Large* (1981), *Keeping in Touch* (1985), and *Making Sense* (1989).

10. Christopher Lasch, a professor of history at the University of Rochester, is the author of *Haven in a Heartless World: The Family Besieged* (1979), *The Culture of Narcissism* (1983), *The Minimal Self: Psychic Survival in Troubled Times* (1985), and *The True and Only Heaven: Progress and its Critics* (1991).

Reflections

1. Neither Michael Novak nor Paula Fomby offer specific definitions of the family, but their reasons for not providing a definition are very different. In his discussion of the potential breakdown of the family under capitalism, Novak assumes a nuclear family model. His family contains middle-class husband, wife, and children, and he does not take into account racial or cultural differences. Paula Fomby also does not provide a specific definition, but that is because she knows that the traditional American family model often fails to reflect American families accurately. Fomby explains that there is no definition of the gay family, although she knows they exist because she grew up in one. At the end of the excerpt, Fomby asserts, "It's time for society to expand the definition of family" so that children will be able to be proud of whatever family they come from. Angela Davis, speaking of the tradition of the African-American family in the United States, also notes that the nuclear family model usually does not apply. Instead, Davis describes an extended-family model, in which grandmothers, grandfathers, aunts, and uncles, are integral to the family. Davis traces this family form back to its roots in the slave era and suggests both the strength and flexibility of the African-American family when she writes, "The creativity with which African-American people improvised family connections is a cultural trait that has spanned the centuries" (para. 3). As students discuss which definition of family makes the most sense to them, they should consider how their own backgrounds affect their preference for a certain definition of "family."

2. Many students will begin to address this question by expressing the assumption that the breakdown of the American family means the loss of working-class and middle-class nuclear families (this is, father, mother, and their biological children) as a result of divorce, economic pressures, and working mothers. This view of American families has become almost commonplace, and it is reflected in several pieces in *Looking at Ourselves*. Michael Novak's piece focuses on middle- and upper-middle-class families that are vulnerable to economic forces that "shear marriages and families apart." William Mattox sees single parenting as indicative of the breakdown of American families. Marilyn Berlin Snell says that the "traditional" family broke up when fathers started leaving home every day to go to work, and Patricia Schroeder says that the family is "breaking down . . . because we don't give it any support." Angela Davis, speaking of African-American families, contends that they are not "breaking down" as some have said, because throughout American history they never matched the white model of the nuclear family. Davis's piece may provide the best point of view for considering the significance of writers' assertions that the American family is "breaking down." In Davis's view, extended

23

families, in which grandmothers raise grandchildren, are not a sign of a family "breaking down," but instead are a sign of the strength and flexibility of families. Novak, Mattox, Schroeder, and Snell all speak of families collapsing, rather than considering the efforts people make to adapt their family structures and daily routines to economic and social pressures — efforts that may be the sign of a strong family, rather than a family on the verge of collapse.

3. Students should be able to collect a long and diverse list of the most valuable functions of family, aside from those mentioned in the pieces included in *Looking at Ourselves*. Michael Novak writes that "the family is the primary teacher of moral development" and is the source of an individual's "creativity, psychic energy, social dynamism." Capitalism, and the individualism and greed capitalism breeds, have prevented families from fulfilling their functions. William Mattox says that two-parent families provide "structure" and that households headed by single mothers fail to do this. He claims that children reared by single mothers are vulnerable to a startlingly comprehensive list of emotional and intellectual deficits, including depression, aggression, mental illness, and gang membership. Patricia Schroeder, more sympathetic to women's efforts to work and raise their families, writes that the family functions as the "basic building block of our society," but that governmental spending on defense, coupled with a widespread lack of regard for the financial needs of families, prevents families from functioning as healthy, strong social units. Davis writes that the extended African-American family "has functioned as a child-care system available to working parents," but that increasing poverty and drug use, caused by the social and economic pressures of racism, make it hard for families to continue functioning. Ellen Goodman writes that the family is "the one social glue strong enough to withstand the centrifuge of special interests." She sees the emphasis on individuality, and especially segregation according to age, as potential obstacles to family connections. And Christopher Lasch, who seems to consider the family as a child-care unit, sees the introduction of group childcare as a menace to the integrity of the individual and the family. Throughout these selections, the family's primary function is defined as raising children. Threats to that function come from the outside, in the form of economic or social pressures, and from the inside, in the form of working mothers, absent fathers, and an emphasis on individuality.

4. Several major disagreements emerge among writers on issues such as childcare and family structure. Christopher Lasch and William Mattox (on the one hand) and Angela Davis and Patricia Schroeder (on the other) are diametrically opposed on the issue of how to manage childcare in the American family. Lasch contends that placing children in childcare may cause them to become incapable "of deciding on their own what [is] good or bad." Although he does not recommend that mothers begin to stay home with children, this is one of the most likely results of decreasing the amount of time children spend in childcare. Single mothers are among those who work while raising children; William Mattox blames them for children's emotional and physical problems and implies that only the two-parent family can resolve the problem. Patricia Schroeder, by contrast, argues that the realities of women's lives demand that they work, and that the government and corporations can and should support their efforts to raise families by helping them with childcare. Angela Davis argues that "society has refused to assume more responsibility for the economic well-being of its members and for the care and education of our children." Some of the problems facing families could be solved, she contends, by making good childcare available to everyone.

24

RIGOBERTA MENCHÚ, Birth Ceremonies (p. 76)

Explorations:

1. Among the Quiché Indians, the parent-child relationship serves as a model for relationships between leaders and community members. The man and woman elected as leaders bear parental responsibility for the entire community and become grandparents to every child born (para. 1). Thinking of the community as an extended family has several advantages for the Quiché. Because they live under harsh conditions as a marginalized group in Guatemala, the Quiché need to maintain close connections with each other, offering each other material and emotional sustenance. The Quiché religion is also based on a parent-child model, in which the sun is father and the moon is mother to the people (12). The ceremonies that introduce the newborn child to family and community integrate him or her "in the universe." The emphasis on parent-child relationships in Quiché society and religion helps to remind people of their close connections with their ancestors, encouraging group solidarity and a deep commitment to traditional values and customs important for physical and psychological survival.

2. Each ceremony for the Quiché child marks an important milestone in her or his progress as a member of the community. Before the baby's birth, the mother and father together inform community leaders that a child is on the way so that leaders can prepare to accept the child into the community (1). Each child is born in the presence of carefully selected couples representing both family and community and is introduced to family and friends with ceremonies and celebrations. For eight days following the birth, the child is left alone with his mother while neighbors bring gifts (7). These gifts, and the feasting and celebration that follow, solidify the child's position as a community member. Other customs, including tying a bag of talismans around the baby's neck, binding the baby's hands and feet, and lighting candles at the four corners of his or her bed, symbolize important aspects of Quiché life that the child will eventually be expected to understand and respect (10, 8). The care with which children are inducted as community members impresses on everyone the need for mutual support if the Quiche are to survive as a culturally intact group.

3. The child's education about future responsibilities begins before birth, when the mother introduces her unborn child to the natural world and to the culture by talking to her or him about Quiché life (2). When the child is eight days old, a ceremony introduces him or her to the community and the parents tell the child about the family's suffering to symbolically prepare him or her to live a hard life with dignity (9). At a large gathering forty days after a child is born, parents and community leaders promise to teach the child to follow Quiché traditions and keep the community's secrets safe from outsiders (11). They voice the expectation that the child will grow up to live as his or her ancestors did and will one day become a parent to help multiply the race. When the child reaches the age of ten, parents and village leaders again reinforce traditional values by talking to the child formally about the necessity of honoring ancestors and carrying out responsibilities toward the community (13). Throughout childhood, boys and girls are introduced to gender-specific responsibilities; girls are taught to care for the family and prepare to become mothers, and boys are prepared for their future responsibilities as heads of the family.

Connections

1. Ellen Goodman invokes an American holiday, Thanksgiving, as a celebration of intergenerational family ties. Family, she says, is the only social institution that may help us to withstand the pressures that categorize each generation as a "special interest group," a tendency that dissolves connections among family members. According to Rigoberta Menchú, the family in Quiché society plays a similar role, but students will need to recognize that the pressures that might pull the Quiché apart are very different from those that affect the middle-class American family Ellen Goodman analyzes. Many of the birth customs Menchú discusses are ways of reinforcing family and community ties to help the Quiché ensure survival and resist oppression and appropriation by the dominant culture. The American family in Goodman's analysis is part of the dominant culture; family unity is threatened not by oppression or material want, but by an emphasis on individualism that segregates family members from one another.

2. In Quiché society, children are integrated into the life of the community, so that no arrangements for formal childcare need be made. Each child belongs not only to his or her parents, but to the community as a whole. Children are not segregated in schools during the day, but are educated at home and in the neighborhood. Even as small children, they work alongside their parents. Although the Quiché solution to the problems of childcare may seem attractive, it would not work in the United States, where most parents must work outside the home. Although the middle-class working mother Pat Schroeder refers to is usually considered to have primary responsibility for childcare, she cannot emulate the Quiché mother and have her children work alongside her. Furthermore, her "community" has no responsibility to provide childcare, and women are expected to give up gainful employment so that they can stay at home to care for children. According to Schroeder, the government's refusal to take some responsibility for childcare pays homage to a "mythical family" in which the mother wants to stay home and can afford to do so, but in reality the lack of government support for childcare tends to pull families apart.

3. Both Novak and Menchú emphasize the importance of the family in teaching values to children. Novak says the family in American culture has a diminishing importance, as post-industrial capitalism promotes liberty and hedonism, values that tend to dissolve emotional bonds between parents and children. Under more ideal conditions, Novak maintains, the family would be the primary social and economic unit, and American children would learn "basic trust." Novak's ideal American family seems to have much in common with the Quiché family Menchú describes. According to Menchú, the primary values children learn in Quiché society are to respect traditions and help support the life of the community through hard work and deep involvement in community affairs. Children are taught to be proud of their family and their people's history and to resist the efforts of outsiders to lure them away from their own culture and religion. One of the problems students may encounter in responding to this question is that, while Menchú's discussion deals with a relatively small and distinct community, Novak's comments on the "American family" may invite generalizations that ignore economic and cultural difference among American families. For instance, it will be important for students to recall that the family Novak is concerned with is "upwardly mobile," and that, as Pat Schroeder points out, in reality many American children live in poverty.

4. Most students will recognize that Rodriguez's and Menchú's accounts of childhood have in common a model of relationships between adults and children. The model is based on the children's familial respect for adults, but it is also based on the children's integration into the life of the community. Both these aspects of childhood might seem unusual to many U.S. students. Menchú discusses how tribal government draws on models of parent-child relationships; the elected leaders, for instance, are regarded as the community's mother and father (see Explorations #1 above). In Rodriguez's account, he recalls that the Catholic priest was called Father, and that the use of familial terms for nuns and priests "implied that a deep bond existed between my teachers and me as fellow Catholics." The sense of extended family, and a tightly knit community in which members share a common world view and spirituality, are factors that influence both Rodriguez's and Menchú's accounts of childhood.

LOUISE ERDRICH (Er-drick), Adam (p. 88)

Explorations

1. For Louise Erdrich, perhaps the hardest part of mothering Adam is achieving enough patience to deal with the day-to-day struggle of living with a child who has Fetal Alcohol Syndrome. She mentions this problem early on (paras. 5, 6), but its full impact becomes most clear when Erdrich relates her conflict with Adam over his refusal to eat dinner (10-37). Nevertheless, Erdrich appreciates the rewards of mothering Adam, including the ease with which he initially accepted her as his mother (10). But the deeper rewards have to do with gaining self-knowledge. Erdrich writes, "In the years I've spent with Adam, I have learned more about my limits than I ever wanted to know," but the pain of that knowledge is offset by the "bond of absolute simplicity, love" that has developed between her and Adam.

2. Most students will understand the poignancy of Erdrich's statement that a day when Adam has a seizure is "no special day" in her family. Erdrich's attitude is one of patience and resignation. Her calm, nurturing treatment of Adam after he falls shows first of all how much she cares, but it also shows how common this event is. The grand mal seizure would be an acute crisis in a family less accustomed to dealing with a major disability, but for Erdrich it is an unremarkable incident.

3. Some students may find the opening paragraphs of Erdrich's essay as confusing as they are intriguing. Until paragraph 5, when Erdrich defines Adam's disability, students will wonder about Adam's seizure and Erdrich's calm response. Erdrich's explanation of Fetal Alcohol Syndrome will take care of any confusion, but to help students think about the choices Erdrich has made about style and organization, it may be helpful to ask them to discuss the shift in Erdrich's tone as she begins to define Fetal Alcohol Syndrome. In paragraph 5, Erdrich gives facts about the syndrome and states her opinion of women who drink while pregnant: "It's a lot of fate to play with for the sake of a moment's relaxation." If Erdrich had begun with this paragraph, her tone would have sounded merely judgmental, since her readers would not have understood that Fetal Alcohol Syndrome has a daily impact on her life and her adopted child's life.

Connections

1. In describing how her family came into being, Erdrich says, "it simply happened" (para. 6), but in fact it was a deliberate process. Her husband, Michael, had adopted Adam and two other children while he was single; Erdrich accepted them into her life along with their father, and she adopted the children a year after she and Michael married. Erdrich doesn't define "family" directly, but many students will understand that it is unlikely she would define it according to the nuclear model of two parents biologically related to their children. In *Looking at Ourselves*, Paula Fomby asserts, "It's time for society to expand the definition of family" so that children will be able to be proud of whatever family they come from. Fomby is concerned with gay families, but her comments would apply equally well to the nontraditional family that Erdrich has helped to create. Angela Davis, in her discussion of African-American families, also refutes the idea that the nuclear family model is superior. Instead, Davis describes an extended-family model, in which grandmothers, grandfathers, aunts, and uncles are integral to the family. This model would probably appeal to Erdrich, because she recognizes that the problems that face the Native American community can best be dealt with by emphasizing tribal values (50).

2. Patricia Schroeder mentions that one of the major problems of childcare is that legislation fails to acknowledge or support the realities of family life in the United States. Although nine out of ten women must work (2), the United States does "less than any other industrialized nation: In terms of tax breaks, we would do better raising thoroughbred dogs or horses than children" (4). Erdrich would probably agree with Schroeder's assessment of the problems of childcare, and she might also argue that the lack of government support for the real needs of women and children contributes to the erosion of family and community in some Native American communities. Erdrich mentions the dedication of Adam's teacher (6), and says she and Michael have provided for Adam's care in their wills (10), but for the most part they seem to have dealt with child-care problems by sharing responsibilities between themselves.

3. It will be a challenge for students to identify the similarities between Erdrich's middle-class Native American family and Rigoberta Menchú's description of Quiché Indian families. A good beginning would be to consider how both Erdrich and Menchú discuss the need for an extended family structure and community involvement in bearing and raising children. Menchú says that children belong not just to the parents but to the entire community (1), an idea Erdrich would agree with because she believes women have a responsibility, not only to their own children but also to the community at large, to have pregnancies free of alcohol (44–49). In Menchú's description of the treatment of pregnant women in the Quiché tribe, she gives many examples of the ways in which the community functions as a large and caring family. Community members monitor the health and nutrition of the pregnant woman, taking responsibility for her welfare: "You must treat her with respect so that she recognizes it and conveys this to the baby inside her" (17).

LIANG HENG and JUDITH SHAPIRO, Chairman Mao's Good Little Boy (p. 97)

Explorations

1. There seems to be no positive definition of Rightist in Mao's China of the 1950s; rather the term refers to anyone who questions the Revolution. The standard definition refers to capitalist tendencies, but the application of the title seems to have little to do with that ideology. A *revolutionary*, unlike a Rightist, conforms to the Revolution unquestioningly. (Some students may recognize the paradox in this interpretation of the term.) The events in this selection suggest that at the time Liang's mother was discredited, the truest test of the revolutionary was his or her denunciation of enemies of the Revolution.

2. Liang's parents either live in dormitories or travel, so the children live with their grandparents. His parents view the Revolution as more important than raising their children. When Liang's mother is disgraced, the children are moved from the maternal to the paternal grandmother's home (really her son's dormitory apartment). Had the father been disgraced, he would have lost the apartment, which was allocated to him as an employee of the *Hunan Daily*. Had this happened, both his mother and his children would have been homeless. By exercising such control over family life, and by providing favored workers with housing, the Party is able to ensure loyalty to the state. The work environment is used in much the same way. When Liang's mother is disgraced, one of her worst punishments is to lose her job and salary. The intrusion into every aspect of an individual's life tightens government control over the individual while discouraging loyalties to anything other than the government, even to family, thus preventing the spread of ideas that might interfere with the Revolution.

3. The absence of understanding and judgment exhibited in the first paragraph indicates that it is being told from the point of view of the child himself. Students may need a bit of encouragement to notice that when he talks of his fear that Waipo has forgotten him, Liang makes no comment on the irrationality of that fear. He also refrains from characterizing the foolishness of his escape. All we see is the experience as it appears to the child. But while limited, his consciousness rebels naturally against the constraints of the child-care center and the society it mimics. In the last sentence we see the value Liang places on freedom; words like "exploded" and "dazzling" raise the experience to a heroic level. The implication is that even a young child can recognize the abuses of human dignity suffered by those subjected to such a regime.

Connections

1. The contexts and outcomes of the estrangements between mother and child are very different in Heng and Shapiro's "Chairman Mao's Good Little Boy," Erdrich's "Adam," and Fomby's selection in *Looking at Ourselves*. The estrangement between Liang and his mother is by far the harshest and longest. Liang's father, family, government, and school system all work to keep Liang and his mother apart. She tries hard to keep contact with her children and to work her way back into the good graces of the Party (paras. 24, 36, 41), but she cannot overcome the effect on her children of hearing their mother constantly condemned. Liang implies that he and his mother eventually had a reconciliation, because he is able to write much of the story from her perspective (19, 20) and because,

as a mature man, he understands that she was unjustly accused and lived an agonizingly isolated life as a result (22). In Erdrich's "Adam," the estrangement between mother and child has to do with the pressures of living with Adam's disability. The specific event that causes Erdrich to tell Adam "Don't call me Mom" is a battle over food (11–37). It takes years to fully mend the rift between them (40). Adam's disability makes it difficult for him to relate to others, but Erdrich's day-to-day care of Adam does much to overcome the distance between them. Paula Fomby's relationship with her gay mother was ambivalent, but not truly estranged. Fomby writes, "In order to live peaceably, I accepted my mother's lifestyle a long time ago; feeling comfortable with it has come more recently" (5). Fomby "grew up in the closet" (1), which made her feel isolated and overly protective of her family, but with maturity she realized that there were many benefits to being raised in a gay family.

2. In the United States, group childcare, especially if it is funded by the government, has sometimes been seen as a step toward communism. For instance, Richard Nixon vetoed the Comprehensive Child Development Act of 1971, which would have provided federal funds for childcare. He argued that it sided with a "communal approach" to childrearing over a "family-centered approach." Issues of childcare have as much to do with national political goals as with families and communities. The goal of the child-care system in China was to produce children who would serve the government obediently; Liang writes that he was "sent off to the child-care center for early training in Socialist thought through collective living, far from the potentially corrupting influence of family life" (3). Pat Schroeder argues that in the United States the family is "an economic unit and basic building block of our society" (5). Affordable, adequate childcare is one essential way of reinforcing the family and preparing children for school, but few would argue that group childcare in the United States is specifically intended to indoctrinate children, either into communism (as Nixon argued) or capitalism.

3. Novak believes that the capitalist system places an emphasis on money and success that makes people neglect their family bonds and look outside the family for emotional satisfaction. Yet Liang and Shapiro's description of a Communist society shows some of the same problems, although in China people do not suffer from "too much emotional space" or a surplus of material goods. In fact, economic scarcity and the desire to succeed, which means obtaining rank in the Communist Party, make people willing to promote Party over family loyalty. Students could argue that many of the members of Liang's family remain close. He has strong attachments to his grandmothers; his maternal uncle defends his mother; and early on he sticks up for his mother as well. But the political stigma faced by the family destroys it as a nuclear group when the mother becomes an outcast. Comparing Liang's family with their own, most students will undoubtedly prefer the system with which they are familiar. While Novak paints a devastating picture of American family life, most students will find it limited to an economically affluent class to which they may not belong. Liang and Shapiro's narrative of Chinese family life pertains to the largest population group. Therefore, "on balance," most students will choose the American system as providing the better climate for families, since family members here are never asked to repudiate their relatives in order to succeed.

4. Liang and Shapiro show that the family in China is composed of several generations and that they interact on a daily basis. While this "social glue" may derive from the traditional arrangement whereby brides moved in with their husbands' families, the great shortage

of housing space in modern China reinforces the necessity of the arrangement. Three generations of Liang's family live together in his grandmother Nai Nai's house. His grandmother Waipo raises him before he goes to day care, and his maternal uncle, along with his wife and three small children, still lives with her. And when Liang's father thinks about divorcing his wife, even though he is a grown man, he consults his mother (40).

WOLE SOYINKA (Woe-lay Shoy-ING-ka), Nigerian Childhood (p. 112)

Explorations

1. The integration of Anglicanism and traditional magic will probably serve as a source of amusement for students. The characters seem to find no contradiction in weaving magic throughout the fabric of the religion they have been taught. In fact, the combination seems to work wonders as far as keeping children in line is concerned: Wild Christian's story of the encounter with the wood sprites is a case in point. Her lament that faith and discipline are no longer valued follows her account of the children's failure to obey the oro's orders to stay away from his place in the woods. Reverend J. J., an Anglican minister, respects the wood sprites, and when the children are chased out of the woods after disobeying the order, he whips them (after, of course, invoking the power of the Christian God to keep off the sprites). Uncle Sanya is punished too, for his stubbornness — one of the greatest of sins. Even the children themselves respond to the twin traditions: They abandon their evening visits to the woods after the incident with the wood sprites. Students may need some guidance in recognizing the essential similarity of the religion and the tradition, namely, that both depend on faith in a power greater than that of any human.

2. The stories of Reverend J. J. emphasize the need for faith (his stand against the wood sprites), perseverance (his refusal to give up preaching despite the egungun's warning), and respect for tradition (his following the old woman's orders when Sanya was ill). An interesting sideline is the narrator's confusion between perseverance and stubbornness: Try as he might, he cannot keep from characterizing Reverend J. J.'s perseverance in the face of warnings as something fearfully close to the "sin" of stubbornness.

3. Although it is sometimes difficult for students to recognize subtle changes in point of view, a close look at the selection will reveal that even though Soyinka speaks in the voice of an adult, he sees things with the eyes of a child. His grasp of history, as well as his ability to articulate his conflicting responses to his mother's stories (the sense that the children's fright was punishment enough for their foray into the woods, the feeling that Reverend J. J.'s perseverance was really stubbornness) are indications that we're hearing this story from an adult. But Bishop Crowther's apparition is definitely the experience of a child: The fact that the author never questions its authenticity allows us to perceive the experience as the child does. His matter-of-fact accounts of his mother's stories reinforce the sense that these are the observations of a child. Even when Lawanle pulls him away for his bath, we feel the reluctance of the child. More perceptive students will also point to Soyinka's mature vocabulary and style as evidence of an adult voice recounting these experiences from the point of view of a child.

31

Connections

1. Many students will be confused initially by young Soyinka's encounters with Bishop Ajayi
    Crowther. Soyinka describes the Bishop not as a dream image or fantasy, but as a figure
    who is as real as the bougainvillea from which he emerges. Students may find it easier
    to accept the interweaving of fantasy and reality in this passage (and, later, in Wild
    Christian's stories) if they are given a term for the technique: magic realism, an approach
    that gives imagination and fantasy the same authority usually accorded to supposedly
    solid, external reality. The story with which Soyinka opens his narrative is extremely
    important because it creates the context for his mother's story about Uncle Sanya. Soyinka
    knows from his own encounters with the Bishop that he should take Wild Christian's story
    seriously, and his respect for her story signals the reader to follow suit. Liang Heng's story
    about his abortive escape from the child-care center also helps to create a context for his
    mother's story of her ostracism at the hands of her community and family. Liang's attempt
    to escape the center, and the fact that Waipo forces him to return, suggests how
    thoroughly politicized the family is. The same revolutionary loyalty (and fear of
    retaliation) that motivates Waipo also causes Liang's father to denounce his supposedly
    Rightist wife and approve of her exile.

2. Children in "Nigerian Childhood" seem to have few responsibilities. Even their gathering
    of firewood, snails, mushrooms, and berries is partly a game (paras. 1, 14, 35, 38).
    Rigoberta Menchú describes significant responsibilities for children in the Quiché
    community, including, for girls, cleaning, mending, and washing, and, for boys, working
    in the fields. Yoruban children, as Soyinka describes them, have more freedom to play
    and are not asked to contribute as much work to the family and community.

3. At the end of his essay Naipaul suggests that Western ways and ideas are overlaid upon
    a much more vibrant and deep-seated indigenous African tradition. When the Westerners
    themselves disappear, the order they have created barely sustains itself. Thus Naipaul
    sees a dichotomy: the "real life . . . in another realm of the spirit," which stems from the
    traditional values versus the "false, arbitrary ritual" of forms that mimic Western ways and
    standards. In Soyinka's story, perhaps because it is narrated from a child's point of view,
    no suggestion of such a dichotomy exists. Instead, Soyinka's story shows how perfectly
    the traditions of American religion and African magic have become intertwined. Wild
    Christian's story demonstrates the intense faith of the Reverend J. J. and the miracles
    worked on behalf of the Christian as well as the continuing existence and powers of the
    African spirit world. The structures of English life — the church and the boarding school
    — continue to flourish without the English presence, and Wild Christian looks back to
    earlier days to lament the loss of the intensity of the early converts' faith, not of her
    forefathers' religion. Unlike Ebony, she does not try to disassociate herself from the
    English colonizers. Like Ebony, she has been influenced by both traditions; however,
    while he denies this influence even as he displays it, Wild Christian has remained
    unaware of a need to analyze her relationship to a Western tradition.

4. How students view Soyinka's extended family will depend to some extent on the
    structure of their own families. Those who have had grandparents, cousins, or informally
    adopted family members living with them will identify with the African tradition. The
    specific evidence in "Nigerian Childhood" that Soyinka's family was part of an extended-
    family tradition is Wild Christian's and Sanya's upbringing in their grand uncle's home
    and the presence of "Auntie" Lawanle as a nanny in Wild Christian's home. Soyinka's

use of quotations around "Auntie" suggests that Lawanle is not a blood relative, but an adopted family member (22). Soyinka does not feel a need to explain the extended family structures in these families, because they are a common feature of African life, as they are in some African-American households.

JOHN DAVID MORLEY, Acquiring a Japanese Family (p. 122)

Explorations

1. Few American students have had the experience of living with the almost complete lack of privacy Boon encounters while living with Sugama, so they will be able to sympathize with Boon's perplexity as he considers how differently he will have to live in a house without firm inside walls. In order to understand the "corporate" concept that defines Japanese family relationships, Morley analyzes the term uchi, which means both "household" and "I." The term suggests the inseparability of self, home, and family; "I" does not mean an individual, but "the representative of my house in the world outside" (para. 35).

2. Responses to this question may vary with students' ethnic backgrounds. Some may recognize the respect accorded adults in the Japanese family, as well as the patronizing attitude that accompanies that respect. (Note Sugama's amusement at his aunt's and uncle's fears.) These students may also understand the older adults' treatment of their young adult relatives: It seems that in Japan, your parents can always tell you what to do, regardless of your age or accomplishments. Those unfamiliar with this relationship will probably find vast differences between the obligations of a young adult Japanese and his or her American counterpart. Whereas the young Japanese are responsible for their parents' welfare, most Americans view themselves as responsible only to themselves and their children. (An interesting discussion may ensue if you ask students which situation they feel is better or more compassionate.)

3. The first-person narrator often makes for a more limited perspective; Morley achieves a broader view of the meeting of cultures by writing through a third-person narrator. Boon's introduction to the apartment reveals him to be a foreigner: He is awed by the open spaces and especially by the concept of family indivisibility that leads to such construction. He must accustom himself to the apparent "classlessness" (36) of most Japanese homes. Perhaps more striking, however, are Boon's comic reaction to meeting Sugama's mother and his overtly Western advice to Sugama that the latter's plans for marriage are nobody else's business. In contrast, Boon's choice of living quarters, his increasing facility with the language, and his preference for Japanese food make him less foreign. By showing all this through Boon's eyes, Morley is able to remain distant. Both he and the reader can judge Boon's reactions and behavior objectively.

4. This question provides a wonderful opportunity to discuss the importance of apparent "sidelights" to the story as a whole. Without the descriptions of the house or the story of the earthquake, we would have to rely on exposition for information about Japanese

notions of family, home, respect for elders, reliance on what Westerners would consider superstition, perceptions of foreigners. The list goes on. Responses to the second part of the question may again underscore the different backgrounds of students; if it does, discussion should be quite lively.

Connections

1. Skeptical students will be surprised that both Morley and Soyinka approach their characters' superstitions in a matter-of-fact way. Sugama tells the story of his great-aunt's faith in her fortune-teller's prediction without ridicule. Morley describes Sugama's relatives and their superstitions with the bemused humor that is characteristic of the entire essay. He notes, for instance that "everything they touched turned to farce" (para. 59), but he describes his initial meetings with Sugama and his mother with similar humor. Soyinka treats his characters' superstitions and their encounters with spirits with a similar respect, but more importantly, Wild Christian has specific reasons for telling her children uncanny tales. She wants to teach her children to respect religion, a motive evident in her story about how J. J. Ransome-Kuti was able to send the *iwin* away because he had a power that comes from faith and discipline (20, 21). To help students talk about their own responses to the superstitions Morley and Soyinka describe, it may be helpful to ask students to talk about superstitions they, or their relatives or friends, believe in. Some of the superstitions they describe will serve purposes similar to those evident in Morley and Soyinka's narrative: to help in dealing with real fears (of earthquakes or strangers, for instance), or to give a feeling of having control over events.

2. Although the problem may be similar, students should recognize at once a few essential differences between the Chinese and Japanese handling of overcrowding: For one thing, the lottery used to award apartments would be anathema to the Chinese, who see it as the duty of the state to house all its citizens. Furthermore, the Chinese would scoff at the apparent ineptitude of the Japanese civil servants, who swallow Sugama's increasingly preposterous explanations of his grandfather's absence. Such behavior, looked upon by Japanese (and Westerners) as inventive if a bit underhanded, would be viewed as a serious crime against the people in China. Yet students should recognize some similarities as well: Both cultures share a healthy respect for the institution of the family (as long as it doesn't interfere with the state in China) and the responsibility of each family member to the others; the multiple uses of each room and the lack of private bedrooms underscore the solidarity of the family. Both cultures also view individual goals and accomplishments in light of the larger good (in China the state, in Japan the family). Although they both foster the concept of family as "social glue," in China the strength of the family is a means to achieve the ultimate goal, the good of the state. In Japan, the family appears to be an end in itself.

3. In both pieces the concept of the family as bastion against the onslaughts of a hostile world is upheld. Novak, of course, laments the undermining of this concept in the United States, whereas Morley reveals that it thrives in Japan (Sugama's response to his aunt and uncle's fear is a case in point). Novak sees the corporate influence, with its constant push for success and its insensitivity to the need for roots, as the culprit in the assault on the American family. That same capitalist concentration on advancement presents Sugama with his dilemma of whether to marry and return to his home or to remain single and successful in the city. But Japan's culture was not built on capitalism or the concept of

free enterprise; students may be surprised to observe a country in which the prevalent economic system is rooted in an entirely different philosophy from the cultural traditions. This cultural base seems to be the force that keeps capitalism from disrupting family life in Japan the way it has in the United States.

GYANRANJAN (Gee-ahn-ran-jan), Our Side of the Fence and Theirs (p. 134)

Explorations

1. It may be difficult for students to appreciate the protective role of the parents, especially the father, with regard to daughters. They can see no real danger confronting the girls in the family; nevertheless, the narrator is appalled by his neighbors' lack of concern for their daughter's safety. According to the story, parents must protect their children, especially the girls, from real or imagined harm and must provide for their future protection by selecting suitable husbands for them. Equally difficult for today's students to appreciate will be the notion of absolute obedience to parents. In the India of this story, children uphold tradition, never questioning their parents. The entire family, it seems, must act (in private as well as in public) according to long-standing rules of appropriate behavior.

2. It's easy to miss, upon first reading the story, that this is an extended family of adults. The narrator is apparently a high-school or college student (his naïveté makes it difficult to tell), and his brother and sister-in-law, as well as his grandmother, live with the family. Instead of concentrating on standard characteristics, the narrator is fascinated with how people relate to one another — he's astounded when he sees the family next door laughing together, for example. He becomes more and more interested in what makes people happy.

3. His fascination with the family is readily apparent, but students may initially miss the evidence of what psychologists call an attraction-aversion response. Some of his judgments involve calling their life-style "unusual" and "careless" in paragraph 3, and "strange" in paragraph 4, criticizing the mother and daughter for failing to notice that the latter's dupatta had fallen from her shoulder, exposing part of her breast in paragraph 6; and commenting on their lack of curiosity about the narrator's family in paragraph 8; among others. Yet all the while that he is criticizing their behavior, we sense his longing to be like them. They are easygoing and self-sufficient, never caring about what others think — they're probably quite Westernized. And the narrator, in comparing his family with theirs, implicitly condemns his family's rigid adherence to tradition, musing at one point, "If only I'd been born in that home!" (15).

4. It's important for students to realize that by taking the dialogue out of context, and simply reporting bits of it as he recounts his narrative of the wedding, the narrator creates the effect of hearing a series of speeches pronouncing judgment on the family next door. Previously, we've been privy only to the narrator's thoughts; his failure to include dialogue until this point preserves the filter through which we see the neighbors. The technique also enhances his increasing feeling of isolation. By using dialogue at the end, he allows us to see where his attitudes come from. More important, however, he creates

an image of solidarity in his family — something he sorely needs now that the primary object of his attraction-aversion has gone. Gyanranjan leaves us with quite a powerful image, as the lone critic joins the "bazaar of neighbor-criticism . . . doing a heated business."

Connections

1. Both Boon and Gyanranjan's narrator place themselves in the position of observers, separating themselves from the views of those around them. Boon is clearly "the American" to Sugama's aunt and uncle, even though he disappoints their expectations. He is an outsider who seeks to understand and adapt himself to a new culture. Gyanranjan's narrator separates himself from his family's values by casting longing glances into the neighbors' yard and imagining what his life would be like if he lived in that happier, more lenient environment. Boon never draws any contrasts, but Gyanranjan's narrator is constantly comparing the rituals of the neighboring household with those of his own and passing judgment. Even after he has learned the neighbor's religion, which seems to temper his enthusiasm for growing up in their household, his final remark passes a harsh judgment on his own family, contrasting their critical gossip with the other household's silence.

2. Focusing on a child narrator allows both Gyanranjan and Liang to look from a fresh viewpoint at family and social pressures to conform. Their child narrators don't fully understand the demands of conformity, and they share their questioning and doubts with the reader. In the first paragraph of "Our Side of the Fence and Theirs," the narrator believes that his family is "respectable, honorable" because of the way they protect their daughters and honor traditional customs. Therefore, the neighbors who do things differently are not to be trusted. But in the same paragraph, he also describes himself as curious about strangers. He has not altogether adopted the prejudices of his elders. He observes the neighbors' daughter laughing without restraint with a mixture of disapproval and fascination (para. 6). Later he recalls how any free show of affection between men and women is considered shameful in his family (12), but nevertheless he is attracted to the freedom and easy affection the neighbor family display for each other. At one point, he thinks, "If only I'd been born in that home!" (15). In Liang and Shapiro's "Chairman Mao's Good Little Boy," Liang learns about the pressures of conformity at the age of three, when he is punished for escaping from the child-care center and reprimanded by the nurses: "you haven't upheld Revolutionary discipline" (11). Liang's youthful innocence and incomprehension about why he is in disgrace helps the authors explore the far more complex problems that beset his mother when she is labelled a rightist and expelled from her job, family, and community, since she is as blameless as her son.

3. Students should immediately recognize the similarity between Novak's plea for a stronger commitment to family and the narrator's fear of anything that seems to shake family traditions. The idea that strongly defined gender roles are essential to family is represented in the selection by Marilyn Berlin Snell; a similar idea is reflected in the sense of danger felt by the narrator's family about the apparent freedom of the women in the neighboring family. Ironically, although the neighbor family seems relatively Westernized, it's difficult to find much similarity between their views and those in *Looking at Ourselves*. There may be some sympathy between them and Fomby, however, who finds

that her family evokes the same kind of anxiety that the narrator experiences in regard to his alien neighbors. Students might enjoy thinking about Goodman's definition of family — "the people who maintain an unreasonable interest in each other," in light of the narrator's "unreasonable" interest in his neighbors.

VED MEHTA (MAY-tah), Pom's Engagement (p. 142)

Explorations

1. It is primarily Daddyji who is responsible for arranging for Pom's engagement to Kakaji. Daddyji says a girl's *parents* investigate prospective grooms and make the selection, but Daddyji alone makes the journey to talk with Kakaji's family, and it is Kakaji's uncle who has the power to accept or refuse the engagement. Both Kakaji and Pom have some power over whether they will marry each other, but both accept their elders' choices (paras. 17, 79).

2. Most American students will find the idea of an arranged marriage disturbing. In order to help them understand Daddyji's views, it would be helpful to begin with his comments in paragraph 77 on Western marriages. He admits that there is some injustice in the Indian system, but he also notes that the Western method of marrying for romantic love probably doesn't work any better. Daddyji's views of marriage come out during his conversation with two of his daughters, Umi and Nimi, who express the feminist view that both men and women should have the right think for themselves and contribute equally to a marriage. Daddyji argues that although Pom may have to suffer for years and make many sacrifices while she tries to get used to living with and serving her husband and his family (69), this will ultimately bring her the greatest happiness, which he describes as "a uniting of ideals and purposes" between husband and wife (71).

3. The process involved in bringing about the marriage of Pom and Kakaji is very different from courtship processes in American cultures. It might be useful to have students make a step-by-step comparison between courtship in their own culture and the one Mehta describes. The process in "Pom's Engagement" begins with Daddyji's investigation of Kakaji and Kakaji's family (1); then he visits the prospective groom and discusses with them the possibility of a marriage. Only months later, when Kakaji and his family have expressed serious interest, do Daddyji and Mamaji tell Pom and her siblings of her impending engagement. There follows a brief meeting between Pom and Kakaji under her parents' watchful eyes (36–45) and a letter from his family making a formal offer of marriage (46). Mamaji then consults an astrologer to set the wedding date (80). Once this is arranged, an engagement ceremony, with prayers, songs, food, an engagement ring for Pom, and an exchange of gifts, formalizes the engagement.

4. The blind child focuses on the sounds and smells of the house when preparations are being made for Kakaji's arrival, and on the sound of the prospective husband's footfall and voice: "His footfall was heavy . . . his greeting was affectionate, and . . . his voice seemed to float up with laughter" (33). He also notices keenly the sound of Pom entering the room and later of tea being served. One of the most profound impressions is made

37

by Pom's hand, newly adorned with her engagement ring, on his neck: "It had something cold and metallic on it, which sent a shiver through me" (83). Like these, most of the other sensory impressions in the narrative involve sound and touch.

Connections

1.   As in the narrator's family in "Our Side of the Fence and Theirs," there are generational differences in Pom's family. The older members of the family are more ready to accept traditional values and customs, especially about sex roles and marriage; the younger members still respect their elders' opinions, but they are more open to new and different ways of running a family. For instance, both Gyanranjan's narrator and two of Mehta's sisters, Umi and Nimi, are intrigued by the idea of women having greater freedom and autonomy. In "Our Side of the Fence and Theirs," the narrator notices with a mixture of approval and surprise how easily the neighbor girl relates to her parents. She goes through with her simple wedding without weeping or any display of unwillingness, which suggests that she is independent of her parents and may have had some power to decide who and when she would marry. Pom's family resembles the family on the other side of the fence in that there is open communication between parents and children. Umi and Nimi disagree with their father. Rather than being shocked or angry, he discusses his own views of marriage frankly and admits the old traditions are not entirely equitable in terms of class and sex (paras. 57, 58, 77).

2.   The mix of emotions Ved Mehta felt when he listened from outside the drawing room to the women's engagement singsong suggests that he realizes he is growing up and is becoming more aware of the differences between the roles of men and women. He realizes that a few years before, he might have been outside playing, or would have been invited into the room, but now that he is barred because he is a growing boy, he is at once captivated by the women and ashamed of his interest. The narrator in Gyanranjan's essay experiences a similar sense of shame and captivation in relation to the girl who lives on the other side of the fence (7). At several points he shows this mix of emotions, as when he realizes that he is probably the only one who has noticed the "movement of her bosom . . . free and unrestrained" (6). When his sister-in-law teases him about his interest in the neighbor girl, he is pleased and embarrassed (20), but by the end of the essay he is wavering between defending the girl's respectability and agreeing that she has behaved badly (28).

3.   Like Pom and Kakaji, Liang's parents do not marry for romance, but because of the similarities in their backgrounds and values. They hardly know each other when they marry, but they agree about politics, and they are prepared to obey the traditions of filial loyalty (7, 8). In "Pom's Engagement," Daddyji argues that the match between Pom and Kakaji will work because Kakaji's "way of life and thinking will be similar to mine. We are of the same caste. . . . The atmosphere in Pom's new home will be very much the same as the atmosphere here" (56).

4.   Birth and marriage customs in the Quiché tribe are very different from the Hindu customs Mehta describes, but to some degree they have the same purpose: to help young women accept traditions and assume their assigned roles as wives and mothers. The closeness between Pom and her mother intensifies when Pom becomes engaged because her mother is helping her through the process of taking on women's responsibilities. In

Menchú's "Birth Ceremonies," the closeness between mother and daughter serves a similar purpose. Menchú describes how a woman teaches her daughter to perform women's tasks. The mother explains everything she does, including how to say prayers, light the fire, and cook the meals. Menchú writes, "She explains all these little details to her daughter, who learns by copying her" (18). Only by spending much time observing and helping her mother can she learn to follow in her footsteps. This method of instruction, according to Menchú, "is all bound up with our commitment to maintain our customs and pass on the secrets of our ancestors" (19).

MARGUERITE DURAS (Durah), Home Making (p. 161)

Explorations

1. Duras sums up a mother's basic identity in this way: "The woman is the home" (para. 28). Once students understand Duras's basic assumption, developing a list of mothers' responsibilities is an easy matter. According to Duras, no matter what a woman does professionally or socially, she "is still responsible for everything in the house" (24). The mother, like the home, provides a "center" for men and children (1). She feeds them, tries to keep them safe (5), and accommodates her schedule to theirs (10). She is responsible not only for the literal running of the home, but also for keeping her family's "ideas, emotional phases, and endless feelings" in order (26). In the same paragraph, Duras says that men build houses rather than make them. Men are good for amusing children, but not for taking care of them, because the men themselves are just like the children (28, 29). Duras reports that she feels "slightly repelled" by a man she knows who does housework and cares for the children (31). In Duras's opinion, this man and his wife have disrupted the proper distribution of responsibility for the home.

2. Duras's description of motherhood reinforces her statement in paragraph 28 that a woman is the home. Earlier in the essay, Duras says that men consider a woman a good mother when her work is "like the rain-bringing clouds" (14). In paragraph 35, Duras describes the mother as part of the environment (she is a hill, a garden, something to eat, something to sleep on). In her portrayal of her own mother, Duras says that "home was simultaneously her and the house — the house around her and her inside the house" (20). Motherhood means sacrificing some part of one's individuality; a good mother "lets herself be devoured" by her family's needs (35).

3. Most students will be able to identify as traditional Duras's idea that women are primarily responsible for running the home and caring for the children. Less conventional, perhaps, is her contention that men are unnecessary to the home (see, for instance, Duras's description in paragraphs 16–18 of how her mother coped with raising her children single-handed). How students respond to Duras's ideas about home and family will depend on their own upbringing and family relationships. In order to help students understand the background for their opinions, it would be good to have them talk about the distribution of responsibilities in their own families.

4. Duras's evidence is entirely subjective. She draws on her own experience of mothering, her memories of her own mother, and her observations of others to support the generalizations she makes about mothers and homemaking. She often makes statements of faith, as in paragraph 22, where she says she believes mothers represent madness, and in paragraph 27, where she says she seriously believes women's position hasn't changed. Duras also admits she may be "idealizing" mothers (33). As students discuss whether her evidence is convincing, it may be helpful to ask them to consider Duras's essay first as an exploration of her own personal philosophy of homemaking and mothering, and then decide whether her subjective observations and interpretations are convincing on a general level.

Connections

1. In both "Pom's Engagement" and "Home Making," women are responsible for day-to-day housekeeping and childcare. There are, however, important differences in how Duras and Mehta approach women's role in the family. Duras writes about women's responsibilities as someone who herself carries them out. For instance, it is clear from her account of buying a house that she identifies strongly with the nine generations of women who once lived in and ran the house that now belongs to her (para. 5). She writes of them, and of her mother and herself, as women who belong to the home, but are independent of the men they care for. Ved Mehta's description of women's responsibilities, on the other hand, comes from his father's point of view. Daddyji says that in their Hindu tradition, Pom's life will be joined with her husband's: "it is she who will forsake her past to build a new future with him" (75). Duras, speaking from the point of view of a woman and a Westerner, would not agree that a woman's life should be dependent on her husband's. Students may have some difficulty identifying similarities in men's roles in "Home Making" and "Pom's Engagement." Although the mother in both Duras's and Mehta's essay is responsible for practical arrangements and decisions, the father in Mehta's essay holds much more authority in the home than Duras believes men really have.

2. In Ved Mehta's essay, Sister Umi accuses her father of "advocating the subservience of women" when he says that a woman should sacrifice her own interests in order to gain her husband's respect (62–65). Duras also argues that women sacrifice for their families; for instance, see her comments in paragraphs 10 and 11 about how women fit their schedules to their families' needs, as well as her comment that "a woman gives her body over to her child" (35). But she is not arguing that women should subordinate themselves to men. In fact, she writes that her mother sacrificed to make a home for her children, but that she never would have done that for a man (26).

3. In *Looking at Ourselves*, William Mattox writes that children "in single-parent homes usually receive less parental attention, affection, and supervision than other children," factors that he believes lead to significant developmental problems. Patricia Schroeder agrees that women, especially those who are single parents, face major problems in trying to balance earning a living and running a home. Christopher Lasch, although he doesn't address the question of mothers' roles directly, argues against childcare, a stance that suggests he believes women should be back in the home rather than in the work force.

Both Mattox and Lasch imply that single mothers and working mothers are to blame for being unable to meet the needs of their children, but Schroeder blames the government for failing to support women's efforts to work and raise their children. Duras's depiction of a mother in France differs in that she has nothing to say about women who work outside the home. Her own working life as a writer is integrated into her housework, as is suggested in her statement that "all I had to do was prepare the vegetables, put the soup on, and write" (4).

GHOLAM-HOSSEIN SA'EDI (Goo-lam-hoo-sane Sah-EE-dee), The Game Is Over (p. 162)

Explorations

1. Students may have some difficulty recognizing the transition, because the entire piece is told in the past tense. But with a little encouragement, they should sense the shift to specific past in "But that night it was different." In paragraph 4 we return to the moment of Hasani's suggestion with "That afternoon, the one before the night I went to Hasani's place, Hasani came out, and he was really low." By intertwining present observations with the past incident, Sa'edi is able to verify some of the story. The boys' traditional greeting by fighting, their fear of their fathers, their forays to the wells — all of this is exposition that is essential for the reader to understand if the tale is to achieve its full impact. If told in chronological order, the tale would suffer first from a long and tedious expository beginning before the action begins and, second, from frequent interruptions at key points, destroying momentum.

2. When the narrator tells us that he and Hasani fear their fathers, and that they greet each other by fighting, hitting each other "hard so it hurt" (para. 1), we begin to sense the violence in their lives. Students should notice a number of other instances in which Sa'edi states or implies that these children live in a world characterized by family abuse. In paragraph 6, for example, the narrator comments in a matter-of-fact tone that "Hasani's dad would beat him every night, but my dad would only beat Ahmad and me once or twice a week." When the boys are at the wells, Hasani takes to hitting his toes with a stick, and when they reach home, they hear Hasani's mother and father calling each other vile names. The parents, in fact, treat each other with contempt. All of this, while it angers the boys, is considered by them to be simply the way things are.

3. Sa'edi has the narrator initially worrying about how Hasani's parents will react (126), what they'll do to him (the narrator) when he tells them that Hasani has fallen into a well (130), what will happen to Hasani while he's hiding out (136), and later worrying about how to effect the return (213–38). The suspense seems to center on whether Hasani will be welcomed back with caresses and tears or another beating, so the ending should be a surprise to all but the most perceptive readers. Some students may be shocked or dismayed by the story's ending, wishing that Hasani had made his triumphant return to the town. But it's difficult to imagine the impact of such an ending: This isn't Hannibal,

41

Missouri, and a joyous reunion seems out of the question for these people. A beating, though, would be anticlimactic. This question may present instructors with the opportunity to discuss consistency in a story, as well as the demands of the art itself. The ending is really the only way that both consistency and artistic integrity can be maintained.

Connections

1. In Marguerite Duras's essay "Home Making," the primary benefit children derive from the home is a sense of emotional and physical security. She writes of her own childhood: "As long as we had a house and our mother, we'd never be abandoned or swept away or taken by surprise" (para. 17). Hasani's house provides no sense of security; it is, in fact, a dangerous place. For Hasani, home is the antithesis of what Duras describes. Mothers, in Duras's estimation, are identified with the home. Hasani's mother is too beaten down to protect her son from his father's beatings, so it is as if he had no home at all. In part, what Hasani seeks when he tries to trick his family into thinking him dead is a more secure place in his own home. He wants them to recognize him as a valued member of the family, worthy of love and protection. Hasani imagines that his family will great him with joy, and his father will not beat him when he returns from the dead (265–269). His desperate attempt to gain his family's attention demonstrates how completely his home had failed to meet his basic needs.

2. In both stories religious values provide a subdued background to the actions and thoughts of the protagonists. Although religious ideas are not overtly referred to by the characters in "Our Side of the Fence and Theirs," religion is quietly integrated into the fabric of everyday life. For example, the narrator notes that his "sister-in-law takes Puppi along even when she goes outside to get flowers for worship" (17), a statement that implies that the family is governed by traditional and religious principles. Hasani's father also appears to be a believer, although no religious principles contain his daily violence. However, in his grief he calls to an Islamic saint to restore his child (187). In "The Game Is Over," the characters turn to religion only in moments of despair or as a last resort. The characters expect their religion to work miracles, to restore the lost Hasani or the "sanity" of the narrator at the end of the story. Perhaps the harsh economic circumstances of Hasani's village accustom its inhabitants to hardship so they seek relief only in the most desperate circumstances. The characters in Gyanranjan's story live under more stable circumstances: They are not abused, completely poverty stricken, or without time for some amenities, including daily religious rituals.

3. The irony in this observation should not be lost on students. Whereas Novak cites capitalism and the desire for success as causes for the disintegration of the family, Sa'edi cites the opposite, poverty. In one case the family suffers because there are too many goods available, too many goals for individual members to strive for. In the other the lack of goods, of realistic goals, provides for a despair that undermines Iranian family life every bit as much as materialism does American life.

ADDITIONAL QUESTIONS AND ASSIGNMENTS

1. In a journal entry or a collection of informal notes, discuss the images of children presented in three or four of these selections. Consider such issues as the rights of children, their responsibilities to their parents, parents' responsibility to protect their children, children's need for the attention and love of a caretaker, their need for independence, and any other issues you find relevant. As you look over your notes, try to discover similarities and differences among the cultures represented. Can you come to any general conclusion about the image of children in a given culture?

2. Interview someone who grew up in a family setting different from your own. As you gather information, consider the kinds of information you're interested in eliciting — do you want to know about sibling relationships? Responsibilities of children to parents? Influence of religious or social values on the family? Roles of males and females in the family? As you write the interview, decide what information is best summarized in your own voice and what is best delivered by your subject in his or her own words.

3. Write your own version of "Our Side of the Fence and Theirs," using one of the more popular television families (from any era) as the neighbors. You may want to begin by listing the distinctive characteristics of a family like the Cleavers, the Cartwrights, the Bunkers, the Ewings, the Simpsons, the Seavers, or the Huxtables and comparing them with the characteristics of a "real-life" family. Then imagine yourself watching them for several weeks. Record what you see, using the same kind of commentary as that provided by Gyanranjan's narrator. Remember that you'll be characterizing yourself as much as your subject family.

4. The issue of children with two working parents is currently receiving a good deal of attention in the media. Some reports focus on the responsibility of the state to provide adequate childcare, some explore the effects of day care on the child, and some investigate the impact of working mothers on society as a whole. Research one of these topics (or choose your own related topic) by consulting magazine and newspaper articles on the subject as well as the opinions of experts found in books and interviews. Write a paper in which you present two opposing interpretations of the issue you've chosen, maintaining neutrality yourself.

5. Conduct further research into one of the cultures represented in this section, focusing specifically on the role of the family. It would be wise to choose a culture about which information is readily available — China, France, Japan, and India are likely candidates. If the selection is an excerpt from a larger work, look first at that work. You can find other sources by consulting the headnotes for other selections from that culture (if there are any) and a general encyclopedia, as well as journals devoted to the study of that culture. Narrow your topic to something manageable — such as religious influences on the family, the place of children in the family, the role of the extended family, or the responsibility of the family to the state — and write an expository paper in which you elaborate on the view of family presented by the original selection.

Part Three

LANDMARKS AND TURNING POINTS:
THE STRUGGLE FOR IDENTITY

INTRODUCTION

The range of cultures covered in this section, from the Hispanic community in Phoenix, Arizona, to the mixed African and Western influences in Abidjan, Ivory Coast, may leave students reeling, but the unifying theme should be eminently familiar to them. Heker, Liu, Orlean, and Tan all relate the experiences of girls on the journey to maturity; Rushdie, Grass, Binur, and Vargas Llosa represent the male experience. Other possible divisions within the unit include the awakening of social and political consciousness (Heker, Liu, Grass, and Binur), the shattering of comforting childhood illusions (Heker, Tan, Liu, and Grass), roles dictated by social class and race (Binur, Grass, Heker, and Liu) and by sex (Vargas Llosa, Tan, and Orlean), and the role of violence as a catalyst for personal growth (Liu, Vargas Llosa, Grass, and Binur).

Students may find the unit more accessible if they first discuss the various rituals involved with turning points in their own culture. They will be able to compare their own rites of initiation with those represented in Orlean, Vargas Llosa, and Grass. Some may identify with the scenes of alienation in selections by Hughes, Cooper, and Baldwin in *Looking at Ourselves*. They will probably have strong responses to the brutality represented in Grass, Binur, and Liu. They may find similarities in their own lives to the complexities and trials of growing up represented in pieces by Vargas Llosa, Tan, and Grass.

Instructors may wish to consult the following familiar works in preparing related selections from *Ourselves Among Others*:

Essays

Maya Angelou, "Graduation" (*I Know Why the Caged Bird Sings*, Random House, 1970).
Nancy Mairs, "On Being Raised by a Daughter" (*Plaintext*, University of Arizona Press, 1986).
George Orwell, "Shooting an Elephant" (*Shooting an Elephant*, Harcourt, 1950).
Lillian Smith, "When I was a Child" (*Killers of the Dream*, Norton, 1949).
Alice Walker, "Beauty: When the Other Dancer is the Self" (*In Search of Our Mothers' Gardens*, Harcourt, 1983).
Alice Walker, "Brothers and Sisters" (*In Search of Our Mothers's Gardens*, Harcourt, 1983).

Short Stories

Chinua Achebe, "Marriage is a Private Affair" (*Girls at War*, Doubleday, 1972).
Toni Cade Bambera, "The Lesson" (*Gorilla, My Love*, Random House, 1972).

Dorothy Canfield, "Sex Education" (*Four-Square*, Harcourt, 1945).

Kate Chopin, "The Story of an Hour" (published as "The Dreams of an Hour," *Vogue*, April 19, 1894); *The Awakening and Selected Stories*, Penguin, 1983.

Ralph Ellison, "Battle Royal" (*Invisible Man*, Random House, 1952).

Louise Erdrich, "The World's Greatest Fisherman" (*Love Medicine*, Holt, Rinehart, 1984).

William Faulkner, "The Bear" (*Go Down, Moses*, Random House, 1942).

Doris Lessing, "A Sunrise on the Veldt" (*African Stories*, Simon and Schuster, 1981).

Doris Lessing, "Through the Tunnel" (*The Habit of Loving*, 1955).

Jeanne Schinto, "Caddies' Day" (*Shadow Bands*, Ontario Review Press, 1988).

John Updike, "A & P" (*New Yorker*, July 22, 1961; *Pigeon Feathers*, Knopf, 1962).

BIOGRAPHICAL NOTES ON LOOKING AT OURSELVES

1. A contributing writer for many magazines, Gail Sheehy has written a novel, *Lovesounds* (1970), and several studies of contemporary American and global life, including *Hustling* (1973), *Pathfinders* (1981), *Character: America's Search for Leadership* (1988), *The Man Who Changed the World: The Lives of Mikhail S. Gorbachev* (1991), and *Silent Passage: Menopause* (1992). The excerpt in *Looking at Ourselves* is taken from Sheehy's *Passages: Predictable Crises of Adult Life* (1974).

2. Michael Dorris, an anthropologist and writer, was the founder and chairman of the Department of Native American Studies at Dartmouth. He is the author of a memoir, *The Broken Cord: A Family's Ongoing Struggle with Fetal Alcohol Syndrome* (1989), and of the novels *A Yellow Raft in Blue Water* (1987) and, with Louise Erdrich, *The Crown of Columbus* (1991).

3. Poet, novelist, and short story writer Langston Hughes has been called the father of the Harlem Renaissance literary movement of the 1920s and 1930s. His "Negro Artist and the Racial Mountain" (1926) was the manifesto of the revival. His autobiographies *The Big Sea* (1940) and *I Wonder as I Wander* (1956) chronicle his worldwide travels during which he was a merchant seaman, waiter, English teacher, and Parisian bohemian.

4. Terry Galloway is the author of two plays, *Heart of a Dog*, which won the Village award in New York, and *A Hamlet in Berlin*; she has also coauthored a public television program for deaf children and published a book of poems, *Buncha Crocs in Search of Snac* (1980).

5. Bernard Cooper lives in Los Angeles and is the author of *Maps to Anywhere* (1990), a collection of autobiographical essays and poems.

6. Alfred Kazin is a prominent literary critic and memoirist whose critical works include *On Native Grounds* (1942) and *Bright Book of Life: American Novelists and Storytellers from Hemingway to Mailer* (1980). He is perhaps best known for his autobiographical trilogy: *A Walker in the City* (1969), *New York Jew* (1978), and *Starting Out in the Thirties* (1989).

7. James Baldwin was widely regarded as one of the preeminent black writers of his time. He is perhaps best known for his novels *Go Tell It on the Mountain* (1953), about the black church, and *Giovanni's Room* (1956), dealing with homosexuality, and for the essays collected in *Notes of a Native Son* (1955) and *Nobody Knows My Name: More Notes of a Native Son* (1961). His searing polemic *The Fire Next Time* appeared in 1963. He died in the south of France in 1989.

8. Joyce Carol Oates, a professor of English at Princeton University, is one of the most versatile, prolific, and acclaimed writers in contemporary America. Among her many works are the novels *them* (National Book Award 1970), *Expensive People* (1982), and *Black Water* (1992) (based on the Chappaquiddick incident); the essay collections *On Boxing* (1989) and *American Appetites* (1990); and the short story collection *Where Are You Going, Where Have You Been: Stories of Young America* (1974). She has also written gothic romances and horror stories and edited the *Oxford Book of American Short Stories* (1992).

9. Malcolm X, born Malcolm Little in 1925, became a Black Muslim in jail and, after his release, advocated black separatism until he was assassinated in 1965. His *Autobiography of Malcolm X* (coauthored with Alex Haley) appeared that same year.

Reflections

1. Issues of honesty are important in selections by Terry Galloway, Bernard Cooper, and Langston Hughes. Students who have difficulty in identifying with the childhood experiences of a deaf woman, a gay man, or an African-American will be better able to engage with this question if they have the opportunity to discuss the relationship between personal honesty and social acceptance in their own lives. Terry Galloway learned that it was better for her to be honest about her deafness after she suffered isolation and severe emotional stress while trying to keep her deafness a secret. She lied about her deafness in college in order to "avoid the stigma of being thought different," a motivation that was also important to Cooper and Hughes. She found it easier to gain acceptance when, as a result of facing up to the hard realities of functioning as a deaf person in a hearing world, she decided to begin to tell people of her hearing disability. Bernard Cooper faced a somewhat similar dilemma when, as a boy, he began to realize that he was gay. He lies to a potential friend, Theresa Sanchez, and his mother about his orientation, in part because he has not yet fully grasped what it means. He also lies because he fears — rightly, in relation to his mother and another boy he has befriended — that he will be rejected if he tells the truth. As an adult, Cooper reflects on this time of his life and regrets not admitting to Theresa, the one person he might have trusted with the truth, that he was gay. Whereas Cooper's situation did not involve any clear solutions to the problem of when and with whom to be honest, Langston Hughes's piece recounts an incident when being honest could not have led to acceptance. His initial refusal to claim that he had seen Jesus during a prayer meeting was an effort to represent himself honestly to his friends and family, but as time goes on and he sees that they will not accept him as he is, he finally gives in to their demands and pretends that he too has seen Jesus. However, he is left feeling bitterly alone and isolated, effects he suffers not only because he was unable to be honest, but also because he has lost faith in his aunt and their religion.

2. Students' responses to this question will depend on their personal perceptions, combined with how their unique cultural and ethnic backgrounds affect their feelings about assuming the rights and responsibilities of adulthood. Some students, recalling how impatient they were to take on the privileges of adulthood, will feel that an abrupt transition to adulthood, marked by a single event in which they could "prove" their maturity, would have been a vast improvement over a long adolescence. Others may argue that the length of time young people in the United States spend in school without taking on major responsibilities is a tremendous waste of talent. Adolescence is often

considered a long-term identity crisis in which one is no longer a child but still has not achieved adulthood; a ritual that would help resolve the crisis and situate the young person as a full adult would be welcome to many. A longer transition might appeal more to middle-class and wealthy students, whose family resources allow them more leisure to attend school, enjoy extra-curricular activities, and explore possible careers. The advantages of a longer transition might be a more complete academic education, more time to enjoy the relative freedom of a youth unencumbered by an adult work load, and more time to learn how to handle family and community responsibilities.

3. Along with considering connections between Langston Hughes's account of being "saved" in the church and Michael Dorris's description of Native American initiation rites, it will be a good idea to have students consider the different purposes of the rituals Hughes and Dorris relate. For both, one purpose is to initiate membership in a social and spiritual group. For Hughes, it is membership in the ranks of those "saved" by Jesus; for Dorris, it is membership in the ranks of adults who have faced the physical and spiritual challenges of entering the wilderness alone. However, the revival Hughes attends emphasizes the authority of the Christian god over the young people who are his "lambs." Dorris, by contrast, describes an initiation that is intended to prove the independence and individual courage of young men and to introduce them to their adult selves. Dorris writes that the insights the initiate gained may have been induced by exhaustion, hunger, or other stresses, but he affirms that the experience was ultimately a positive one. Hughes, on the other hand, must face spiritual disillusionment and the disappointment of not having experienced the transformation his aunt expected of him. The other young people at the revival, either by the force of their own convictions or because of social pressures, "went to Jesus" without resistance. It may be that for some initiates undergoing the wilderness ritual Dorris describes, a sudden transformation was achieved for similar reasons: because of pressures to conform to the expectations of family and community, along with a desire to be accepted as an adult.

4. Hughes employs biblical phrases and the repetitive, rhythmic style of revival preachers to evoke the mood of the prayer meeting. He describes the songs and sermon, and quotes the preacher imploring the children: "'Won't you come? Won't you come to Jesus? Young lambs, won't you come?'" The congregation prays "in a mighty wail of moans and voices," and when all the children had arisen, "Then joyous singing filled the room." Hughes contrasts these lyrical and biblical passages with a more conversational style that suggests the inauthenticity of the religious experience for him. He begins the piece, for instance, by saying, "I was saved from sin when I was going on thirteen. But not really saved." Hughes employs a similarly conversational style whenever he describes his inner reactions to the meeting, as when he finally gets up after deciding "that maybe to save further trouble, I'd better lie. . . ." Baldwin uses repetition for a different effect. His opening paragraph repeats the phrase, "it comes as a great shock" in order to emphasize the severity and permanence of the trauma a young black child experiences when she or he discovers that, because of racism, the mainstream culture will attempt to situate her or him as "other" — and as inferior. Later in the piece, Baldwin uses repetition to imply that the damage is felt not only by the individual child, but also by the nation as a whole. He writes, "It is a terrible thing for an entire people to surrender to the notion that one-ninth of its population is beneath them," and re-emphasizes this point in his last sentence by repeating the sentence structure: "it is a very grave moment. . . ." Cooper employs a very different style to describe his experience of growing up gay. His piece begins with

a physical description of Theresa Sanchez that suggests the narrator's keen sense of sensual detail. Later in the piece, with his description of Grady's body and behavior, the personal significance of his acute awareness of bodies becomes clear, because this passage describes his awakening awareness of his homosexuality. His awareness of bodies also has a defensive function; he writes that he emulated Grady's behavior and was not, therefore, "singled out as a sissy." The need for defenses is even more apparent in his description of his body as "The Visible Man in our science class." Cooper completes his essay with a sensual moment he enjoys as an adult with his lover, a passage that affirms that he has come to terms with his body and his sexuality.

SUSAN ORLEAN, Quinceañera (p. 200)

Explorations

1. Students may have some trouble understanding how Azteca Plaza, the formal-wear shopping center where parents shop for the gowns their fifteen-year-old daughters will wear to their quinceañeras, represents the dual nature of the Hispanic culture in Phoenix. They may find it easier if they begin by considering the dual meanings of "plaza." A plaza is a traditional outdoor marketplace and central meeting place, but it also denotes a modern shopping center. The Aztec culture thrived in Mexico until Cortés arrived in the sixteenth century. Invoking the Aztecs for a formal wear shop may be taken as an indication of the place of quinceañeras in traditional Mexican culture. Azteca Plaza, like the Hispanic culture Orlean describes, represents a mixture of traditional Mexican and contemporary Hispanic influences.

2. Quinceañeras were originally meant to mark a girl's initiation into womanhood and society, and to affirm her commitment to the Catholic church (para. 1). Students will find plenty of evidence that quinceañeras still serve as a social debut. Whether the event is held for an individual girl or for groups of girls, it brings the community together to recognize the girls' passage from childhood to young womanhood. But some members of the Hispanic community are concerned that quinceañeras no longer serve as a meaningful religious rite. One of Orlean's informants tells her that the ethnic and religious significance of the quinceañera is irrelevent to today's young people (5). Father Sotelo tells Orlean that the quinceañera has become an empty ceremony (8). Some girls seemed to regard the event as an opportunity simply to be the center of attention at a fancy party, and some parents seemed to consider that it was their duty to go into debt to sponsor the most opulent party possible. Father Sotelo believes that the event should be primarily a religious celebration; hence his unwillingness to give masses for girls who are not religious or obedient to church doctrine. Father Peacock, on the other hand, believes that the church should work to meet people on their own terms (12) and to help them come together to celebrate family and community in any way they choose. Students will be able to come up with many reasons for the changes that have taken place in the ceremony since its Mexican origins. Most of these reasons may have to do with the impact of Anglo culture, which could be viewed as a threat to traditional values. The new deemphasis on the religious aspects of the event, the modern gowns the girls wear, the mix of Mexican

music with rock 'n' roll (27), and the emphasis on spending extravagantly to impress others, are all changes that might be put down to the negative influence of Anglo values.

3. Orlean's selection of sources is so broad that most students will have trouble thinking of other sources she might have included. She observes firsthand Azteca Plaza, the Vesta Club quinceañeras mass, and the country club party that follows. She interviews adult community members who are involved in planning quinceañeras and two priests, Father Peacock and Father Sotelo, who have very different opinions of the meaning of the quinceañera celebration. She consults Father Sotelo's guidebook (7), written for girls who want to celebrate the mass, and she watches videotapes of quinceañera masses with Father Peacock (10). There are three sources, however, she does not cite directly. She has not consulted the elderly, who might have participated in quinceañeras in the early twentieth century and would, therefore, have a better grasp of some of the changes that have taken place. Nor does she speak with Mexican nationals, who would be able to provide a unique commentary on the ethnic significance of the celebration. And lastly, she does not include interviews with any of the sixteen girls who are taking part in the quinceañera she attends. This last omission is especially curious since the event is for them.

4. Orlean is present as an interested observer rather than as a participant in the stories she tells. If she were closely involved, her story would dominate the essay and limit its scope. In the role she plays, Orlean is able to gather together stories from numerous informants and give a multifaceted presentation of events and opinions. Orlean's own opinions come through in the choices she makes about what scenes to include. For instance, late in the essay Orlean records a significant exchange between a girl and her mother at the quinceañera party. The girl asks when the "debutante of the year" will be announced, and her stepmother replies curtly, "Later" (27). It is a small moment, one among many Orlean might have chosen to include, but it suggests that Orlean believes that quinceañeras can be competitive and a source of parent-child tension. If Orlean were not present in the stories she tells, such a moment could not be recorded. Her essay would be a dry composite of the history and current customs related to the quinceañeras, rather than the lively piece it is.

Connections

1. The fifteen-year-old girls who have quinceañeras are in some senses very much connected to their families, as their participation in a traditional Hispanic celebration indicates. But like the young teenagers Sheehy discusses, these girls are also trying to redefine the celebration — and their relationship to their families — by modifying it to better suit their needs and desires. Although the original intent of the quinceañeras was to formalize a girl's "passage into womanhood" and "commitment to Catholicism," as well as her personal social debut (para. 1), for many, the emphasis is now on the last objective. Father Sotelo, for instance, complained about the "queen-for-a-day" attitude of many girls (6). In addition, for some girls, planning the quinceañera is an opportunity to exert their individuality through conflicts with family (7). Their refusal of the traditional religious meaning, and their desire to include rock 'n' roll along with traditional Mexican music (27), suggest that they are working at differentiating themselves from their families.

2. It will be important for students to appreciate the historical, ethnic, and sex differences between the Native American male initiation rites Dorris describes and the quinceañera celebration. Young Plains Indian men were expected to challenge themselves physically and spiritually in order to become men. It was a private rite of passage, marking not only an external change in how an initiate would fit into his community, but also an internal change in which he would discover a personal vision and vocation. The quinceañera celebration also has a spiritual component. The emphasis, however, is not on a personal spiritual vision, but on a public affirmation of a girl's commitment to the Catholic Church (1). It is not a private ritual, and although mild physical challenges are involved (negotiating the intricate waltz, for instance), the fifteen-year-old Hispanic girl is not expected to endure privation or fend for her life. However, the two very different initiation rituals do have in common the idea that a single event can mark a profound change in how a young person relates to his or her community. Both are meant to celebrate the beginning of adulthood.

3. Rodriguez mentions that he was "struck by diminished family closeness and the necessity of public life," and that the Catholic Church served a mediating role between his private and public lives (1). Attending mass made him feel connected to other Catholics, whether or not he wanted the connection. The girls who celebrate quinceañeras in Orlean's essay might express some of the same ambivalence about the role of the church in their lives. Father Sotelo reports that some girls expected to have a mass said for them even though they were never in church and disobeyed the church's doctrines (6), a problem that suggests some girls were not willing to establish the close connection to the church Rodriguez recalls. Father Sotelo complained that "when these girls would walk down the aisle with their parents at the mass, you could tell that quite often the girls and their parents couldn't stand one another"(7). Rodriguez recalls that he felt distanced from his family, due to generational, educational, and cultural differences. But the church served at least to bring him and his family together for the purpose of worship. Father Peacock mentions a similar purpose for the quinceañera mass. Some families, "have experienced child abuse, sexual abuse, divorce . . . [Father Peacock] loves seeing such families together at the occasional happy affair like a quinceañera " (12).

LILIANA HEKER (HEH-kur), The Stolen Party (p. 212)

Explorations

1. A few students will recognize that the "theft" of the party happens in two ways. Ines steals the party from Rosaura by demonstrating that the girl was invited not as a guest, but as a servant. Rosaura, at least from Ines' point of view, steals the party by stepping outside her prescribed role and insisting on being treated as a guest. Most students, however, will be so thoroughly in sympathy with Rosaura's perspective that the dual meaning of the title will go unnoticed. The fact that the party has been "stolen" from Rosaura only becomes clear at the end, when the thing she most values, a sense of belonging and respect, is taken from her.

2. Some students may be surprised to find two central conflicts in the same story; the two in this story are defined clearly enough, however, that students should be able to identify

them readily. By introducing the mother-daughter conflict in the first paragraph, Heker sees to it that the reader is taken in, as is Rosaura, by the seeming importance of this conflict. She sees herself and her friend as allies against the intolerance of her mother. Unlike Rosaura, however, the reader senses the legitimacy of the conflict between rich and poor introduced in the second paragraph. By constructing the story this way, Heker diverts the reader's attention from the primary conflict, clouding the issues and preventing a premature anticipation of the ending. While the reader knows that Rosaura's mother is probably right in questioning the invitation, the child's perception is so appealing that the reader willfully suspends skepticism and hopes, with Rosaura, to prove the mother wrong.

3.   While Señora Ines's ignorance and class bias allow her to think she's being generous in giving Rosaura money rather than a trinket, the child recognizes the insult for what it is and immediately presses close to her true ally, her mother. Rosaura's refusal to take the bills, as well as her stare, reveal to Ines that she has erred; however, she is paralyzed, unable to withdraw the offer but incapable of making any other gesture. Both characters realize at this point that they've been involved in a charade, and that realization makes any further pretense impossible.

4.   Among the possible responses to this question are Rosaura's certainty that her mother knows nothing about friendship (para. 8), her criticism of her mother's intolerance of rich people (13), her sense of superiority to the other children in the careful handling of dishes (19), her perception of power in being chosen to distribute the cake (39) and to hold the monkey (52), and her misinterpretation of Señora Ines's comment that she is a "marvelous daughter" (68). In each case she's attempting to repress any sense of inferiority to the rich children and to reinforce her own sense of importance. And she is indeed an accomplished child — she is an achiever in school and is interesting enough to intrigue her rich friend. But regardless of the legitimacy of her pride, her naïveté blinds her to the perceptions of society. She fails to recognize the fact that to Señora Ines her accomplishments are no more meaningful than the antics of the monkey; she may be clever, but she's still the maid's daughter.

Connections

1.   Luciana's mother gives her a fancy birthday party that will impress the parents of the children who attend and reinforce her social position. The inclusion of Rosaura, who gracefully helps to keep things running smoothly, is part of her effort to bring off a perfect party. Luciana, like Rosaura, is too young and naïve to understand how the party might be an occasion to reinforce class divisions by displaying wealth. She only wants to enjoy herself and to be sure her guests, including Rosaura, enjoy the party too. The different goals of mother and daughter are in some ways analogous to the different goals of mothers and daughters in Susan Orlean's "Quinceañera." Quinceañeras are opportunities to impress friends and relatives with a extravagant show of clothes, money, music, and food. While the daughters enjoy receiving the attention and gifts, the mothers may use the occasion to be recognized for their social and organizational talents.

2.   Rosaura's friendship with Luciana demonstrates that she is between two worlds: the working-class world of her mother, where education and social etiquette are considered luxuries, and the upper-class world of her mother's employer. When Rosaura attends Luciana's party, she shows she is ready to take a step further into Luciana's world. She

can only do that by distancing herself from her mother's world. In spite of Ines's gesture, which is an attempt to put Rosaura squarely back in the disadvantaged place Rosaura's mother holds, Rosaura may eventually be able to use her education to move into the middle class. Mphahlele writes that when an African mother sends her son to high school, "dialogue between her and the child decreases and eventually stays on the level of basic essentials" (para. 4). A similar gulf is opening up between Rosaura and her mother as Rosaura's education progresses. However, Rosaura's mother is proud of her accomplishments and helps her prepare for the party even though she knows it will create distance between them. Less relevant to Rosaura's situation are Mphahlele's comments about the African writer's relationship to tradition (5). Rosaura would not be leaving behind her traditional cultural roots if she succeeds in moving up the socioeconomic hierarchy. The distance between her mother and her has not been opened up because of the intrusion of what Mphahlele calls an "alien" language and culture (7). Instead, it is due to the class differences that will separate them as Rosaura gains an education and enters the middle class within her own culture.

3.   It may be difficult for students to appreciate the differences in the problems with racism Baldwin is addressing and the more class-based problems Rosaura confronts. Baldwin mentions the shock an African-American child feels when he is forced to realize that, although he has given his loyalty to the United States and adopted its values, the United States has not "evolved any place" for him (1). Although the exclusion Baldwin notices has serious economic consequences, it is based on skin color (1). At the end of "The Stolen Party," Rosaura, too, is shocked to discover that she has not been accepted as the equal of the other children. However, unlike the African-American child, Rosaura is excluded because of her class status.

SOPHRONIA LIU (Loo), So Tsi-fai (p. 219)

Explorations

1.   In her description of So Tsi-fai in paragraph 3, Liu seems to echo the teacher's feelings: All she can see are dirty clothes, the sneering grin, the shuffling gait. But after his suicide, as she remembers him the reasons for his behavior become clear. She intersperses her own account of his hardships with the scorn and criticism of the teacher, revealing the frustration that So Tsi-fai faced daily. The ghost that comes to claim his rightful place is the product of Liu's own mind, born of her guilt. As she ponders those events during the next twenty years, she begins to question the fickleness of fate, wondering why she was chosen to be successful while he was doomed to failure.

2.   Paragraphs 6, 7, and 8 make it quite clear that Liu blames fate in the larger sense but the social system in particular for So Tsi-fai's death. When we hear Sister Marie's criticisms after we've read about the responsibilities heaped on the boy, we cannot help condemning an educational system that ignores the student's life outside the classroom. Liu seems to suggest that a more compassionate approach to education is needed, one that looks into the problems students may face out of school and attempts to help students rather than simply condemning them. (It might be interesting to compare students' sympathy with So Tsi-fai with their response to "problem students" in American

classrooms. Are we as willing to sympathize with the real person who's disrupting our classroom as we are with the character we know only from the printed page?)

3. This question should provide quite a jolt for those students who have been told that sentence fragments are among the great crimes against humanity. Regardless, exploring this question will prove enlightening. The musing effect that Liu achieves by using fragments in her first three paragraphs suggests the uncertainty — even the desperation — of the sixth-grader confronted with the suicide of a peer. The questioning, the incompleteness of the thoughts is reflected in the sentence structure. When she begins paragraph 4 with the standard "It was a Monday in late November," the reader sits back, ready to hear the story behind the questions.

Connections

1. The similarities are numerous: Both children suffer the consequences of poverty and lower-class status in their superficial rejection by those more privileged than they. Both accept the power of authority figures either to lift them from their present state or to condemn them to a life of insignificance. So Tsi-fai is condemned by his teacher's judgment of him as "incorrigible" (para. 3); Rosaura feels exalted by her preferential treatment at the party — until the devastating revelation that Señora Ines has been using her as a maid. Rosaura's eyes, however, reveal her strength. The cold stare she levels at Señora Ines in the end suggests that she will not only survive but also will overcome the handicaps of poverty. She does not despair as does So Tsi-fai, in part because she can rely on the strength of her mother, who stands ready to protect her. In addition, her poverty and its demands are not as harsh as his. As a result, we can expect Rosaura to prevail.

2. As eldest sons, both So Tsi-fai and Sugama are expected to take on major responsibility for the welfare of the families, especially to provide for their parents and younger siblings. Sugama, a young professional in Tokyo, will be expected to live with his parents and grandfather. His dilemma is that he cannot live with and support his parents in Tokyo, since it would be too expensive for them all to live there (45). Instead, if he plans to honor his familial obligation, he will have to give up his city job and go home to take a dead-end job. So Tsi-fai's family differs from Sugama's in that they are extremely poor, making it even harder for So Tsi-fai to fulfill family obligations. As the oldest son, So Tsi-fai has had no older siblings to care for him, but he "helped in the fields, cooked for the family, and washed his own clothes" (6). With so many responsibilities, he has little time to give to studies. This is the dilemma So Tsi-fai faces: If he devoted himself to doing well in school, he would not be able to contribute to his family's immediate needs. But because he had so little support for his schooling from teachers and parents (4, 7) and because he gave his time to responsibilities in the home, he has failed in school — which means that he will be unable to fulfill his parents' expectation that he help them more substantially in the future.

3. Although the roles played by the ghosts in the two narratives are quite different, their acceptance suggests an acknowledgment of supernatural forces, probably stemming from ancient traditions. In "Nigerian Childhood" (p. 112) the ghost serves as instructor to children, reinforcing traditional values. In "So Tsi-fai" the message is the opposite: The ghost assails the status quo, condemning a tradition that contributes to the suicide of a young boy. The dramatic roles of the two ghosts differ as well: Whereas Soyinka's ghost

is a component of legend, an integral part of his heritage, Liu's ghost arises from guilt, a personification of values and ideas, and comes from within to condemn the behavior of society. Thus Liu's ghost can be viewed in two ways: If her ghost is considered less literal than Soyinka's, more of a literary technique, then perhaps it is less frightening. Conversely, if her ghost is considered to be rooted in the hearts of Liu and her classmates, then it is more frightening than Soyinka's — you can't run home to escape the ghost from within.

MARIO VARGAS LLOSA (YOH-sa), On Sunday (p. 224)

Explorations

1. Some students may be reluctant to extrapolate, having been warned in the past to stick to the story. But if they're encouraged to imagine relationships and situations that are consistent with the characters and themes in the story, they should be able to handle this question. Miguel has apparently been loving Flora "pure and chaste from afar" until this point. He clearly suspects that Rubén too has been with her; perhaps his rival has even told Flora of his (Miguel's) love for her. The key word here is rival: Until this situation presented itself, Miguel and Rubén had been friends, members of the same gang. Now love and competition for the same young woman have turned Miguel's comradely feeling for Rubén into enmity.

2. Students may be a bit confused by this ending, failing to understand fully the implications of the contest. Miguel and Rubén have obviously shared an accomplishment by undergoing their ordeal, but they have also settled their rivalry. What Miguel and Rubén seem to realize is that their rivalry over Flora need not undermine the bond between them nor the bright future promised by their youth, strength, and support for each other.

A less appealing but probably accurate interpretation might emphasize that the unspoken agreement between the two is that Flora (or any woman, for that matter) is simply not worth the fight. The bond between men is far stronger than the attraction of women. (Some students may find this interpretation particularly unsavory, but it is consistent with the view of women in the story.)

3. Many students will be able to identify with Miguel's fantasy of personal victory and the humiliation of his rival Rubén, although the specifics of the fantasy (a military parade) may seem foreign to them. Miguel's fantasy arises out of his suspicion that he is less of a man than Rubén. Whereas the fantasy can only temporarily help him deal with those fears, saving his friend from drowning dispels Miguel's apprehensions about his manhood. In Miguel's fantasy, Rubén is publicly shamed and Miguel is glorified. But in reality, when he has the opportunity to shame Rubén by revealing his rival's physical weakness and fear, Miguel chooses to allow Rubén to keep his dignity. In this way, he can feel better about himself and renew his friendship with Rubén.

4. This question should precipitate some lively discussion. In a traditional composition class, most of the men and many of the women will fail even to notice that Flora is merely a prize to be fought for. Some students, upon recognizing this, may not find this view

of women disquieting. Regardless, a close reading of the story should reveal to all students that while Flora shows some compassion for Miguel, she also lies about meeting Rubén. Beyond that, we get very little sense of a personality. Both young men seem more interested in winning her than in understanding her. For her part, Flora seems little more than a pawn: It seems not to matter at all what she does or how she acts; Miguel and Rubén will still spar. The quest itself wholly ignores Flora's wishes. The role that Flora plays is dictated by the rules governing male-female behavior in her society. Under those rules the female's role is a passive one.

Connections

1. In entering the swimming match, Miguel behaves in a self-destructive and life-threatening fashion. This foolish act, along with his drinking to excess in the bar and his taunting of Rubén, shows that he has not yet gained enough maturity to behave responsibly. However, the disaster that might have occurred did not; Miguel still can believe that "Before him was opening a golden future" (para. 188). So Tsi-fai, like Miguel, behaves self-destructively in order to get attention, but in every other way their situations are very different. If So Tsi-fai had survived, he could not have looked forward to a "golden future." Miguel's actions are thoughtless, but he experiences none of the deep despair that causes So Tsi-fai to seek actively to destroy himself. Miguel is an accepted member of a community; he has every reason to think he will be able to have good friendships and even "win" a girl. So Tsi-fai is an outsider to others of his own generation, and he tries to be responsible for his family in ways that even an older and more able person would find hard.

2. Miguel's experience during the swimming match with Rubén gives him new insights similar to those described by Michael Dorris in his discussion of the initiation of young males in Plains Indian tribes. The personal, spiritual turning point Dorris describes takes place as a result of "Fear, fatigue, reliance on strange foods, the anguish of loneliness, stress, and the expectation of ultimate success . . ." (3). Miguel experiences many of these psychologically transformative pressures when he finds himself floundering at sea. However, when he decides to save Rubén, he ceases to call on God to save him and begins to act capably. He reacts with authority during a real emergency, wins Rubén's grudging admiration, and is recognized upon his return as having "becom[e] a man" (187). This accords with the goals for the Plains Indian initiation, which for a young man included a "foresight of . . . his adult persona" (3).

3. Students should find a number of familiar scenes in this story: Miguel's awkwardness in his meeting with Flora, his insistence on drinking despite his fear that he won't be able to hold the beer, his bold plunge into the sea followed by his "certainty that God was going to punish him by drowning him," and the resulting comic bargaining with God for his life (165). Students' ability to identify with such attempts to be adult, countered by feelings of inadequacy, should help them to grasp some of the implications of Miguel's epiphany.

SALMAN RUSHDIE, The Broken Mirror (p. 240)

Explorations

1. Students may be better able to explore the dual meaning of the mirror if they first consider how Rushdie compares the old black-and-white photograph of his father's home with the house he sees when he visits it. His vision of his past, like the photograph, is apparently stable and fixed. When he sees the house in person, he is "assaulted by colors," and the vividness of his new vision forces him to consider how partial — how "monochromatic" — his former vision of his childhood had been (para. 2). In paragraph 6, Rushdie mentions that the narrator for his book *Midnight's Children* has a "fallible memory . . . and his vision is fragmentary." He generalizes from the narrator to expatriated Indian writers, asserting that they cannot reflect an intact vision of India because they are working with "broken mirrors, some of whose fragments have been irretrievably lost" (6). This is, however, a valuable way of viewing the past and of viewing India. Rushdie argues, in regard to his own partial memories of images from India, that "fragmentation made trivial things seem like symbols, and the mundane acquired numinous qualities" (8).

2. Reflecting on his childhood in India and his later life in the West, Rushdie feels that "it's my present that is foreign, and that the past is home" (1). Nevertheless his Western influences affect his vision of India and his childhood. He makes reference in the first paragraph to British writer L. P. Hartley while he is exploring the idea of a foreign present and later refers to John Fowles, another British writer, on the topic of whole versus partial vision (11). He wrote *Midnight's Children* in North London, a fact that caused him to consider how his life in the West has changed his vision of India (5). Western influences affect his memories of India in more direct ways as well; Rushdie recalls seeing as a child billboards and ads for Western products (7). Rushdie makes two biblical references, the first when he alludes to Lot's wife in paragraph four and the second in the conclusion, when he addresses the issue of Western influences directly, by calling up an image of the expatriated Indian writer as "fallen" — an image that derives from Christianity (12).

3. Although Rushdie distinguishes between the Western and Indian parts of his identity in historical terms, as when he writes that "the past is a foreign country" (1), his strongest statements about expatriate Indian writers have to do with the mix of cultures they represent: "Our identity is both plural and partial" (12). He considers his "ambiguous and shifting" position between cultures potentially productive. Rushdie wants to reclaim his Indian past (2, 3), but he also realizes that his life in the West has given him a perspective on India that is unique and unavailable to those who remained in India. He uses his knowledge of Western culture, and his memories of Indian culture, to reject the "guru-illusion" that "writers are . . . sages, dispensing the wisdom of the centuries"(11).

4. Students may need help interpreting Rushdie's reference to Lot's wife when he writes that writers in exile who look back "risk . . . being mutated into pillars of salt"(4). Like Lot's wife, Rushdie implies, expatriate Indian writers have failed to keep their eyes on the present and future; by looking back at a doomed past instead of forward to a living future, they can become static and unable to progress. If they are "haunted" by the past, writers in exile will not be able to recognize that they are creating "imaginary homelands," not reclaiming the literal India.

Connections

1.   Students may have trouble with this question until they have considered some of the basic differences between Rushdie's and Vargas Llosa's writing. Rushdie's essay elaborates on a complex of ideas about the fiction writer's process and the functions of memory. "On Sunday," on the other hand, is a narrative. Whereas Rushdie uses the device of the broken mirror to describe the problems and advantages for the expatriate writer of partial memory, Vargas Llosa uses the figure of the mirror to reveal something about his main character Miguel. In paragraph 16, Miguel's vivid fantasy of his victorious march at the Naval Academy parade vanishes "like steam wiped off a mirror," replaced by an equally vivid fantasy of his rival with the girl Miguel wants. The device of the mirror in this sequence functions to show us Miguel's youthful, overactive imagination and his fears of being humiliated. In the same instant, he recalls having told Flora that he loved her — a memory that, in view of his unhappy fantasy, now makes him feel angry and ashamed. In the next paragraph, Miguel sees an image of himself in the mirror: "a face both ravaged and livid." The device of the mirror, reflecting both his fantasies and himself, demonstrates how Miguel has allowed fantasy and reality to become mixed. In this sense Vargas Llosa and Rushdie use the devices of mirror and memory in similar ways; both are concerned with how memory and fiction — or fantasy — work together to influence a person's psychological state.

2.   Rushdie's broken-mirror metaphor describes both the richness and the partial nature of the memory of former places and former selves. Terry Galloway describes a breakdown she underwent when she had trouble facing the ways in which her deafness would affect her life. As a result of the breakdown, however, she developed some skills she could use to help her create a new and happier life. Therefore, her memory of herself before the breakdown, and before she became completely deaf, is influenced by her current situation. As hard as her early life was, it is now evident to the mature Galloway that her young self had every reason to be confident that she would learn to cope well with her disability. At the end of his reflections on his early problems confronting his homosexuality, Bernard Cooper uses an image from earlier in the piece to form a contrast and a connection between his adult self and himself as a boy. The adult Cooper touches his lover's back and feels "the pleasure a diver feels the instant he enters a body of water." As a boy, he swam with his best friend and felt — but couldn't allow himself to admit — pleasure and desire. Cooper concludes by saying that his only regret is that he hadn't been able to admit his homosexuality when he was a boy, a regret that simultaneously indicates his current acceptance of himself and affirms that his young self had every reason to believe that he would one day be able to value himself as a gay man. Malcolm X suggests a mirror analogy when he writes that he "often reflected upon the new vistas" that learning to read offered him. What he sees reflected in his own past is a man with a "long dormant craving to be mentally alive," but this realization about his former self is only possible because he can look back from the point of view of a self-educated man.

3.   It is interesting that both Rushdie and Mphahlele use the image of a man with his legs spread to suggest their dual position between their cultures of origin and the Western world. Mphahlele says in paragraph 2, "It is not as if I were pinned on a rock, my legs stretched in opposite directions." Rushdie claims that expatriate Indian writers sometimes "feel that we straddle two cultures; at other times, that we fall between two stools" (12). Although Rushdie and Mphahlele appear to disagree about whether Western educations

57

create psychological rifts for writers, in fact both agree that there are significant advantages for writers who "straddle two cultures." Rushdie claims that since literature provides one way to "enter reality," the expatriate writer is in an especially good position since his dualism allows him to see from new angles. Mphahlele writes that a Western education creates conflicts for the writer, but that depending on his "innate personality equipment," the writer must "strive toward some workable reconciliation inside himself" (2). Both Rushdie and Mphahlele, then, see that the conflicts felt by a writer between cultures also provide opportunities for a new and stronger understanding of the self and the world.

AMY TAN, Two Kinds (p. 246)

Explorations

1. Students will find it easy to come up with several meanings for the story's title. One of the most obvious meanings is revealed late in the story, when Jing-mei's mother shouts "Only two kinds of daughters. . . . Those who are obedient and those who follow their own mind!" (para. 75). The mother's denial that Jing-mei could be obedient in some ways and independent in others reflects the all-or-nothing thinking that affects every aspect of her relationship with Jing-mei. The mother believes that one is either a genius or "not trying." Initially, Jing-mei accepts her mother's view and thinks that she "would soon become perfect" (10). At times Jing-mei views herself as divided into two kinds — the prodigy and the failure. This interpretation of "two kinds" is reinforced by the contrast between Jing-mei and Waverly, who tells Jing-mei, "You aren't a genius like me" (62). But Jing-mei has already had a moment when she sees herself as "angry, powerful" (19). She realizes that the "prodigy side" of her is someone who can resist her mother. This doesn't resolve the conflicts embedded in the idea that there are "two kinds of daughters," but it is an important step toward integrating herself. Only much later, as an adult, can Jing-mei resolve the conflicts she and her mother battled over. In the closing paragraph, Jing-mei returns to the idea of "two kinds" when she looks back at "Pleading Child," the music she tried to play at the recital, and sees that opposite it is another piece, "Perfectly Contented." She recognizes that "they were two halves of the same song," a realization that helps her put to rest the conflicts between her mother and herself.

2. The top goal of Jing-mei Woo's mother is to make her daughter become a prodigy. Most of her actions during the story show that her life focuses on this goal. She constantly watches television or combs magazines for stories about prodigies to see which possibilities are open to her daughter (4, 12). She drills Jing-mei every evening. Finally, she exchanges cleaning chores for piano lessons and scrapes together money to buy a secondhand piano. Although students may find the mother a domineering and repellent figure, understanding her motivations will help them see the issue of meeting parental expectations from alternate points of view. The mother sees America as a magical place where anyone can be whatever she wants to be: rich, famous, a prodigy (1, 2). From her point of view, she is asking her daughter to achieve a very reasonable goal that will help Jing-mei experience a happier life than she herself has known.

3. After only one reading, students will probably interpret this story as an example of mother-daughter or parent-child conflict. However, thoughtful students who reread it will notice that the narrator herself has different feelings about being a child prodigy. Because she often shares her mother's feelings, abandoning them only after she feels incapable of meeting her mother's expectations, the conflict between Jing-mei and her mother could be interpreted as an externalization of Jing-mei's own inner struggle. At first she "is just as excited as [her] mother, maybe even more so" (9). Her parents will adore her (10). But she also is anxious that the prodigy in her will disappear (11) and she will turn out to be an ordinary person. Her failure to succeed at her mother's examinations confirms her sense of being ordinary and makes her lose faith in the possibility of becoming a genius. At that point, she says, "something inside of me began to die" (18).

4. As long as her mother retains her faith in Jing-mei's ability to become a prodigy, Jing-mei does not completely give up hope for her own success. But her mother's abandonment of hope confirms Jing-mei's inability to escape being ordinary. Furthermore, the mother is so constantly hopeful, so convinced that "there were so many ways for things to get better" (3), that the loss of this faith implies she has been defeated. By offering the piano back to her daughter, she makes Jing-mei feel that she can never completely lose faith in her.

Connections

1. Rushdie uses the device of the broken mirror to convey the quality of the emigrant's memory, which he believes achieves a partial view of former places and former selves. The emigrant's memory mixes reality and fiction to create "imaginary homelands." Early in "Two Kinds," the narrator Jing-mei recalls her mother's life in China, where she had lost her entire family and her home (para. 3). This tragic part of her mother's history is significant to Jing-mei in part because it means that she, Jing-mei, will be expected to fulfill "all my mother's hopes." This is, of course, far too big a burden for Jing-mei to carry. The mother's selective vision allows her to see America only as a place to become "anything you wanted to be," which demonstrates that she is seeing the present, as well as her past, reflected in a "broken mirror" that gives back only a partial image. Jing-mei uses the little she knows about her mother's former life to separate herself from her mother. She tells herself, "I wasn't her slave. This wasn't China" (67). And, most painfully, she recalls the children her mother lost in China and uses this to further distance herself from her mother. After telling her "I wish you weren't my mother," Jing-mei shouts, "I wish I were dead! Like them" (78).

2. Like So Tsi-fai, Jing-mei Woo cannot realistically meet her parents' expectations. Jing-mei's mother is unrealistic in her belief that her daughter already possesses the answers to the grueling nightly quizzes (12–20) or that just working hard produces a prodigy (28). The concept of talent does not exist for her. Like Jing-mei Woo, So Tsi-fai is his family's "biggest hope" (6). His education might liberate him from a life of poverty and toil. Listing the conditions that make her feel that he could not succeed in escaping his condition, Liu describes him as "poor, undisciplined, and lack[ing] the training and support to pass his exams" (18). Both Jing-mei Woo and So Tsi-fai appear to be lazy and rebellious but behave this way to provide excuses for failure. So Tsi-fai commits suicide by drinking insecticide (9); Jing-mei Woo figuratively destroys herself by a humiliating display of her lack of achievement (54–56).

3. Jing-mei Woo's mother in "Two Kinds," Sister Marie in "So Tsi-fai," and Rosaura's mother in "The Stolen Party" try to change the outlook of the central character in each story. They belittle the children's inability to accept their adult point of view and try, through disparaging comments, to reduce them to obedience. Although Rosaura's mother seems the most sympathetic to the feelings of her child, wanting to spare her humiliation at the hands of outsiders, Herminia sneers at Rosaura's belief in the monkey (1) and criticizes her for thinking too highly of herself (4). Sister Marie, having no sympathy for So Tsi-fai, constantly criticizes him, calling him lazy and good for nothing. She exercises her authority by standing him in the corner and making him report to the principal's office, yet can't make him change his behavior (3). Jing-mei Woo's mother also criticizes her daughter, convinced she is not trying (28). Like Sister Marie, she does not hesitate to react with physical punishment (33) in an equally vain attempt to control the situation. Students can see that explanations for the adults' failure would vary from culture to culture. In our culture, we would probably feel that people respond better to positive incentives.

4. Students will easily pick out points of comparison between the two, for Jing-mei Woo seems to fit Sheehy's description of an adolescent who seeks and fears autonomy. Just as described by Sheehy, Jing-mei covers her fear of failure "with acts of defiance and mimicked confidence." She has "thoughts filled with lots of won'ts" (19), and her whole piano performance mimics the behavior of the girl on "The Ed Sullivan Show." Like the adolescent Sheehy describes who pretends to know what she wants, Jing-mei has made up her mind to assert her own identity, vowing "I won't let her change me" (19). But she still feels very much a part of her family, sharing the shame she inflicts on them (56). Jing-mei can consciously reject her mother, trying to hurt her by saying she wishes she wasn't her daughter, but this statement also scares her, since she is not ready to break all of her family ties (75).

CHRISTOPHER REYNOLDS, Cultural Journey to Africa (p. 258)

Explorations

1. This will be an easy question for most students because Reynolds begins his essay by defining Culturefest and its purposes. Culturefest 1992 was designed to establish cultural connections between African-Americans and the continent of Africa. Reynolds follows several African-Americans at Culturefest as they seek "roots and cultural resonances," (para. 2) and he quotes one participant who defines Africa as "the final link to the souls of our ancestors" (5). Their search for that link is complicated, since they find Abidjan a rich, chaotic mix of contemporary western and African influences (2). Students will also readily find information about the tactics participants use to discover connections between Africa and themselves. The Americans search through Abidjan (12), take a tour of working-class areas (17-20), try to get to know local people (24), and attend an initiation (29-32). One woman decides to buy property on the Ivory Coast (26), and another successfully barters at the market (27).

2. Perhaps the best reason for choosing the Ivory Coast as the site for Culturefest is its position as a "continental crossroads" where sixty ethnic groups and over 2 million

migrants from other West African countries have made their homes. "On this ground," Reynolds says, "a black American inevitably stands among distant kin" (8). In discussing the question of why a luxurious, Western-style hotel was chosen as the tour's headquarters, students who have also read Atwood's "A View from Canada" or Octavio Paz's "Hygiene and Repression," both in this volume, will recall that, unlike travelers from some other nations, people from the United States are often uncomfortable unless they feel they have brought their own culture and environment with them. One of the tour organizers comments that Americans need "an adjustment period" when they arrive (11), but it may be that the tour organizers realized that they would attract more participants if the Americans knew they would be staying in a modern hotel with all the amenities (9).

3. Reynolds does not go into the history and geography of the Ivory Coast until after he has introduced Culturefest and some of its American participants (1–6). He offers more background information on Abidjan and its economy in paragraphs 9 and 14. Most students will easily see that if Reynolds had discussed the "facts" first, readers would have been lost and unable to understand why this background information would be significant or interesting. In analyzing the rhetorical impact of Reynolds's organizational choices, it will also be important to point out that Reynolds is economical in his use of history and geography, selecting only those facts that contribute to the purpose of his essay, which is to follow the cultural journey of African-Americans as they seek a link to the Africa their ancestors left on slave ships.

Connections

1. To help students get into the spirit of this question, it may be helpful to begin by asking them to reflect on their own immigrant heritage. Most students will be able to identify one or more homelands from which their ancestors came. Jing-mei Woo has powerful connections to China because of her mother's history, but even those students who no longer have immediate ties to a far-away homeland may be able to comment on how their ancestors' origins in (for instance) Asia, Europe, or Africa have contributed to their own identity and sense of kinship. Ironically, Jing-mei Woo experiences her ancestral homeland, China, as something that separates her and her mother. The memory of the children and other family her mother lost before she left China (paras. 3, 78) is a burden Jing-mei carries, because she feels that she can never be as good or as worthy as those her mother loved in China. Some of those who joined Culturefest 92 expressed the benefits of re-establishing ties to Africa: "cultural resonance" (2), spiritual awakening (5), sense of kinship (4), and a more tangible connection to history (6).

2. Unlike those who came to the Ivory Coast for Culturefest, Rushdie has memories of Bombay from his own childhood. However, he wants to "restore the past to myself . . . in CinemaScope and glorious Technicolor" (2). Rushdie readjusts his vision to accommodate the differences between his expectations of reality and what he actually finds in Bombay; similarly the African-Americans who went to Africa have to adjust their expectations — sometimes drastically — in order to comprehend the realities of Abidjan (11). Rushdie describes Bombay as "a city built by foreigners upon reclaimed land" (3); Abidjan also shows the effects of Western and Asian influences (2), a factor that some African-American visitors found disorienting initially. Rushdie, however, affirms the validity of "imaginary homelands," (4) which arise because physical alienation from his

nation of origin sets him free to construct "'my' India" (5). Similarly, one of the African Americans who visited the Ivory Coast later realized that "I found my Africa" (32).

3. Western, African, and other cultural influences overlap in Reynolds's depiction of Abidjan, beginning in paragraph 3 with the mention of skyscrapers, taxis, urban streets, and French restaurants intermingled with coconut trees, fishermen, and a woman bearing her laundry on her head. Later in the essay, Reynolds again demonstrates how Western and African influences intermingle when he mentions the French boulevards and American billboards amid "an enduring pattern of village life" (12). But perhaps the most important Western influence is the Hotel Ivoire, where the American participants in Culturefest stay. They venture out to investigate the African landscape and sample its culture, but at night they return to a familiar environment. Similarly, V. S. Naipaul begins his essay, "Entering the New World," by recounting his meeting in an Abidjan hotel with Ebony, and he ends his essay with a scene at a French restaurant in another part of the city. Like Reynolds, Naipaul sees Western and African cultural influences as interwoven, but for Naipaul it is Ebony himself who brings the two cultures together. In Naipaul's eyes, the mix of cultural influences in Ebony has produced uneasy results. Ebony has entered the "new world," but Naipaul does not believe Ebony takes seriously the effects of the Western influence on the Ivory Coast (18). By the end of the essay Naipaul is beginning to doubt that the "new world" has really made an impact: "Remove those men [the Europeans], and their ideas — which after all had no finality — would disappear" (22).

    Students should have few problems locating the features Western visitors might find most and least attractive about Abidjan, because Reynolds has summed them up in the comments of two African-American Culturefest participants. One says that her visit to the Ivory Coast is "like a vacation from racism" (15), but in the next paragraph another woman lists the problems: squalor, deprivation, and the oppression of women. Naipaul conveys his opinions of the Ivory Coast through his observations of Ebony, whom he finds to be sociable (5) and "relaxed, a whole man" (18), even as he is irritated by Ebony's apparent intellectual dilettantism (10, 18). The more difficult problem, for most students, will be interpreting the differences in Reynolds's and Naipaul's assessments. One way to approach this question is to consider the differences in how Reynolds and Naipaul represent themselves in their essays. Reynolds says nothing about his own experience in Abidjan and does not give his opinions directly. He uses quotes from others, conveying their sense of the attractions and problems of the Ivory Coast. Naipaul, on the other hand, is a participant in the events he describes, and his emotions and opinions are apparent throughout "Entering the New World." Another way to approach this problem is to have students consider the cultural differences between the writers. Naipaul was originally from Trinidad but now lives in England. His focus is on European influences and their effects on African culture. Reynolds takes an American perspective, seeing the Ivory Coast through the eyes of people whose ancestors were once slaves in the United States and who now want to regain a sense of connection to African culture.

4. In "The Westernization of the World," Paul Harrison writes that China, Japan, and Turkey began to study and even embrace Western culture and technology as a way of dealing with the threat of Western military power and obtaining some of the benefits of industrialization (14, 15), but he also argues that the adoption of Western culture in many nations is producing "world uniformity" (6). In Reynolds's essay, Culturefest 1992 also represents a form of cultural borrowing, but the motivations and the results are very

different. The African-American visitors to the Ivory Coast are not seeking to draw power from a dominant but alien culture by adopting its ways; many are looking for general connections to their ancestors, who were enslaved by one of the most powerful Western powers, the United States. Their "borrowing" from African culture is not a movement toward "world uniformity," but an attempt to understand and appreciate the highly diverse mixture of cultures in Ivory Coast.

GÜNTER GRASS (Grahss), After Auschwitz (p. 264)

Explorations

1. Most students will know that Auschwitz was one of the concentration camps where the Germans interned about 4 million people, most of whom were Jews. Many Jews were exterminated at Auschwitz by phenol injections, gas, and other means. For these reasons, Auschwitz has come to symbolize the appalling crimes of the Holocaust as a whole. Günter Grass calls up vivid images of the horror of Auschwitz when he describes photographs of dead bodies and piles of hair and shoes he was forced to view in an American prison camp (para. 6). The personal meaning that Auschwitz has for Grass arises from his confrontation with the realities of what occurred there. He thinks of Auschwitz as a "monstrous phenomenon" that goes "beyond facts and figures, beyond the cushioning academic study, a thing inaccessible . . ." (8). For Grass, Auschwitz marks the beginning of his adulthood, the point in his own life when he had to rid himself of the illusions of his youth (7) and begin to consider the social and political responsibilities of himself as a writer (9).

2. Students will be better able to discuss Grass's involvement with National Socialism if they first understand that "National Socialism" is synonymous with "Nazi" (the German acronym for the party). Its main goal was to establish Aryans as a "master race" under the leadership of the Führer, who would purify the "race" by exterminating Jews and Communists, among others. As a boy, Grass was a member of the Hitler Youth (7) and recalls "campfires, flag drills, shooting practice with small-caliber weapons (25). By the time World War II began, he had been "rendered stupid by dogma" (3) — a reference to the ideologies of National Socialism. He marks the Nuremburg trials as symbolic of his disillusionment with the party (7), but his artistic impulses had already caused him, earlier in his life, to doubt his commitment to the Hitler Youth (10). After World War II, Grass rejected National Socialism completely: "the anti-Semitism of one's youth was exchanged for philo-Semitism, and one defined oneself unquestioningly and without risk as antifascist" (15). National Socialism became identified with Auschwitz, which strongly influenced the development of Grass's literary and artistic career. He agreed with Theodor Adorno that it was an "irreparable tear in the history of civilization" (16), and he considered himself to be implicated in the crimes that the Nazis committed (22). In many of his books, Grass promoted the "demonization of the Nazi period" (29), and he became involved in politics (30).

3. Grass asserts that efforts to reunify Germany took impetus from a general desire among people in Eastern and Central Europe for the economic and political advantages that "solidarity and freedom" would bring (36). But he believes that this general hope for European unity was "twisted into German aspirations. Once again the call is heard for 'all of Germany'" (37). Grass opposed reunification because Auschwitz would not have been possible without "a strong, unified Germany" (38).

4. Students should be able to come up with multiple responses to this question, but they should begin by considering the occasion and audience for Grass's speech. In paragraph 2, Grass identifies his audience as students. He is speaking at a Frankfurt university. Grass describes his audience as "innocent" because they did not grow up under an active Nazi influence as Grass did. Grass considers himself a "witness" (1) to the Nazi era, and in that role he is able to give Germany's young people a vivid and firsthand account of what it was like to go through a conversion from the Aryan supremacist ideologies of National Socialism to his mature, solidly antifascist stance. The university evidently invited Grass as a famous writer to talk about his professional and personal development. They may also have asked him to speak because "those who do not learn from history are condemned to repeat it." Concerned about the possibility of a resurgence of Nazi sympathies in a unified Germany, the West German university may have invited Grass because he could speak out against the Nazis from the unique position of someone who once accepted Nazi ideology unquestioningly. Grass represents the process by which he was converted as a process of maturing. It was as an embarrassingly credulous boy that he was indoctrinated (25); as he became a man, he learned to recognize the truth and reject the propaganda he was force-fed as a member of the Hitler Youth. This perspective might appeal to university students who are themselves in the process of becoming adults and learning to recognize and accept the harsher realities of their own history.

Connections

1. One way to approach a discussion of the basic differences between Grass's efforts to reclaim a lost heritage and the efforts of African-Americans to seek their roots in Africa is to ask students to compare the different ways that racism is relevant to Grass and African-Americans. African-Americans — even the middle-to-upper class people who could afford the trip to Africa — cope on a daily basis with the economic, psychological, and social effects of racism directed against them. Grass, on the other hand, has not been on the receiving end of racism. Instead, in his youth he was a member of the National Socialist Party, which is founded on racist principles. Grass suffers guilt and embarrassment over his personal involvement (para. 25), and he lives with the knowledge that he belonged to a party that inflicted terrible harm on Jews and other groups. Some students may think that his task is the harder one, since he has spent his life seeking to keep alive a history that makes him feel ashamed. Others may think African-Americans have the harder task, since they are reaching back into a history and a homeland that was stolen from them when their ancestors were enslaved. Most will never be able to retrieve their personal heritage. Ultimately, it will be less important for students to debate the question of whose task is harder than to consider how the unique social and historical circumstances of Grass and African-Americans influence their efforts to reclaim a lost heritage.

2. Sophronia Liu, Liang Heng, and Günter Grass all look back with a certain amount of guilt and regret at the tragic injustices they were associated with as children. Grass declares that he and other poets of his generation "belonged to the Auschwitz generation — not as criminals, to be sure, but in the camp of the criminals" (21). As an adult he has not renounced that sense of responsibility, but he has turned it to positive use, actively seeking to prevent National Socialism from rising to power again. Liang Heng suffered personally as a result of his mother's ostracism and the family conflicts that arose over her misfortune. In the last paragraph, Liang recalls that "over the years, I came to resent my mother for making my life so miserable. . . . I cut her out of my life just as I had been told to do." But as an adult, Liang understands that his mother was not responsible for what happened. He realizes, for instance, that she made every effort to mother her children in spite of her husband's abuse of her and her own difficult circumstances (36). Sophronia Liu felt deeply the impact of So Tsi-fai's death when she was in school, but as an adult she still confronts the ghost of So Tsi-fai (19) and asks herself "Is there anything I can do to lay it to rest?" In writing about his life and death from a sympathetic perspective, and refusing to write him off as unworthy of support and respect, Liu is taking an important step toward letting go of her own sense that she was, somehow, implicated in the tragedy.

3. Among the revealing comments Rushdie makes about expatriate writers is that they "are haunted by some sense of loss, some urge to reclaim, to look back, even at the risk of being mutated into pillars of salt" (4). In the case of Sophronia Liu and Liang Heng, leaving their homelands may have left them with a sense of being haunted by the past (see Connections #2, above), but it has also given them enough distance to explore their memories from a clearer perspective than they might have had if they had stayed. Spending much of his life in the West has given Liang a more detached, but also more comprehensive, view of the political circumstances that caused his mother to be exiled. Similarly, Sophronia Liu uses the perspective gained in the process of maturing and coming to the United States for graduate school to reassess the tragedy that "close[ed] off a young boy's life at fourteen just because he was poor, undisciplined, and lacked the training and support to pass his exams" (18). Günter Grass's situation is very different from Liang's and Liu's, since he stayed in his homeland. Like Liang and Liu, Grass lost his youthful innocence because he was confronted with unthinkable injustices. Grass may have been, in fact, more in danger of being "haunted by a sense of loss" than Liu or Liang, since he continued to live amid the memories of Nazi Germany and has devoted so much of his artistic and political life to interpreting that era and its aftereffects.

Yoram Binur (Bee-NOOR), Palestinian Like Me (p. 275)

Explorations

1. Binur began his impersonation in the hope of bringing a "fresh perspective" to his journalism (para. 3) but soon learned that when his perspective changed, he reevaluated what he already knew. As he puts it, "It wasn't a question of discovering new facts, but of discovering what it meant to *feel* the facts" (6). Suddenly he learns that Arab fear of

military patrols is not just an exaggeration (6); he becomes an "invisible" man (8, 9). By the end of the essay, he has developed a sympathy for the Palestinians and accepts that the Israelis mistreat them. Yet he does not conclude by pointing a finger or affixing blame. Instead, he uses his picture of the fear and mistrust on both sides to argue that continued Israeli occupation will lead only to an oppressive society and more bloodshed (52).

2. This essay presents a picture of the Israelis radically different from the one most people in the United States have encountered. Depending on the composition of the class, responses could include anger, disbelief, and a sense of vindication. To prevent students from limiting discussion to an emotional debate on the virtues of Jews versus Arabs, they might be asked to examine the feelings of Jews and Arabs in any given situation. (Their reactions are rarely based only on the situation at hand.) Binur concludes that Jews rule "without the least curiosity about how the other side lives" (52). If students can remain curious, without immediately taking sides, they may better understand how nationalism and religious and cultural differences contribute to the explosive situation in Israel. For instance, *sumud* and *intifada* would be defined quite differently by Jews and Arabs, depending whether these acts are viewed as threat or resistance. According to Binur, *sumud* is the most basic form of Arab resistance, based on the idea that to exist and not to be driven from one's land "is an act of defiance" (36). *Sumud* uses surreptitious actions to express hostility toward the Jews. For example, the Israeli government has housing erected on occupied lands as a symbol that they will never be returned to Palestinians. Palestinian workers build the houses, then damage them in a symbolic action (42). The *intifada* is a movement of anti-Israeli demonstrations in the Palestinian refugee camps. Binur presents the Arab view when he calls the *intifada* "the anguished cry of a minority trying to call attention to the discrimination that is being practiced against it." According to Binur, the Israelis see the *intifada* as riots (45).

3. Since Binur reports as a Jew disguised as an Arab, readers would not expect him to have a pro-Arab bias. If he corroborates Palestinians' statement of their position in Israeli society, he cannot be accused of exaggerating or fomenting discontent in support of a political cause. His evaluation is more devastating because his heritage and culture have trained him to reject this point of view. Had he written from a third-person point of view his essay would have been far less convincing. Binur had an intellectual awareness of the facts of Palestinians' lives, but he could not feel what those facts meant (6). By writing in the first person, he makes his readers share his experiences so that they can reach a new awareness of what it means to be a Palestinian in Israel.

Connections

1. Binur is angry when he hears Abd Al Karim deny that Hitler killed the Jews, but he remembers that his Palestinian friends grew up in refugee camps, where they endured unrelenting violence and privation at the hands of Israeli Jews. Through his examples of his own and Muhriz's beatings by Israeli soldiers and policemen, Binur makes clear that what the Palestinians endure under Israeli rule has left them no room for understanding or tolerance. The German denial that the Holocaust took place has very different motivations. According to Günter Grass, when the facts about Auschwitz came out, many Germans said to each other, "Germans would never do a thing like that" (para. 5). They denied German responsibility because the Holocaust overturned the Germans' view of themselves as just and compassionate.

2.	The relationship between "symbol" and "substance" in Binur's essay is complex because Binur conceals the "substance" of his Jewish identity behind the "symbols" that differentiate Palestinians from Jews. Binur uses his knowledge of the Arabic language and the Palestinian culture as a mask in order to pass as a Palestinian. In a sense, Binur himself begins to mistake symbols for substance when, in the course of his undercover research, he internalizes "that paralyzing fear" that Palestinians live with daily (6). His ability to identify with Palestinians, and indeed his entire project, depends upon the tendency of people to judge identities by superficial evidence such as clothing. For instance, radical Jewish right-wingers — marked by beards and skullcaps — accost him at their demonstration because he is dressed in Arab clothes (22). They misidentify him as an alien because of the symbolic content of his apparel. Police discover the keffiyeh and take it as a further proof of his Palestinian identity; in fact, they are skeptical about the authenticity of his Israeli I.D. because they are misled by the symbols of his Palestinian identity (29). On the basis of these symbols, Binur is harrassed, beaten, and denied his civil rights. Another manifestation of the misinterpretation of symbols is suggested in Binur's account of the demonstrators' singing the Israeli national anthem. When Binur writes that they raise Israeli flags and sing the anthem as a "gesture in support of Jewish terrorists" (35), he indicates that he believes they are mistaking the symbol for the substance of patriotism.

3.	Students should easily be able to see the parallel between the shocking discoveries Baldwin and Binur make about the social and economic privations of minorities. Both recognize that the minority is exploited by the dominant group. In his Palestinian identity, Binur works in restaurants and garages (5); even Arabs with professional degrees are forced to do manual labor (37). Palestinians have to be able to "prove" their right to be on the streets at any given moment, as when Hussein checks to make sure he has his Israeli I.D. before going out to buy pita bread (11). What Baldwin discovers is similar to the displacement exemplified in the harrassment of Palestinians by the Israeli police; Baldwin writes, "It comes as a great shock . . . to discover that the flag to which you have pledged allegiance, along with everybody else, has not pledged allegiance to you" (1). Similarly, Binur writes that young Palestinians "get a whiff of the democratic privileges that Israeli citizens enjoy, but they cannot share in them" (51). One of the most basic differences in the kinds of racism Baldwin and Binur describe is demonstrated in Binur's ability to pose as an Arab. Binur, once he learns the language and something about the culture, can "pass" into Palestinian communities. The color-based racism Baldwin describes does not permit this kind of contact. Israeli racism has a religious and nationalist basis that American racism does not demonstrate.

ADDITIONAL QUESTIONS AND ASSIGNMENTS

1.	In a journal entry or a collection of informal notes, refer to two or three of these selections to discuss initiation rituals as they apply to women. Consider such issues as perceptions of women's ability to assume responsibility, rules governing their behavior, support (or lack of it) from other women, and their obligations toward men. As you look over your notes, try to discover similarities and differences among the cultures represented. Can you come to any general conclusion about the image of women in a given culture?

2. Many of the selections in Part 3 deal with how individuals break with the traditions and expectations of their culture as way of defining a new self or marking their entry into a new stage of maturity. Günter Grass's break with the National Socialist Party comes at a time when he is mature enough to face the harsh realities of nazism. As part of his process of maturing, he realizes that he cannot conform to the ideologies of the party. Yoram Binur discovers he can no longer conform to conventional Jewish attitudes about the Jewish-Palestinian conflict after he lives as a Palestinian. As a result, he redefines his Jewish identity. In a personal essay, discuss what role issues of conformity have played in your process of maturing. Using Grass, Binur, Tan, or Vargas-Llosa as a model, consider at what points in your life issues of conformity and nonconformity to conventional attitudes and beliefs have become important to your self-definition.

3. One of the laments heard frequently today is that children are growing up too fast. Statistics reveal that problems with sexuality and substance abuse that used to be found in high schools now plague junior highs and middle schools. Parents complain that everything from rock videos to advertising encourages children to imitate adults. Using magazines and newspapers from the 1950s or the 1960s and from the present, compile information on what young people were wearing, doing, listening to, and buying. Organize the information into a paper in which you compare the attitudes and life-styles of young people in the two periods, focusing on two or three of the categories you've set up (for example, clothing, musical tastes, recreation). Emphasize in your paper the positive and negative features of the experience of young people in each period.

4. Conduct further research into one of the cultures represented in this section, focusing specifically on the emergence from childhood to adulthood. It would be wise to choose a culture about which information is readily available — Germany, Argentina, China, and India are likely candidates. If the selection is an excerpt from a larger work, look first at that work. You can find other sources by consulting the headnotes for other selections from that culture (if there are any) and a general encyclopedia, as well as journals devoted to the study of that culture. Narrow your topic to something manageable — such as a particular rite of passage, the influences of religion on the culture's rites of passage, or the differences in rites depending on class or sex — and write an expository paper in which you elaborate on the culture's treatment of initiation from childhood to adulthood.

Part Four

WOMEN AND MEN:
IMAGES OF THE OPPOSITE SEX

INTRODUCTION

Given the backlash against feminism in recent years and the discomfort some college-age students feel about discussing gender issues, teaching this section may require a bit more energy than others. But the rewards will be well worth the effort. One of the more interesting characteristics of the section may serve as a useful introduction to the selections. The subtitle, "Images of the Opposite Sex," suggests that we don't always perceive men and women in realistic terms, choosing instead to affix labels to them. Among the excerpts in *Looking at Ourselves*, students will find references to "the madonna" as a "female prototype" (Allen); "Dead White European Males" (Jacobs); "female chauvinists" (Wright); and "the weaker sex" (Weitz). A class discussion of various contemporary terms for men and women may prove enlightening, easing the way into more complex analyses of related images in other cultures.

Among the selections themselves the story by Kemal may cause difficulties. It presents the same problem of stereotyping as does Sa'edi's in Part Two. The tendency to view Middle-Eastern women as victims and perpetuators of sex-based oppression can be countered, however, by assigning Cooke's selection before Kemal's. Her comparison of western perceptions of veiling with Islamic women's own perceptions should help balance stereotypes students may develop when they read about the abhorrent behavior exhibited by the villagers of Chukurova.

Within the section there are several possible subthemes, among them romantic visions of relationships (Silko, Kazantzakis, and Moravia), the role of women in Islam (Minai, Cooke, and Kemal), European versus Islamic views of sexuality (the preceding, as well as Fuentes, Bugul, Kazantzakis, Beauvoir, and Moravia), and state-controlled sexuality (Minai and Cooke).

Instructors may wish to consult the following familiar works in preparing related selections from *Ourselves Among Others*:

Essays

Judy Brady, "I Want a Wife" (*Ms. Magazine*, Dec. 1971).
Annie Dillard, "The Deer at Providencia" (*Teaching a Stone to Talk*, Harper, 1982).
Gretel Ehrlich, "About Men" (*The Solace of Open Spaces*, Viking, 1985).
Barbara Lawrence, "Four-Letter Words Can Hurt You" (New York Times, Oct. 27, 1973).
S. J. Perelman, "The Machismo Mystique" (*Vinegar Puss*, Simon and Schuster, 1975).
Katherine Anne Porter, "The Necessary Enemy" (*Collected Essays and Occasional Writings of Katherine Anne Porter*, Delacorte, 1970).

287–401 (Text pages)

Scott Russell Sanders, "The Men We Carry in Our Minds" (*The Paradise of Bombs*, University of Georgia Press, 1987).
Susan Sontag, "Beauty: How Will It Change Next" (*Vogue*, May 1975).
Deborah Tannen, "Different Words, Different Worlds" (*You Just Don't Understand*, Morrow, 1990).
Paul Theroux, "On Being a Man" (*Sunrise With Seamonsters*, Houghton Mifflin, 1985).
James Thurber, "Courtship Through the Ages" (*My World — And Welcome to It*, Harcourt, 1942*)*.

Short Stories

Margaret Atwood, "Rape Fantasies" (*Dancing Girls*, McClelland and Stewart, 1977).
Kay Boyle, "The Astronomer's Wife" (*Life Being the Best*, New Directions, 1988).
John Cheever, "The Country Husband" (*The Stories of John Cheever*, Knopf, 1978).
William Faulkner, "A Rose for Emily" (*Collected Stories of William Faulkner*, Random House, 1950).
James Joyce, "The Dead" (*Dubliners*, Viking, 1982).
D. H. Lawrence, "The Horse Dealer's Daughter" (*Complete Short Stories*, Penguin, 1976).
D. H. Lawrence, "Tickets, Please" (*Complete Short Stories*, Penguin, 1976).
Doris Lessing, "A Woman on a Roof" (*A Man and Two Women*, Simon and Schuster, 1963).
Alice Munro, "Meneseteung" (*Friends of My Youth*, Knopf, 1990).
Katherine Anne Porter, "Rope" (*Flowering Judas*, Harcourt, 1930).
Eudora Welty, "Petrified Man" (*The Collected Stories of Eudora Welty*, Harcourt, 1980).

BIOGRAPHICAL NOTES ON LOOKING AT OURSELVES

1. Paula Gunn Allen, professor of English and American Indian Literature at the University of California, Los Angeles, is of Laguna-Pueblo-Sioux-Lebanese descent. She has written a novel *The Woman Who Owned the Shadows* (1983), a book of poems *Skins and Bones* (1988), a collection of essays *The Sacred Hoop: Recovering the Feminine in American Indian Tradition* (1986), and edited *Spider Woman's Granddaughters: Traditional Tales and Contemporary Writing by Native American Women* (1989) and *Grandmother of the Light: A Medicine Woman's Sourcebook* (1991).

2. Daniel Evan Weiss is the author of *The Great Divide: How Females and Males Really Differ* (1991).

3. The founder of *Ms.* magazine, Gloria Steinem is the author of a biography of Marilyn Monroe, *Marilyn* (1986), a collection of essays, *Outrageous Acts and Everyday Rebellions* (1983), and the controversial *Revolution from Within: A Book of Self-Esteem* (1992).

4. Joe Kane is a free-lance writer living in San Francisco.

5. Sally Jacobs writes for the *Boston Globe*.

6. Camille Paglia teaches humanities at the University of the Arts in Philadelphia. She is the author of *Sexual Personae: Art and Decadence from Nefertiti to Emily Dickinson* (1990) and *Sex, Art, and American Culture* (1992).

7. Lawrence Wright has taught at the American University of Cairo and been a staff writer for the *Race Relations Reporter*. He is the author of *In the New World: Growing Up with America from the Sixties to the Eighties* (1987) and *Peace Report* (1991).

8. A professor of sociology at Arizona State University, Rose Weitz is the author of *Labor Pains: Modern Midwives and Home Birth* (1988) and *Life with AIDS* (1991).

9. Richard Goldstein, arts editor for the *Village Voice*, writes frequently about sexual politics. He is the author of *The Poetry of Rock* (a collection of rock lyrics) (1969) and more recently, *Reporting the Counterculture* (1989) and *Superstars and Screwballs: 100 Years of Brooklyn Baseball* (1992).

10. A professor of linguistics at Georgetown Univeristy, Deborah Tannen has written both scholarly works (*Conversational Style*, 1984; *Talking Voice*, 1989) and popular books (*That's Not What I Meant*, 1986; *You Just Don't Understand: Women and Men in Conversation*, 1990).

Reflections

1. Two common ideas emerge in these three pieces. The first is the importance of personal and social relationships in defining women's identities. Paula Gunn Allen writes that for an American Indian woman, "her sense of herself as a woman is first and foremost prescribed by her tribe." Rose Weitz implies that among lesbians, involvement in the feminist movement and the possibility of establishing egalitarian love relationships suggests a greater sense of connectedness than is possible for heterosexual women who are involved in hierarchical relationships. And Deborah Tannen, defining the differences between her and her husband's world view, writes that she approaches "the world as many woman do: as an individual in a network of connections." Unlike Weitz, Tannen sees the tendency to relate hierarchically in personal and social situations as a matter of gender rather than sexual orientation. The second common idea is developed in Allen's and Weitz's pieces. Both writers posit a contrast between Christian (or Western) images of "woman" and realities of women's lives. Allen remarks that the "female prototype" in the Christian world is "essentially passive;" women are portrayed as "mindless, helpless, simple, or oppressed." In American Indian cultures, by contrast, women are viewed "variously . . . as fearful, sometimes peaceful, sometimes omnipotent or omniscient. . . ." Weitz also points to the passivity and weakness inherent in images of women in Western culture and contrasts those images to the realities of lesbians' lives, since lesbians use their strengths to survive without "even the illusion of male protection that marriage provides." Weitz writes that the ability of lesbians to live without men "suggests the potential strength of all women" and implies that they can rise above stereotypical views of women as "the weaker sex."

2. Richard Goldstein, writing about the history of male homosexual marriage, describes the common "image of homosexuals as emotional nomads." His piece attempts to balance that stereotype by offering evidence of attempts to establish long-term, publicly acknowledged relationships between male partners. By implication, Goldstein's description of the image of gay men as incapable of emotional commitment and sensitivity extends to heterosexual men as well, a stereotype Wright addresses in his piece about his relationship with his daughter. Wright sums up the stereotyped view of men with a quote from Barbara Jordan, who said that "women have a capacity for understanding and

compassion which a man structurally does not have. . . ." Both Wright and Goldstein believe that the stereotypes of men are not accurate; that the campaign to legalize male-to-male marriage (Goldstein) and the efforts of men to nurture children (Wright) are evidence of men's attempts to achieve emotional intimacy in stable relationships.

3. Lawrence Wright ascribes the positive traits (and negative traits) of being male to genes and hormones. He writes that men are naturally more assertive sexually, tolerate pain well, are tenacious, and adept at spatial reasoning. He goes on to say that "nature and human history have rewarded" men's strength and ability to act. Many of the pieces in *Looking At Ourselves* suggest that being a man entails many privileges, including greater representation in the media (Weiss), "greater opportunity and unparalleled privilege" in comparison with all women and men of color (Julian Bond, quoted by Jacobs), and far greater freedom to experience "solitary adventure" (Paglia). Most writers seem to depend for the most part on what they believe are obvious or commonplace truisms about being a white male in western society. Wright bases some of his ideas on interpretations of scientific evidence about the effects of androgens, and Weiss simply offers the facts of gender-differentiated representation on television. Paglia relies on personal opinion and anecdote. Jacobs uses interviews with both men and women to back up her generalizations about the advantages of being white and male.

4. Students will be able to elaborate on their responses to Question #1 as they consider the positive qualities of women and the advantages of being female. Allen, Weitz, and Tannen make the case that women are able to function well as members of families and communities because they value connectedness and see themselves as situated within networks of relationships rather than in hierarchies. Although he is critical of some feminists, Lawrence Wright makes some positive generalizations about women, saying they have brought "humanity" into business and politics and they have a greater ability to survive physically because of their genetic makeup. Gloria Steinem and Sally Jacobs imply that all women, because they deal with gender oppression, are more sensitive to the ways in which other people are oppressed.

CARLOS FUENTES (Fwen-tays), Matador & Madonna (p. 303)

Explorations

1. Students may tend to differentiate between the qualities that make the figure of the matador a model of Hispanic manhood and those qualities that make him Christlike, but Fuentes implies early in his essay that they share qualities. In paragraph 4, Fuentes asks, "Who is the matador?" and immediately responds, "a man of the people." The bullfight is a popular phenomenon. The matador, like Christ, represents a sacrifice made for the common people rather than the aristocracy (paras. 2, 4). In that sense he unites the qualities associated with Jesus Christ and the gentler qualities that are associated with Hispanic manhood, such as courage, grace, and self-sacrifice. Fuentes goes on to describe the sexual energy of the matador and the blood lust of the ritual bullfight (5) — qualities not associated with Christ — but in the next paragraph he again connects the qualities of Hispanic masculinity with Christ, declaring that the matador is "a prince

of the people" and the bullfight "an opening to the possibility of death." In paragraph 9, Fuentes makes the connection more explicit, describing Goya's painting of matador Pedro Romero and associating "the virgin body of this perfect bullfighter" with the wounded and dying Jesus Christ.

2. Both la Dama de Baza and la Dama de Elche are pre-Christian Spanish mother figures (10, 11), making them antecedents to the Virgin Mary, the figure in whom their qualities were later embodied. La Dama de Baza is an earth goddess, a figure of "maternal authority" (10), while la Dama de Elche is an erotically powerful figure (11). However, the quality Fuentes most wants to highlight in the pre-Christian earth goddesses is their ambiguity — they are all "mysterious, two-faced, tender and demanding, mother and lover . . ." (12). The Virgin Mary inherited these qualities from her precursors (13). Fuentes sees this ability to adapt, to blend the pagan and the Christian, as inherently "Andalusian" (Andalusia is a region of Spain).

3. As students read this essay, they may become confused about what Fuentes is trying to accomplish by drawing connections among such disparate cultural and religious expressions as flamenco dancing, the bullfight, Jesus Christ, the Virgin Mary, and pre-Christian mother figures. In paragraph 8, Fuentes intimates his purpose when he describes as a "circle" the confluence of events on the Sunday of Resurrection, which inaugurates the season of bullfighting, prominently features flamenco dancing, and celebrates the Virgin Mary and Jesus Christ. Fuentes makes these connections conceptually, on the basis of the shared sense of redemption and resurrection, but he also makes them apparent in his use of certain words and images. The flamenco dancer is "inviolately chaste" (22) like the "virgin body" (9) of the matador. Both, nevertheless, appear in finery that emphasizes their sexual presence; the dancers' "bodies are swathed in frills, satins, silks, lace, complicated girdles, unimaginable underwear" (21) and the matador presents himself dressed in the "effrontery of the suit of lights, its tight-hugging breeches, the flaunting of the male sexual organ . . ." (5). The flamenco dancer embodies also the qualities of the Virgin Mary, being both "chaste" and erotically charged. In paragraph 24, Fuentes makes the analogy between the flamenco dancer and the Virgin explicit, writing that the dancer is "sexual turbulence clad in saintly longings, as exhibited by the Virgin figures carried through the streets of Seville."

Connections

1. Students will be immediately able to identify the similarities between Fuentes's and Paula Gunn Allen's description of the madonna. Allen mentions the sexually charged quality of Western images of women, and she cites the madonna as the Christian (i.e., Western) "female prototype." She also emphasizes the passivity of the madonna, a quality immediately apparent in Fuentes's description of the sumptuously dressed effigies of the Virgin Mary men carry through Seville during the Easter week celebration (paras. 15–17). However, whereas Allen sees the madonna as representing a limited power of birth, Fuentes sees in her maternity a greater range of meanings and powers. These meanings are most apparent in Fuentes's description of the pre-Christian mother/temptress figures from whom the Virgin Mary inherited many of her qualities. The madonna is associated with birth and death (10); she actively demands loyalty and obedience (10, 12) and is a sexually powerful figure (12). The differences between Allen's and Fuentes's characterization of the madonna is due in part to their cultural differences. Allen attaches

greater value to mythic Native American female figures because her purpose is to resist the assimilation of those figures into the madonna. As a figure that represents the dominant Western European culture, the madonna, in Allen's view, personifies the repression of strong powers associated with female figures in some traditional Native American tribes.

2. In order to help students evaluate the cross-cultural connections and differences among male initiation customs, discussion might begin with students describing the ways in which the young men in their communities "prove" their masculinity. It is unlikely that American boys fight bulls in the dark, as Fuentes says Spanish villagers do, or compete to see whose body and spirit will give out first swimming out to sea, as Miguel and Rubén do in "On Sunday," but chances are many students will recognize in American male initiation customs the quality these feats share: bravado, competitiveness, and disregard for personal safety. Fuentes describes how amateur bullfighters partake of the "incredible arrogance" of the bullfighter by stealing into rich men's fields to fight the bulls at night, when neither the bulls nor the toreros can see their opponents well. In "On Sunday," the drunken Miguel and Rubén goad each other into a swimming contest on a cold night when they cannot see the surf or judge direction.

3. Both the *quinceañera* and Holy Week celebrate an ideal, Christian femininity. Orlean describes the basic events of the quinceañera as an affirmation of a girl's commitment to the Catholic Church and her introduction into society — emphasizing the significance of the quinceañera as both a religious and a social initiation for girls (2). The girls are dressed up for the occasion in expensive gowns for which their parents sometimes go into debt (12). The Holy Week custom of dressing effigies of the Mother of God in finery such as "A great triangular cape contrived with the most elaborate ornamentations of ivory and precious stones . . ." (17) also presents an image of ideal, virginal femininity exalted by opulent clothes and a public celebration.

LESLIE MARMON SILKO, Yellow Woman (p. 312)

Explorations

1. The difficulty for students in this story lies in understanding the reason the narrator, a married woman, decides to follow a stranger to his home. Students may be too easily satisfied with believing she is coerced by his strength, which he demonstrates when he holds her wrist and says, "Let's go" (para. 26). However, students should not discount her uncertainty that he may be a character from the mythical world, an idea that possesses power over the narrator. She does not dismiss the tales of her culture as mere stories, as students may do. She hopes to meet someone along the way — a mythical character who would not reveal himself to anyone but her. Silva presents himself as a mythical figure, reinforcing her tendency to believe. Later, when they both meet the rancher, the nonmythical world intrudes. Suspicion that Silva murders the rancher, coupled with her fear of his strength, outweighs her desire for him, and she decides to return home.

2. Silva is presented through the eyes of the narrator, whose only title here is "Yellow Woman," a reference suggesting that Silko, too, may view her as a character in a myth.

74

The narrator sees Silva as physically strong, acquainted with the stories of his culture, and adept at the traditional skills of riding and hunting. She fears his strength yet finds him sexually attractive (56). Later on she finds him "strange" (90), a term that applies equally well to mythical figures and social misfits. The rancher considers Silva a thief and rightly fears for his own life (81, 85).

3. At several points the narrator directly states her feelings about Silva. In paragraph 56 she says she is afraid of him and also mentions a desire to kiss him. At the story's end she states she is sad to leave him (90) and wants to go back and kiss him (91). She conveys her feeling indirectly on other occasions. Her heavy breathing in paragraph 52 reveals her sexual excitement. In paragraph 88 she states, "I went that way because I thought it was safer." Since it was not safer for the horse, she must be talking about her own safety and implying her desire to flee from Silva and the violent encounter.

4. At the end of the story, as she returns to the ordinary world of her home and family, the narrator has almost buried the mythic identity of "Yellow Woman." Silva is no longer present to address her by this name; her family will call her by "another name" (21). She decides to tell her family the realistic story, knowing that only her grandfather would believe in the "Yellow Woman" story. However, even as she confronts the mundane aspects of the "real" world — her mother and grandmother discussing Jell-O, the smell of cooking, her husband Al — she still believes in the mythic truth of her story. The time she spent with Silva will remain for her a rich mix of myth and everyday reality, bringing her closer to her Laguna heritage.

Connections

1. References to Yellow Woman and the ka'tsina appear throughout Silko's story, and students will be able to draw a variety of meanings from them. Silva first calls the narrator "Yellow Woman" in paragraph 12, playfully refusing to give in to her more prosaic view of their encounter. Later, she asks if he always uses the same tricks to lure women to his house (34). Judging from these comments, the ka'tsina is a trickster who uses his wit to get what he wants. Silva also seems to have the power to captivate. He uses song (28), sex, and the old stories to entice her to stay with him. But his seduction is interlaced with coercion (55, 56), making him a complex and disturbing representation of the ka'tsina. Yellow Woman is also a fluid figure, appearing in stories as a desirable and desiring sexual being (19), as being settled in her own home (19) and ready to run away with a man (22). Both live out of time; as the narrator feels herself drawn further into the myth, she has to make an the effort to remember the reality of "yesterday and the day before" (40). Silva displays much of the "incredible arrogance" and sexual powers shown by the matador Fuentes describes (5). Like the torerillos in Fuentes' essay who illegally fight rich men's bulls by night (5), Silva takes advantage of the rich when he steals and butchers their cattle (44–46). The narrator, by contrast, plays a passive role. Even when Silva leaves her alone in the cabin, she doesn't go, mesmerized by the myth of Yellow Woman and her desire for him. Yellow Woman, like the Spanish mother figures (including the Virgin Mary) Fuentes describes (10–12), displays a certain passivity, sexual fascination, and a generous nature (19).

2. Jacobs describes the stereotype of white men as "imbued with privilege" and "out of touch" with the rest of the world (7). She quotes Playboy columnist Asa Baber, who says that white men are defined as "healthy, wealthy, and oppressive" (8). Jacobs herself

points out that white men are indeed still occupying most positions of power (9) in our society. However, the main point of Jacobs's piece is that white men are afraid of all the "others," who they believe are trying to usurp their power (15). The white rancher in Silko's story is fat, suggesting wealth and the greedy consumption of resources. He invokes the law (84) and tries to assert the symbolic power of his race over the Indian, whom he looks down on for being a thief. The Indian feels no respect for the white man's law. He is well armed and confronts the rancher fearlessly, epitomizing the threat feared by the white men in Jacob's piece who worry that those who are not like them will appropriate their privileges.

3. Both Yellow Woman and Soyinka accept the idea that mythical and physical worlds coexist. But Yellow Woman looks positively on the appearance of a "mythical" figure. She would prefer Silva to be a ka'tsina spirit; she worries that he may be a real, and perhaps dangerous, man. In Soyinka's story, spirits appear as part of the child's daily life, but he fears them and sees them as dangerous. The different reactions most logically result from the attitudes handed down by each narrator's family. Yellow Woman's grandfather loved the stories he told. Also the tales told within Silko's story do not show that human beings are threatened by mythical ones. However, Soyinka's family has a great fear of the spirit world and warn the children to keep away from the place the spirits inhabit. Soyinka's mother later relates the harm spirits can cause when not obeyed.

NIKOS KAZANTZAKIS (Kah-zahn-zah-kis), The Isle of Aphrodite (p. 322)

Explorations

1. This question will help students clarify Kazantzakis's premises, which might be difficult for some students to identify, given his lyrical style of writing. In paragraph 4, Kazantzakis describes passing "from Jehovah's camp to the bed of Aphrodite," a phrase that explicitly identifies the deities involved and suggests their differences. Jehovah, the Judean god, is in Kazantzakis's representation harsh and demanding, while Aphrodite, Greek goddess of love, is earthy and ready to be pleased with humanity. The journey through the Judean mountains — Jehovah's camp — was "abrasive," while the destination, Aphrodite's bed, is inviting. He defines the water over which he makes the final leg of this journey as giving rise to the "feminine" mystery of Aphrodite, suggesting the gender differences between the two deities and their relation to the natural world (para. 4). The "feminine" force associated with Aphrodite is natural and inevitable; he equates it with gravity and the tendency of things and people to return to the earth (5). The force he associates with Jehovah is opposed to the feminine; it is "contrary to nature," urging people to overcome human nature and rise above earthly concerns.

2. All through "The Isle of Aphrodite," Kazantzakis is looking for evidence of the goddess. He sees her reflected in the face of Maria, from whom he seeks directions to one of the holy places associated with Aphrodite. Kazantzakis also identifies the proprietor of a tavern as an "earthy, all-enchanting Aphrodite" (27), but soon he seeks a more personal experience of the goddess. As he approaches the temple, he finds that Aphrodite has been "resurrected" within him and feels that when he enters the temple he is coming

home (39). Thus, although he identifies Aphrodite as his "mistress," in a sense he becomes the goddess.

3. Students will be able to build on their responses to the previous questions as a way of discerning the meaning to Kazantzakis's dream. He associates Aphrodite with the earth, and therefore with mortality; Jehovah is a god concerned only with the afterlife, but Aphrodite inhabits the earth and, as he comes closer to her temple, seems to inhabit the narrator as well. The memory of the headless male insect being eaten by the female reinforces the idea of his vulnerability and mortality; the image of the warrior's head on the ring stone (46) once again reminds him of this disturbing memory. The dream in the last paragraph contains the image of a rose, a symbol of love and therefore, also a symbol of Aphrodite. It is a black rose, associated with death, an image that recalls associations Kazantzakis has made throughout the essay between the inevitable forces of the earth (gravity and mortality) and the promises and demands of love (the goddess Aphrodite).

4. There is evidence in the first three paragraphs that Kazantzakis belongs to a Christian religion. He mentions "sin" and uses biblical phrases such as "the will of God" (2) and "glorify the Lord" (3). In paragraph 21, he asks a woman whether "religion" can identify the clay models of women found at Kouklia as either gods or devils. This question suggests that he is accustomed to seeking explanations from religious sources. However, Kazantzakis does not have complete faith in conventional religion, as his search for Aphrodite implies. When the woman he questions replies that their "poor religion" cannot explain the female gods, Kazantzakis does not refute her criticism. As he hovers between the two forces, the Judaic and the pagan, Kazantzakis continues to think in terms of the Judaic traditions. In paragraph 6, Kazantzakis wonders what his free will (a Christian concept) will lead him to do; he wants to distinguish between good and evil, and he continues to be concerned with establishing hierarchies of "virtues and passions."

Connections

1. Both Silko and Kazantzakis begin their pieces with a moment in which the narrator is overwhelmed by the sense of being in a dream. Kazantzakis writes that "drowsiness and sweetness" overtook him and so he felt ready to let go and allow his heart to break loose (para. 1). Silko begins her story with the moment of her awakening at dawn and imagining that she is leaving Silva. She stays, however, and gives into the myth of Yellow Woman he enacts with her. She realizes that she has "no thought beyond the moment" (24) and only because of this can she give in to her own desires. The dreamlike openings of both Silko's and Kazantzakis's pieces creates an atmosphere of abandonment of the self and of everyday reality, allowing the narrators to be sexually aware and open.

2. In "Matador and Madonna," Fuentes describes la Dama de Baza, a pre-Christian earth goddess, as a figure of "maternal authority" (10). La Dama de Elche, on the other hand, is an erotically powerful figure (11). Either goddess might be compared to Kazantzakis's Pandemos Aphrodite, because both embody qualities similar to Aphrodite's. Fuentes describes them as "mysterious, two-faced, tender and demanding, mother and lover . . ." (12), while Kazantzakis describes Aphrodite, when she "lifts her veil" to him, as "unfathomable." He implies that her demands cannot be understood by human beings any more than by animals; she, like the pre-Christian goddesses Fuentes describes, is "two-faced" in that she represents both birth and death (43).

77

3. Both Paglia and Kazantzakis subscribe to the view that the sexes are in opposition to each other. Paglia says simply that "the sexes are at war," and Kazantzakis describes two opposing forces, one that pulls us toward earth (the feminine) and one that pulls us upward (the masculine) (5). Furthermore, Paglia describes male psychological development as a matter of overcoming "the overwhelming power of their mothers," a view confirmed in Kazantzakis's piece by his fear of being eaten alive by the feminine force represented by Aphrodite. However, Paglia identifies male sexuality as aggressive, while Kazantzakis identifies Aphrodite, a symbol of feminine sexuality, as voracious and demanding (41–43).

4. When the boys run to the beach, their feet obey "only a mysterious force which [seems] to come from deep in the earth" (Llosa, 131). But when Miguel dives into the water, he abides by the second of the two forces Kazantzakis describes; he strives to "conquer weight" (Kazantzakis, 5) and the limitations of his body. Llosa writes that Miguel had "forgotten how to ride the water without using force" and at first cannot let go and allow the waves to carry him out. In a sense, Llosa favors the first of Kazantzakis's "torrents," which is associated with giving in to natural forces. If Miguel was able to give in to the force of the water, he would be better able to stay afloat. Instead he fights it, allying himself with the second of the "torrents" Kazantzakis describes, which is associated with a struggle to leave the earth behind.

SIMONE de BEAUVOIR (See-MONE deh BOW-vwar), Woman as Other (p. 329)

Explorations

1. Students should find it interesting to note the many changes in attitudes since Beauvoir wrote her essay. Many will be unaware of the extent to which the position of modern women has changed from that of women of even twenty-five years ago, let alone those who were contemporaries of Beauvoir. Her plea for women to dispute male sovereignty was considered radical when she wrote it; now it's seen as a relatively moderate position. Similarly, her call to women "to refuse to be a party to the deal . . . to renounce all the advantages conferred upon them by their alliance with the superior caste" (para. 13) is now a standard of middle-class feminism. But students may also be surprised to see how many current issues have been the subjects of long-standing debate. While inroads have certainly been made, the resurgence of fundamentalism in the United States, coupled with the Catholic Church's vigorous denouncement of abortion and artificial birth control, has kept the issue of a woman's control over her body alive. Recent reports also suggest that while white, middle-class women in the job market are better off than they were ten years ago, they still earn substantially less than men for similar jobs. Thus the professional status of women has yet to be established. Furthermore, such recent developments as surrogate motherhood raise new questions about a woman's legal rights.

2. Students are sure to find many loaded expressions in the selection. A few of them are "woman represents only the negative" and "A man is in the right in being a man; it is the woman who is in the wrong" (2); the litany of antifeminists, beginning with Aristotle (2–

4); the comparison between women and Jews, blacks, and the proletariat (5, 8, 9); the analogy of the master-slave relationship (12); and the use of the term *castes* (13). Beauvoir's references, as well as her language and style, suggest that she is writing for an intellectual audience that may not accept her views. That she expects men to be reluctant to relinquish their power and women their comfort is clear in her frequent references to the collaboration of women in their own oppression.

3. It might be helpful for students to review their responses to the previous question before exploring this one. Audience is important here; although interviews allow us to identify with the subject more readily, and are normally more entertaining, they don't carry the same weight as references to classical scholars, respected authors, and renowned philosophers. Beauvoir is stating an intellectual case here; thus if she included interviews or eliminated references, she could be dismissed by her audience as a single voice arguing a case that may have a few current supporters but lacks broad, long-term merit.

Connections

1. Kazantzakis would probably agree with Beauvoir's model of woman as Other, a model that implies that the existence of men needs no explanation or justification (para. 2), but that the existence of women must be explained and accounted for. Beauvoir recalls that "it is often said she [woman] thinks with her glands" (2) and that woman are associated with sex (3). Kazantzakis's representation of Aphrodite strongly associates her with nature, the physical body, and sexuality, as is suggested in his description of a woman he compares with Aphrodite. He describes her as "earthy" and "full-bodied with ample buttocks" (27). Throughout his essay, Kazantzakis uses images of women to help him understand his own fears and desires better, rather than considering women as subjects in their own right. This strategy accords with Beauvoir's contention that, from the point of view of men, "woman" exists only in relation to men (3).

2. In "Yellow Woman," the narrator moves between two worlds, that of her home with her husband and family, and that of the myths of the ka'tsina spirit and Yellow Woman. The narrator allows Silva to define her as "Yellow Woman," since he calls her by this name and she willingly plays the role of the woman who leaves her home and follows the orders of the ka'tsina spirit. Silva articulates her relationship to him when he tells her "You will do what I want" (55). This statement and the many commands he issues make their relationship resemble the master-slave relationship defined by Beauvoir. Still, the narrator does not seem to be entirely under Silva's control. Women in this story do not appear as the completely passive beings Beauvoir describes. The narrator has no qualms about leaving either her husband or Silva when she finds it convenient, showing she is not a possession of either. She is self-sufficient enough to arrive home on her own. Furthermore, the narrator would probably reject Beauvoir's reading of her situation. By identifying her story with the archetypal one, the narrator acquires in her own eyes some of the myth's power. She does not try to define herself against a male figure, but in terms of her culture, which places her in opposition to the white culture of the rancher.

3. Sally Jacobs quotes white men who view not only white women, but all people who differ from them, as Other. This oppositional thinking comes through in the first few paragraphs, where men discuss how women and minorities no longer care what white men think. Lawrence Wright opposes himself to "female chauvinists" who denigrate men (4). Camille Paglia maintains that young women have been misled by feminism to believe

that men and women are the same (1). She says, "The sexes are at war" (4) and puts the responsibility on women to protect themselves from naturally aggressive males (5). Gloria Steinem's story implies the discomfort men feel in the presence of female sexuality. Some may place Steinem in both categories, because the woman in her story clearly feels that the men she's in front of haven't experienced anything real in ages. Deborah Tannen differentiates her "connected" way of dealing with the world from her husband's "one-up or one-down" method. The recommendations are diverse: Steinem suggests positive thinking; Lawrence Wright believes that being a loving father to his daughter may help her to appreciate the differences between men and women; Rose Weitz, more radically, argues that lesbians, in allying themselves with other women, overturn the system that defines the hierarchy of sex-based power.

4. The opening of Weitz's observation almost seems to summarize and paraphrase Beauvoir's interpretation of the division of power in the traditional male-female relationship and women's tendency to view each other as rivals rather than allies. Beauvoir argues for a realignment of power, for she implies that men and women need to exist in a complementary relationship. Weitz makes no such assumption about the necessity of male-female relationships. She argues that the "deeply ingrained traditional sex roles" make it unlikely that power will shift in heterosexual relationships. Weitz sees lesbian and gay relationships as possible, and indeed preferable, alternatives. She argues that when both partners are of the same sex, neither partner is assumed to be superior and egalitarian relationships are possible. When Beauvoir wrote her essay, she did not believe that a woman could feel more allegiance to another woman than to a man.

ALBERTO MORAVIA (Mo-RAH-vee-ya), The Chase (p. 337)

Explorations

1. This selection provides an excellent example of the use of seemingly irrelevant material to establish the groundwork for the story itself. In the long opening section, Moravia introduces his narrator's love for wildness, as well as his conclusion that males destroy the very thing they profess to love. Without this section readers would have less of a sense of the narrator's celebration of life. His actions at the end of the story would seem incomprehensible.

2. As he watches his wife board the bus in paragraph 8, the narrator recalls the hunting incident, and he does so again in paragraph 17 as he realizes that he can't confront her. In his present position he is like his father was at the hunt: He has the power to destroy the wild creature — and he is well aware of what comes of shooting a wild bird. He first thinks that he has no choice, that nature's mandate is to kill, but then he realizes what would result if he were to confront his wife and her lover. Ultimately he chooses the role of life giver rather than taker. In doing this he preserves a sense of power, but he also avoids the consequences he recalls from the hunting incident.

3. It can be dangerous to ask students to extrapolate; too often they rely on their own experience and desires, rather than on the evidence in the story, to create sequels. If this question is handled carefully, however, the exercise will be valuable. A close reading of

the last sentence and the third paragraph make it quite clear that the narrator will never again follow his wife. He's giving in to her "wildness" in much the same way she is, refusing either to tame or to be tamed. He probably thinks that his knowledge will bring new vitality to his marriage.

Connections

1. That the narrator compares his wife to a wild bird is clear evidence of his perception of woman as Other. He is enthralled by her unpredictability and laments his newfound ability to understand her and predict her behavior. He wants his wife to be Other; he finds this quality highly erotic. He sees his wife's otherness in terms of power, which he possesses. (His decision to withhold his knowledge of her affair gives him tremendous power over her.) His wife would probably share his perception; when she senses the predictability of their marriage and the resultant waning of eroticism, she seeks eroticism elsewhere. Also, the manner of the meeting between her and her lover accentuates her desire to be perceived as wild and untamed.

2. The key to this comparison probably lies more in the attitudes of the men about their marriages, even though the women are the partners who have temporarily left their husbands. Silko's narrator is attracted to Silva, but like the original Yellow Woman, will return home after her escapade. Indeed, in the myth Yellow Woman is rescued by her husband, who desires her return. Their marriage defines them as a continuing unit. The husband of the narrator in Silko's story may be upset by his wife's absence, but after hearing her explanation that she was kidnapped by a Navajo, he will not resent her departure and will welcome her back. The wife in "The Chase" is only temporarily unfaithful, but her husband cannot be satisfied with her unless she manifests wildness. Yet this quality depends on the narrator's seeing her actions as unpredictable, a situation unlikely to result in the context of a marriage which renders her behavior quite familiar. Therefore, students will probably conclude that the marriage in the Silko story shows more promise of continuing successfully.

3. Both Moravia's and Kazantzakis's narrators are pursuing a feminine being; in both cases, the revelations they make at the end of the pursuit are disturbing and unanticipated. The narrator's revelation in "The Chase" has to do with the independence and unpredictability of his wife, who is not at all as "domesticated" as he believed her to be before he follows her to her assignation with another man. He accepts this revelation in part because it excites him to realize that his wife is still a passionate woman and he does not have the power to deprive her of her "wildness." The goddess Aphrodite that Kazantzakis pursues in his essay is similar to Moravia's representation of the narrator's wife as a mysterious, dangerous entity who is the essence of feminine unpredictability. The wife's wildness, however, is no more personal than Aphrodite's. Moravia writes that "wildness, always and everywhere, is directed against everything and everybody" (17). It is, therefore, a destructive force, although it makes her more desirable in the narrator's eyes.

81

KEN BUGUL (Boo-gull), The Artist's Life in Brussels (p. 353)

Explorations

1. The most important element in Ken Bugul's definition of "bourgeois" is the idea that middle-class people lead a life of privilege. She learns from Jean how to be "liberal," but she is always observing "the artist's life" from the position of a partial outsider (para. 19). Ken Bugul finds the privileged life of Westerners "decadent" (45). She defines the life of the artist as "bourgeois" (41). For the most part, the "artists" Ken Bugul comes into contact with attend gallery openings, make small talk, and are more concerned with fashionable lifestyles than with the production of art (36). The economically privileged life of the middle class allows Jean to pursue at least the appearance of an artist's life, but it also allows him the freedom to leave behind tradition and experiment with unconventional relationships.

2. Students will be able to build on their discussion of Explorations #1 in responding to this question. The fact that Jean and Ken Bugul have never before had a serious talk (27) suggests the superficial nature of the life they are leading. Their life together is too fragile and lacking in trust to allow for serious explorations of their inner lives, so Jean's attempts to live out his homosexuality with Ken Bugul's cooperation and understanding is doomed. Ken Bugul's discomfort with the bohemian life and with Jean's homosexuality comes through, however, when she says that "all that had been so foreign to me remained foreign" (37). Many of her comments reveal discomfort and disillusionment. Soon, she recalls, "I had reached a point where I no longer knew where I stood at all. . . . I was the pawn whom these people needed to break free from an unacknowledged guilt" (44). Having smoked hashish for the first time, Ken Bugul begins to laugh, but it seems more like sobs (52). At last, after Jean explodes over François's interest in Ken Bugul, she feels that "these beings" are "no longer human" (69).

3. Ken Bugul's references to diverse social groups abound; she spends a good deal of time among gays and artists (38, 39). Western feminists receive a brief mention (54). She describes a restaurant where intellectuals, left-wing students, and hippies meet (46) and a party where she encounters people of many different nationalities living communally (48–50). Ken Bugul feels comfortable socializing with homosexual men, and she identifies in some ways with women like Laure, with whom she speaks "the same language" (40). But for the most part, Ken Bugul feels herself an outsider to Western culture. She says that her "compatriots seemed far away to me" (39), and she continues to think of Westerners in general as "them" (45).

4. In the first simile Ken Bugul uses in this section, the morning after she has waited all night for Jean dawns "like an erotic dream" (24), but she compares herself to an unused broom on a rainy day. It is significant that she compares herself to a homely, domestic tool; she feels neglected, like part of the furniture of Jean's home. The erotic dream, by contrast, belongs to the outside world, the world Jean moves in. In the next paragraph, Ken Bugul uses the metaphor of a bleeding wound to describe her heart. The shift from simile to metaphor, along with the vividness of the image, suggests that she is moving toward a more deeply felt expression of her unhappiness. In the following paragraph, she observes the steps Jean has painted black, and then she asks, "Had someone died?" The implication is that it is she, with her heart an open wound, whose death Jean's arrival has brought about.

Connections

1. Moravia defines as wild anything that "is autonomous and unpredictable and does not depend upon us" (para. 2). Near the end of "The Chase," after he observes his wife kissing another man, he elaborates: "wildness, always and everywhere, is directed against everything and everybody" (17). Ken Bugul notices that Jean and François behave savagely when their triangle becomes more complicated with François's interest in Ken Bugul; her autonomy and unpredictability Sharpen Jean's possessive interest, and the men are "wrangling with each other from within their most primitive instincts" (68). The wildness that comes out in each case is primitive, heedless, and potentially destructive, but it is also a quality that allows their deepest desires and fears to be expressed openly.

2. In Beauvoir's terms, Ken Bugul is very much the "Other" to Jean and François's "One." She is "the one they needed to better pass off their homosexuality" (62); she is, by the men's definition, a person who is significant not in her own right, but in relation to them and their needs. Jean's anger is not directed at Ken Bugul, because Jean cannot imagine that Ken Bugul has what Beauvoir terms an "authentic existence" (13). According to the philosophy of gender Beauvoir describes, authenticity belongs only to men, who are capable of self-determination. For this reason, Jean holds François, but not Ken Bugul, responsible for the night he and Ken Bugul spend together.

3. Both Senegal and the Ivory Coast gained independence from France in 1960. Ken Bugul's statement that she is not descended from the Gauls (the Roman name for the French) is the equivalent of Ebony's statement that Charlemagne is not his ancestor. Naipaul's rejoinder that he'd heard it said before is well supported by Ken Bugul's restatement of the idea. Both Ebony and Ken Bugul seek to define themselves as independent of French colonial influences that have distanced them from their own cultures. Both are also attracted by Western cultures, however, and both have received an education that has allowed them to enter the "new world."

MARJORIE SHOSTAK, Nisa's Marriage (p. 354)

Explorations

1. In response to Nisa's running away from her marriage, people tell her that a husband "becomes like your father or your older brother" (para. 8). At first, far from seeming like a member of her family, Tashay seems like someone who is trying to steal her away from her family. She asks her father, "Do I own [Tashay] that he follows me everywhere?" (20) But her father is quick to correct her, telling her that a woman follows her husband. Nisa refers to Tashay as "that person" and "this man," reinforcing the sense that he is a stranger. But eventually, after she begins to mature sexually and gets used to Tashay, she finds that she loves him and misses him when he goes away (48).

2. The beads and ornaments adorning her, the dancing and music, the ceremonial oil, the building of the hut, all the rituals of marriage are designed to signal the transition from child to woman. Bedecking the bride signals the change that is to come over her; the dancing signifies joy; the building of the hut symbolizes the creation of a new family unit.

The anointing with oil solemnizes the union of two people. (Students may wish to continue discussion of this question by considering the symbolic significance of the wedding rituals in their own culture.)

3. That the tribe relies on hunting can be seen in the community's informing Nisa that Tashay will not let her eat the meat of the animals he kills if she keeps crying (8). They are apparently a peaceful people whose main enemies are not other people but rather the animals around them (note that Nisa is frequently warned of the dangers of running away into the forest). The hunting-meat metaphor appears in Nisa's mother's lament that she will stick herself with a poison arrow (29) and in Nisa's comparing herself as a sexual being to food (43).

4. Students should enjoy this question: Nisa's mother is echoing the age-old lament of mothers: "You frustrate and shame me so, I could kill myself," adding that the only thing preventing her from doing so is the weakness of the flesh. There should be quite a variety of responses to the second part of the question, including the threat of getting on a plane or a train, of jumping off a bridge, of driving over a cliff.

Connections

1. The differences between customs and concepts of marriage in "Nisa's Marriage" and "The Artist's Life in Brussels" may strike students more strongly than their similarities. Ken Bugul recalls village life, but she has imbibed Western culture and is living a life far away from the village and its customs. She remembers best the customs about polygamy (paras. 22, 42, 57), which she found straightforward and respectful of all parties. Nisa, on the other hand, mentions nothing about polygamous marriages. In both Ken Bugul's and Nisa's descriptions of the customs of the people of their original cultures, however, there is the sense that marriage is an orderly process that supports the social organization of the community and reinforces connections between and among families. Ken Bugul, having left her village, has a hard time accepting the disorganized and selfish way Jean approaches love relationships. Ken Bugul's knowledge and acceptance of polygamy has partially prepared her for Jean's spending time with other women, and she tries to see his homosexual relationships in the same light, but it remains foreign to her (38).

2. Although Pom acquiesces to her parents' wishes, her silence, tears, and lack of enthusiasm suggest that she shares Nisa's fear and reluctance. Pom cries only at the announcement, however, whereas Nisa not only cries often but also runs away from her husband every chance she gets. Their ultimate compliance never seems to be in question; in each case all the unwritten laws of the society demand that they obey their parents. They simply have no alternatives.

3. By the end of her narrative, we see Nisa's acceptance of her adult role; she shows love for and pride in her husband, mentioning how she misses him when he is away. In "On Sunday" Miguel ultimately accepts his newfound maturity when he admits to feelings of "confidence" and "good spirits" as a result of saving Rubén (174) and when he looks to the future at the end of the story. Both believe that they have finally made that split between themselves and their parents (in Miguel's case, of course, this is only implied). Gender differences dictate the adult roles each is permitted to assume; Nisa's early efforts at independent action (refusing the marriage) were defeated, so she learns to find satisfaction through her relationship with her husband. Because of his sex, Miguel

encounters no familial opposition to his efforts to establish independence as an aspect of his adulthood.

NAILA MINAI (Mee-Nye), Women in Early Islam (p. 361)

Explorations

1. Students will probably be surprised to discover the range of responsibilities shouldered by women in what is considered a backward age. Women in the tribes looked after the herds and engaged in commerce by both producing and trading items of value. They were allowed the privilege of airing their views, enjoyed the power inherent in a matriarchal society allowing polygamy for women, and in general were valued and protected. Their only real risk was of being kidnapped for ransom.

2. The entire tribe gained stability, an easier life, and increased power and wealth. These changes, however, meant that women were no longer needed as they had been; thus they came to be valued less. They were not protected, and they lost their right to polygamy while men retained theirs. A monotheistic religion became the primary means of uniting previously separate tribes, and a social code protecting women and children was gradually established, because the previous incentives for protecting them had been eliminated with the abandonment of nomadic existence.

3. Khadija's wealth and position provided the support Muhammad needed to found his religion. She contributed to the social code of Islam by acquainting her husband with the needs of younger, less powerful women. When he married the young Aysha he began to appreciate the rights of girls, and the scandal concerning her journey with the young man convinced him of a woman's need for protection against false claims of adultery, resulting in the requirement of four witnesses before the charge could be leveled.

4. Some students may encounter difficulty in distinguishing between fictitious and factual elements in an anecdote like this; they may be prone to consider everything they read as fact. This question will allow them to explore the reasons behind and the benefits of embellishment. In opening her essay this way, Minai humanizes the story, allowing the reader to identify with a figure otherwise considered too lofty for human concerns. Her accounts of the family's response to the marriage, the courtship of the couple, and Khadija's infatuation with the young employee are probably fabrications. But she hasn't gone too far; all these elements are plausible, none alters the known facts, and more important all serve the *truth* of the story.

Connections

1. Minai reports that under Islamic law, a woman could not be married without her permission, but that it occurred in practice, since many brides were still children when they were betrothed (para. 14). This is the case with Nisa, whose parents offer her no choice but to marry Tashay. She is given to him before she starts menstruating, and before she understands the responsibilities of marriage. Minai offers one reason that early marriage for women was considered desirable among the early Muslims when she says

85

that Muhammad believed that sexual instincts were natural for both men and women, but they would lead to adultery unless they were fully satisfied within marriage (18). Added to this is the role of marriage in supporting the patriarchal system (16). Nisa's early marriage, and the fact that she was given no choice but to marry Tashay, suggest that similar reasons might prevail among the Zhun/twasi. However, Shostak's book about Nisa describes how Nisa later went on to take a number of lovers, apparently a common practice among Zhun/twasi, whose hunter and gatherer economy cause them to move around a great deal. Thus Nisa's experience is in some ways closer to the marital system in the nomadic tribes before the birth of Islam. Minai describes how a woman might have several husbands, and have children by any of them, but maintained primary loyalty to her birth family (5). Nisa's father tells her she must follow her husband (20), and eventually Nisa does so willingly, but nevertheless she achieves a sexual and economic autonomy that would be difficult to attain for women living under the Islamic laws Minai describes.

2. Students may be surprised by the author's thesis that the implementation of the Islamic code actually conferred upon women an improved position, which gave them "a modicum of security and independence in the patriarchal family" (23). Minai's analysis suggests that the successful continuation of marriages depended more on the desire to maximize the economic benefits than on sexual desire. While the Islamic code did recognize the fact of sexual desire on the part of both the male and the female, the disparate treatment of women suggests that their sexuality could be threatening unless harnessed to the institution of marriage. The Koran advises men to marry only as many women as they can satisfy sexually (17), implying that an unsatisfied woman would seek satisfaction outside her marriage. Thus her sexuality could threaten the family's stability and a male's clearly established line of descent. Both men and women were to be punished equally for adultery, but women still seemed to be singled out more frequently, although Minai attributes this fact to ingrained social prejudices and not the Islamic code. Still, while four witnesses are necessary to establish a woman's adultery, the conditions for establishing male guilt are not discussed. The author suggests this situation rarely occurs, perhaps because men can structure polygamous experience into their marriages. Although the attitudes toward women's sexuality in these two readings are very different, both Moravia's narrator and the Islamic code suggest that marriage defuses women's sexuality.

3. In patriarchal societies such as these, women are seen as subservient to men. Thus even if the existing rules are designed to protect women, they are made by men according to their view of women's role in society. A woman's responsibilities include maintaining the home and becoming a part of her husband's family. If we consider Beauvoir's assessment of male-female relationships, we see both cultures as supporting her view. In each case women are seen as lesser creatures than men, as incomplete beings to be cared for rather than independent beings able to act on their own initiative. Each society uses the male as the norm and thus relegates women to the status of Other.

Miriam Cooke, The Veil Does Not Prevent Women from Working (p. 372)

Explorations

1. The Western image of Islamic women during the European colonial period was a variation of Victorian images of women in general. Islamic women embodied the contradiction of being "cloistered and oppressed" and "seductive and mysterious" (para. 5). The stereotypic American image of the veiled Islamic woman has changed little; Cooke describes the image as one of "anonymous black shapes gliding along high walls, sensuous odalisques reclining against the harem's soft pillows" (4). Such an image, Cooke suggests through a discussion of Edward Said's essay "Orientalism," is the product of male erotic and chivalric fantasies, and has little to do with the reality of women's lives (5, 6).

2. Cooke counters the assumption that the veiling of women is due to sexual oppression by arguing that the veil may signify "class and status . . . religious and political affiliation . . . [or] the current awakening of feminist consciousness. . . ." (12.) She further suggests that the traditional reasons for veiling — class status and social standing — are not necessarily in conflict with contemporary, political/feminist reasons (13). Aside from religious reasons, the veil was important to men because it signified ownership of women and served as a form of protection, either of the woman herself, or of men from women's sexuality (14). Early in the twentieth century, Islamic intellectuals interpreted veiling and seclusion as forms of sexual oppression (15), and some countries banned veiling. Some women have resumed wearing the veil in the last two decades, both as a way of declaring their faith and as a way of gaining some freedom to go into the streets (17, 18).

3. Students will be able to begin to respond to this question by referring to their responses to Explorations #2. Some of the advantages in veiling and in segregating men and women in Islamic countries have to do with women negotiating for rights and freedoms — without betraying their Islamic faith — that allow them to embark on otherwise unavailable professional opportunities. Cooke mentions the women's section of the Riyadh newspaper, where women are segregated physically but are "functionally integrated," not necessarily writing solely on "women's issues" (20). Most students of western backgrounds will only be able to see advantages in segregation and veiling if they are able to respect the religious devotion of women in Islamic countries and if they believe that women can build a satisfying and productive life under these circumstances.

4. Cooke's reasons for opening her essay with a discussion of Western stereotypes regarding Islamic women are significant because of the audience her essay addresses (a Western one) and the point she is trying to make (that Westerners are ignorant of the complex reasons for the segregation and veiling of women in Islamic countries). Part of her strategy for overturning Western stereotypes is to open her essay with an ironic account of American concerns about — and hopes for — the encounter between oppressed Islamic women and "liberated" American women serving in the armed forces. She implies that the expected sexual revolution could not materialize following such an encounter because of Islamic women's "own agency" — their social perspective and religious commitment — that would dictate their behaviors far more powerfully than seeing "tough women soldiers driving juggernauts" (3). If she opened her essay from the Saudi perspective, she would have had to pass up the opportunity of drawing in her Western readers with an anecdote that plays upon their biases and stereotypical images

of Islamic women. She sets up an implicit comparison between the fantasies of the West and the realities of the East, a comparison she exploits throughout her essay.

Connections

1. According to Minai, at its inception Islam represented an extensive reform of women's rights under the law. It provided for women's education and ability to manage personal finances. Women could inherit property and were legally entitled to sexual satisfaction in marriage; divorce was regulated to protect women (para. 2). Muhammad did, however, support patriarchy (12). His laws tended to reinforce male privilege while giving women greater rights than they had previously enjoyed. But the laws were not always put into practice. For instance, a woman cannot be married without her permission, but many brides are still children when the decision about their marriage is made (14).

2. Many students will focus on veiling as the most obvious Islamic practice that supports Beauvoir's contention that men view women as Other. The veil marks women as "Other" simply because men are not required to wear it; the veil is a sign of women's different social and sexual position. In spite of her insistence that women are willing to be veiled and secluded, Cooke admits that the practice originally had to do with men's fear of women's sexuality (14). Simone de Beauvoir wrote that in the eyes of men, woman "is sex — absolute sex, no less" (4). The practice of veiling and seclusion also served men's desire to protect women as their "property" (14). Similarly, Beauvoir associates women's economic "dependence" on men with a master-slave relationship (13) — in other words, a relationship based on the ownership of the "Other" by the "One." Further, Beauvoir writes that women have found it necessary to cooperate in those practices that reinforce sex-based inequalities because refusal to cooperate made it hard to survive: "To decline to be the Other, to refuse to be a party to the deal — this would be for women to renounce all the advantages conferred upon them by their alliance with the superior caste" (13). Islamic women are attempting to use the veil as a way to gain greater personal freedom and more political clout (see Explorations #1 and #2, above), but their desire to retain the advantages of being defined as men's property also tends to reinforce the patriarchal system that inhibits their full participation (16).

3. Students will be able to build on discussions of Beauvoir's concept of Woman-as-Other (see Connections #2, above) in order to consider the significance of associating wildness with women's sexuality. The veil prevents men from viewing women's bodies and faces directly, leaving men free to create fantasies about the sexuality of women in which women are figured as "Other." Cooke contends that the early European view of veiled Islamic women "was a crass image that differentiated women from men chiefly in relationship to lust" (4). Rendered mysterious because of the veil, Islamic women were imagined to embody the elements of "wildness" that Moravia appreciates in his wife: "intimacy, privacy, secrecy." At the same time, however, veiling had come to represent the sexual and social oppression of Islamic women, in that "Islam, it is thought . . . has imposed eternal stagnation on women" (7). Therefore, to the Western mind veiling represents two opposing ideas: the wildness and sexual mystery of women and their oppressively domesticated lives. Both these ideas are also expressed in Moravia's story through the image of the wife, who seems to be "stagnant" and thoroughly predictable, but who becomes in her husband's eyes "wild" and unpredictable. This dual image of

women is also reflected in the original Islamic motivations for veiling women, which were to enforce their domestication and to conceal their sexuality (14, 16).

YASHAR KEMAL (Keh-MAL), A Dirty Story (p. 380)

Explorations

1. A fruitful way of approaching this question might be to ask students what they think of when they hear the term *dirty story*. The common response will be something like "a story about sex." If they then attempt to explain the title of this story, they'll be in for a surprise. It's not the sex itself that makes this a dirty story; in fact, any compassionate reader will find the sexual practices of the town boys repellent. The realization may come slowly, but students should be able to determine that it's the town itself that is dirty. Kemal blames the entire town for Fadik's tragedy: The pettiness of the villagers, their lust for gossip, their attitudes toward women, and their jealousy of Huru — all these factors contribute to a general poverty of spirit fostered by economic poverty in the town. Implicit in the story is a condemnation not only of the social attitudes of the townspeople but also of the economic conditions that give rise to such mean spiritedness as well. It is not surprising that Kemal offers no simple remedies for these problems; he seems to recommend greater tolerance and compassion as the only hope — and there is a ray of hope, however dim, in the final image of Osman carrying Fadik away from her tormentors as the earth renews itself in spring.

2. This scene reveals a classic perception of women as chattel, commodities to be used for work or pleasure. That the discussion among the men reveals no maliciousness toward women in general should be emphasized; they never even consider the plight of the women involved, any more than they would consider the feelings of animals or insects. It is essential that we believe this if we are to accept the horror that emerges in the rest of the story. Thus the attitude must be articulated by the people themselves; if the author provided it for us as an explanation of their subsequent behavior, readers would have a difficult time giving credence to it.

3. That men see strength and domination of women as vital to success should be clear to most students. How women view men is less clear, although much of their behavior indicates that they too respect a strong, domineering man. Their deference to males regardless of age or relationship is revealed in Hatije's inability to control her son's behavior. Women's views of themselves are more complicated. They expect a man to dominate, and they're quite willing to ignore Fadik's humanity. They apparently neither feel empathy toward nor express any solidarity with the victim. It seems that they have adopted the view found in the Swat Valley, namely that Fadik is at fault for the boys' lust. Their behavior is a phenomenon common to oppressed groups: In the interest of self-preservation, they try to separate themselves from members of their group who are currently being persecuted. (Perceptive students might make the connection between Fadik's predicament and that of the rape victim characterized as a seductress. If we acknowledge our solidarity with the victim, then we have to face the fact that we too are at risk.) Probably the only clear difference between men's views of women and their own

self-image lies in this paradox: Men see all women as seductresses, while women see only those unfortunate enough to have been exploited in that light.

4. The women's lust for gossip is evident in their interpretation of the situation. The child has clearly described a rape, commenting that "Uncle Osman's wife . . . was sobbing away all the time" (para. 26), but the women immediately (and gleefully) inform Osman that his wife has turned his home into a brothel and that "anyone can come in and have her" (32). The utter absurdity of their implication that the animals are also at fault for the boys' playing with them makes clear the women's refusal to place the blame where it belongs. At this point Fadik is being exploited, Osman is confused and helpless, and Huru is trying to convince him of the truth, namely that the rumor is based on jealousy of her power and Fadik's beauty. That there is probably no truth to the rumor is clear from the child's story and from the women's jealous tirades against Huru. The truth instead comes out in their story of Esheh, the last woman to have been subjected to the brutality of the young men in the village. Now that she is dead they can sympathize with her, but they obviously offered her no protection during her ordeal.

Connections

1. Kemal's fictional account seems to be consistent with Cooke's observation that men are expected to dominate. Saudi women are veiled in part because they are perceived by men to be dangerously seductive. In each community we also see women circumventing their assigned roles — in Saudi Arabia by using religious laws and the custom of veiling to gain access to social and professional opportunities previously denied women and in Chukurova by using gossip to control men's actions subtly. Most students will recognize that Western women would object strongly to the characterization of women as weak, sex-driven commodities, but they may need to be reminded that evidence in "A Dirty Story" and "The Veil Does Not Prevent Women From Working" reveals that women accept their role, acting out rebellions within the constraints of the role itself. In both pieces, male honor is perceived to be dependent on women's chastity, and women are held responsible for the sexual behavior of men. The class differences evident in Kemal's and Cooke's pieces may account for the contrast in how each portrays sex role divisions. In Kemal's story, poverty, an agrarian economy, lack of education, and cultural isolation prevent men from being compassionate and women from unifying to stop the abuse; on the other hand, as Cooke's essay demonstrates, middle-class Saudi women enjoy the benefits of education, a small amount of economic freedom, and some professional opportunities.

2. In each case the government and religion clearly regulate the sexual and social behavior of women. Cooke describes how governments have either banned or required women to wear the veil, based on the (male-dominated) government and religion in power at any given time (para. 11). The delegation of legal power to the local agha in Kemal's story allows such offenses as the sale of women, gang rape, and slander against women to go unpunished. The only talk of government occurs when the women are speculating about a cure for lice and when Osman worries about the police getting hold of Fadik. It is significant that he worries less about the legal ramifications than about what fate will befall her in the hands of the gendarmes. Religion does little more to protect women. In Chukurova, the villagers, in part at least because they are so poor, seem to have no time for religion. In Saudi Arabia, middle-class women cooperate with religious and legal

restrictions as a way of gaining whatever protection and opportunities the system will allow them. Cooke, although an outsider, seeks to understand the advantages of veiling. Kemal suggests that while the misogyny behind veiling is misguided (because it is men, not women, whose sexual appetites are to be feared), veiling's central purpose — protecting women — is well-founded. Given Kemal's unsympathetic depiction of both Huru (witch) and Fadik (victim), as well as of the village women, some may argue that he'd prefer the protection of veiling to the "woman-as-beast" system.

3. Recalling Beauvoir's explanation of why women collaborate with men's treatment of them should help students to understand how the women of Chukurova behave. Beauvoir emphasizes that women are unable to unite because they have no shared history or identity and thus opt for the few benefits that accrue from a discriminatory system. This is precisely what the women in "A Dirty Story" do. With the exception of the wealthy Huru (who, by the way, keeps the villagers in line by threatening to notify her tax-collecter nephew), women in the village have no real power to resist men. If they support Fadik, then they must condemn the boys. But because their protection depends upon men, they decline to antagonize the boys. Another reason for their compliance suggests the Catch-22 situation outlined in Explorations #3: If they stand by Fadik, then they must declare solidarity with a woman denounced as a whore. Because tradition contends that all women are latent whores, they must collaborate (in denouncing the woman who has been raped) with the very custom that stigmatizes them in order to keep from being associated with the fallen woman. They are in a no-win situation.

ADDITIONAL QUESTIONS AND ASSIGNMENTS

1. In a journal entry or a collection of informal notes, discuss the images of the opposite sex (male students write about female images and vice versa) presented in selections representing two or three different cultures. Consider such issues as rights, responsibilities, innate characteristics, fantasy images, and power. As you look over your notes, try to discover similarities and differences among the cultures represented. Then compare notes with students of the opposite sex. Can you come to any general conclusion about the way we view those considered Other? (If you have answered Question 1 under *Additional Questions* in Part Three, you may wish to compare your responses to that question and this one.)

2. Interview someone who engaged in a courtship ritual different from your own; in other words, talk to someone at least a generation older or younger than you or from a foreign country. Compile a list of the details of the ritual, paying close attention to the characterization of sex roles, the outside forces that interfered with the couple, and the particular joys offered by the ritual. As you write up the interview, try to provide your reader with enough detail of setting and dialogue from your subject to create a vivid impression.

3. Create your own myth to characterize your fantasy mate. Using Silko (and perhaps Moravia) as a guide, list the characteristics you find intriguing in members of the opposite sex. Then write a story in which those characteristics become embodied in a mythic figure. Your story should include both high and low points and should leave the reader with a definite impression of your ultimate response to this Other.

91

4. One of the most interesting phenomena in the recent assault on pornography has been the alliance of feminists with right-wing members of the "moral majority." From congressional hearings on the subject matter of rock music to scientific studies of men's reactions to violent pornography, much has been said and written about pornography's insidious contribution to the degradation of women. Considering the statement implicit in Kemal's story — that inherent danger lurks in seemingly harmless attitudes (in this case viewing women as sex objects) — explore some of the articles in magazines and newspapers over the past ten years that examine pornography's effect on the treatment of women. Using this material as evidence, write a persuasive paper in which you argue either that pornography is harmful or that it is not.

5. Conduct further research into one of the cultures represented in this section, focusing specifically on sex roles. It would be wise to choose a culture about which information is readily available — Western Europe, the Islamic Middle East, or a particular culture in Africa are likely candidates. If the selection is an excerpt from a larger work, look first at that work. You can find other sources by consulting the headnotes for other selections from that culture (if there are any) and a general encyclopedia, as well as journals devoted to the study of that culture. Narrow your topic to something manageable — such as the evolution of sex roles over time, the influence of religion on sex roles, the role of government in determining or perpetuating certain sex roles or courtship rituals in the culture — and write an expository paper in which you elaborate on the images of men and women presented by the original selection.

Part Five

WORK:
WE ARE WHAT WE DO

INTRODUCTION

Students should thoroughly enjoy all the selections in this section. They are readily accessible and will surely evoke laughter, pity, excitement, surprise, and anger. A college classroom is the perfect setting for a discussion of work. While some students may not have clear career goals in mind, most at least recognize their desire for something beyond a dead-end job. A profitable way to introduce the section is to compare students' own goals with those set by their parents. In *Looking at Ourselves*, Baker offers some thoughts on the abstract nature of many current job descriptions and how they affect children's career ambitions and relationships with parents. In Liebow's and Terkel's pieces we see the vast gulf between those who view their work as inconsequential and those who view themselves as moving forces in social change. A discussion of their own ambitions will provide students with a focal point from which to assess the various ambitions and frustrations they'll encounter in the main selections.

Among possible subthemes in this chapter are "men's work" versus "women's work" (O'Brien, Hayslip, Angelou, and Bonner), the dignity of one's profession (Abram, Angelou, Levi, and Iwashita), and exploitation of workers (Hayslip, Angelou, Iwashita, Ishikawa, and Bonner).

Instructors may wish to consult the following familiar works in preparing related selections from *Ourselves Among Others*:

Essays

John R. Coleman, "Blue-Collar Journal" (*Blue-Collar Journal*, Collier, 1974).
Patrick Fenton, "Confessions of a Working Stiff" (*New York Magazine*, 1973).
Erich Fromm, "Work in an Alienated Society" (*The Sane Society*, Henry Holt, 1955).
Ellen Goodman, "The Company Man" (*Close to Home*, Simon and Schuster, 1979).
Jan Halvorsen, "How It Feels to Be Out of Work" (*Newsweek*, 1975).
Malcolm X, "The Shoeshine Boy" (*The Autobiography of Malcolm X*, Random House, 1965).
George Orwell, "Hotel Kitchens" (*Down and Out in Paris and London*, Harcourt, Brace, 1933).
Gloria Steinem, "The Importance of Work" (*Outrageous Acts and Everyday Rebellions*, Holt, Rinehart, 1983).
Lewis Thomas, "Nurses" (*The Youngest Science*, Viking, 1983).
Seymour Wishman, "A Lawyer's Guilty Secret" (*Newsweek*, Nov. 9, 1981).
Virginia Woolf, "Professions for Women" (*Death of a Moth*, Harcourt, 1942).

403–504 (Text pages)

Short Stories

Rick De Marinis, "The Flowers of Boredom" (*Antioch Review,* Winter 1988; *The Coming Triumph of the Free World,* Viking, 1988).
Arthur Conan Doyle, "A Scandal in Bohemia" (*The Adventures of Sherlock Holmes,* Schocken, 1976).
William Faulkner, "Barn Burning" (*Collected Stories of William Faulkner,* Random House, 1950).
Nathaniel Hawthorne, "The Birthmark" (*Mosses from an Old Manse,* Wiley and Putnam, 1846).
James Joyce, "Counterparts" (*Dubliners,* B. W. Huebsch, 1916).
Herman Melville, "Bartleby, the Scrivener" (*Piazza Tales,* Dix and Edwards, 1856).
Eudora Welty, "The Whistle" (*Collected Stories of Eudora Welty,* Harcourt, 1980).

BIOGRAPHICAL NOTES ON *LOOKING AT OURSELVES*

1. Linda Hasselstrom has written both poetry (*Roadkill,* 1987; *Caught by One Wing,* 1990) and nonfiction (*Windbreak: A Woman Rancher on the Northern Plains,* 1987). The excerpt in *Looking at Ourselves* is taken from *Last Circle: Writings Collected From the Land* (1991).

2. Six-foot-nine Larry Bird is a nationally known basketball player whose honors include three years as the NBA's Most Valuable Player. After graduation from Indiana State in 1979, Bird went on to play thirteen seasons as a forward with the Boston Celtics. He retired in 1992.

3   Fred Moody is a free-lance journalist who contributes to the *Baltimore City Paper.*

4. Sociologist Elliot Liebow has been a director of the National Institute of Mental Health. This selection is taken from his book *Tally's Corner: A Study of Negro Streetcorner Men* (1967).

5. Stephen Blackburn is a free-lance reporter. His article originally appeared in the alternative weekly *Kansas City Pitch* in February 1991.

6. Russell Baker, Pulitzer Prize-winning columnist for the *New York Times Magazine,* has published *The Good Times* (1989) and several collections of his wry essays. His memoir *Growing Up* was a best-seller in 1983.

7. The interview with the former Ronald McDonald clown was conducted at the Sixth Annual Vegetarian Food Fair in Toronto. It was published in *ACT: Artists for Cultural Terrorism.*

8. A member of the Creek Tribe, Joy Harjo is a professor of English at the University of New Mexico. In addition to being a screenwriter and musician, she has published several collections of poetry, most recently *She Had Some Horses* (1983) and *In Mad Love and War* (1990).

9. Vladimir Nabokov was a Russian-born author of postmodern novels in both Russian and English. He achieved fame with *Lolita* (1955).

10. John Updike, whose minutely observed sketches of American life are often associated with the *New Yorker,* is perhaps best known for short story collections such as *Pigeon Feathers* (1962); novels such as *The Centaur* (National Book Award 1963) and the Rabbit tetralogy: *Rabbit Run* (1960); *Rabbit Redux* (1971); *Rabbit is Rich* (Pulitzer Prize 1982); *Rabbit at Rest* (Pulitzer Prize 1991); and several volumes of art and literary criticism.

11. Studs Terkel interviewed political organizer Bill Talcott in *Working* (1972). Terkel's other popular "oral histories" include *Hard Times: An Oral History of the Great Depression* (1970), and *The Great Divide: Second Thoughts on the American Dream* (1988). He won a Pulitzer Prize for *The Good War: An Oral History of World War Two* (1984).

Reflections

1. Linda Hasselstrom is most pleased about the variety of work in her life. She says she is "often tired, but never bored" by the combination of running a ranch and being a writer. She believes that having a wide range of work keeps the mind from becoming too rigid: the benefits of working the ranch are specifically that it counteracts the effects of an otherwise sedentary lifestyle, which Hasselstrom believes "is literally killing a lot of us." Physical labor provides a challenge to the body that keeps us healthy. Joy Harjo begins her piece by mentioning that her mother "had already worked hard for her short life," a comment that suggests Harjo not only honors her mother's hard work but also realizes that the challenges of hard physical labor can be as wearing as they may be health-giving. Harjo, like Hasselstrom, values taking a risk, but Harjo focuses on the challenges of writing poetry rather than on physical challenges. She implies, however, that writing poetry is not sedentary, but very active: "Each poem is a jumping-off edge. . . ." Both women value the breadth of vision a varied life brings; Harjo writes that she has decided that "more than one vision . . . is a blessing"; Hasselstrom writes that a person "must look both near and far off" in order to be intellectually healthy.

2. Because college students are often thinking seriously about career decisions, they should be able to engage in a spirited debate about the advantages and disadvantages of "being one's own boss." Although many students will have worked at menial jobs such as those mentioned by Elliot Liebow, few will be able to identify with the sense of having no future that many workers struggle with. However, they will realize that most menial jobs involve long hours, poor pay, and little room for independent decision-making. Many of those whose pieces appear in *Looking At Ourselves* are writers, including Vladimir Nabokov, Linda Hasselstrom, John Updike, and Joy Harjo. All of them suggest that being a writer brings a great deal of independence. Updike's comment about the role of artist in society implies that her or his task is to ignore the dictates of literary culture and see the world in a unique way; Nabokov writes of the author as a man who must create his own values. Both Hasselstrom and Harjo, however, represent their writing as more connected to their own history and their other interests. This suggests another kind of independence, in that their work is tailored to fit in with the rest of their lives. For many, it is more often the case that one's personal life has to be tailored to fit one's work. For instance, Bill Talcott,

95

the labor organizer, is exceptionally dedicated to his work. He says — exaggerating only slightly — that he works 24 hours a day, and he travels a great deal. He also has a family, but chances are his family life has had to be adjusted to his long hours. Students may want to discuss why some people are attracted to an all-consuming career and others are more interested in work that doesn't distract from other interests.

3. Most students will have a hard time coming up with significant advantages to the kind of work mentioned by Elliot Liebow. He writes about low-paying, menial work that "promises to deliver no more tomorrow . . . than it does today." They may be able to see a certain freedom in having no commitment to a job, but this will probably be offset because Liebow emphasizes that that "freedom" comes from lacking a future. Fred Moody also writes negatively about work, but his topic is the yuppie mentality that prizes hard work over family or spirituality. Students will be able to see that the advantages of working that hard at a career are mainly material. Moody mentions technological toys that bring work into one's personal life and remarks that many people admire those who work "right up to the point of self-destruction." Russell Baker, like Moody, writes about corporate work, placing it in a negative light since this kind of work is beyond the understanding of most children. However, many students may believe that the complexities involved in being a "systems analyst" would make the work more interesting than being a person who "makes horse collars," though the latter would be more easily comprehended by one's children.

4. Elliot Liebow probably offers the most significant comment on which factors affect one's ability to choose what kind of work to do. He writes that "it is the apprentice who becomes the journeyman electrician . . . not the common unskilled Negro laborer." The class and race into which one is born are probably the most important factors in determining what work one will do. This fact will surprise students who have been raised to believe that personal ability is a far more important factor than class background or race. The class issue is implicit in pieces by Fred Moody and Russell Baker, who write about forms of work most easily available to those who come from middle class backgrounds and who have college educations. The class discussion about this question may help prepare students to consider how race and class determine the working lives represented in the essays in this section.

MAYA ANGELOU (Mye-uh AHN-zhuh-lo), Mary (p. 415)

Explorations

1. The innocent, but misplaced, sympathy of the young Angelou for her imperious employer makes readers appreciate the girl's kind and gentle nature. During her employment she grows from a naïve girl into a person of accurate moral judgment. Her final retaliation wins readers' admiration since it is motivated by principle and not a mean disposition. After her arrival, Angelou refers to her employer at least three times as "poor" Mrs. Cullinan (paras. 12, 13, 17) because she pities her lack of children. She works hard to compensate for Mrs. Cullinan's unhappiness (13). Her pity is replaced by anger when

Mrs. Cullinan, acting on her friend's suggestion, decides to call Angelou "Mary" to suit her convenience. Rather than stay and compromise, Angelou decides to get fired (34). Mrs. Cullinan's final reaction to Angelou marks Angelou's moment of triumph since Mrs. Cullinan reaffirms her maid's true identity by using her given name twice (42).

2. Angelou writes that any black she knew would find being "called out of his name" an insult (30). Like other blacks, Angelou could interpret the casual arrogance of her employer as a racial slur. Her employer, fastidious about the disposition of her belongings, feels no compulsion to recognize the personal identity of her maid. After Glory recounts that she has been renamed, Angelou wonders about the former and present names of Mrs. Randall's maid. Angelou decides not to tolerate being stripped of her individuality.

3. Angelou recounts her experiences as a maid with a sly humor, which shows she no longer holds her early innocent view of her employer. Many observations in the story demonstrate both the young girl's naïveté and the mature Angelou's merciless mockery. The young Angelou ostensibly decides to write her poem out of pity and sympathy for her employer. However, by writing about Mrs. Cullinan in her autobiography, Angelou shows how little Mrs. Cullinan deserved any sympathy. The literal description of her employer as "white, fat, old" (24) emphasizes her unappealing appearance. Students can find many examples of irony that make Mrs. Cullinan an object of ridicule, including her efforts to "embalm" herself (10) and her inability to claim the Coleman girls as daughters (11, 12). By including these incidents in her autobiography, Angelou recounts an important turning point in her life, demonstrates the false superiority of her employer, and proves that the best revenge is writing well.

Connections

1. Elliot Liebow defines a menial job as one that poses no interesting challenges and offers no opportunities for advancement. Marguerite's job certainly matches Liebow's description, but she is young enough to feel she has something to learn from it, even if all she can learn is how to differentiate dishes. Initially, Marguerite is "fascinated with the novelty" of her new surroundings and duties. She also feels sorry for Mrs. Cullinan, and tries to be good to her (paras. 12, 13) out of pity and a sense of her own worth. This is the most tangible satisfaction of the job; Mrs. Cullinan is so clearly ineffectual (her "barrenness" symbolizes the general futility of her life) that Marguerite cannot help but notice how much more productive she is than her employer. Not until Mrs. Cullinan insults her by calling her "Mary" does Marguerite begin to approach her job with the disregard Liebow describes. Marguerite possesses the "future orientation" Liebow mentions, and she recognizes that if she stays with this job she will end up like Glory, "letting some white woman rename you for her convenience" (34).

2. It will be important for students to understand that Beauvoir's discussion of the master-slave relationship need not be taken literally; she uses the master-slave relationship as a metaphor to describe relationships between the working class and the bourgeoisie. Beauvoir's main point is that the master-slave relationship is reciprocal; that is, each party is dependent on the other. However, the relationship "always works in favor of the oppressor" (12). In "Mary," Mrs. Cullinan is dependent on Glory and Marguerite, as Marguerite realizes most fully when she reflects on how Mrs. Cullinan needs her "to run a thousand errands" (13). Glory, also, seems to have acquiesced to the master-slave

relationship, even to the point of identifying her own interests with those of Mrs. Cullinan (39). Marguerite, however, has not bought into this mutual dependency, and her resistance is demonstrated in her readiness to leave the job when Mrs. Cullinan tries to take away her dignity by renaming her Mary.

3. Naipaul suggests that without the French manager present, the native employees are incapable of running the restaurant in an orderly fashion. But Angelou suggests that employees do not always share their employers' values and may quite consciously reject them. Naipaul reacts in a way that might be expected of a Westerner who feels superior to the inhabitants of the Third World country he visits. Yet perhaps "the whole restaurant idea" (20) has vanished because it is not part of the waiters' cultural heritage. The waiters may attach little importance to their lucrative jobs and the structure that supports them. They, too, may see the restaurant as a "charade" (20).

DAVID ABRAM, Making Magic (p. 422)

Explorations

1. Because we live in a culture that relegates magic to the realm of entertainment, students may be unfamiliar with the great respect and fear accorded magicians in other cultures. Although this essay clearly conveys the role of the magician in other cultures, students will most likely miss the connection between the magician and an underlying ecological balance that ensures the success of the ceremony. They may also find Abram's lack of skepticism hard to accept. Abram consistently refuses to limit the power of his magic to his knowledge of how the tricks are accomplished. Even though he characterizes his own magic as "sleight-of-hand tricks," he does not reduce it to tricks alone. Some unknown aspect of his performance mystifies him as well as his audience (para. 3). This attitude explains his ability to entertain the suggestion in the opening sentence that he may have real powers. Most important, his understanding of the magic used to change Gedé's luck, although it employs tricks, places him in contact with "the particular powers of earth to be found only there" (17). His sense of this contact and his later matter-of-fact acceptance of his magic's success (24) convince readers that Abram takes his experience seriously and does not dismiss the successful results as coincidences.

2. When first approached by Gedé, Abram produces explanations to convince him that his magic would not be powerful enough to accomplish the desired end. Approached a second time, later in the night, Abram leaves "without hesitation" (15). He now seems to be looking forward to the "challenge" of the experience, as if he thinks a chance exists that his magic will work. Students may puzzle about this dramatic change in his attitude. However, Abram plants a clue that helps to explain it. He says at first that he is "reluctant to play very deeply within the dream-space of a culture" not his own (12). When Gedé arrives at his door, Abram has entered this dream-space, quite literally, since he has dreamed of entertaining sea monsters. Although he gathers up some props, the flashpaper and a Coke bottle, ritualistically anoints the boat with sand, and mutters a prayer, his most meaningful "tactic" is making contact with "the particular powers of earth

to be found only there" (17). Paragraph 19 describes the moment Abram attunes himself to his surroundings, finding a harmonious spot within the system. He uses his magic to develop an ecological relationship with the universe.

3.   Abram uses the descriptive and expository passages about his Balinese environment to create an atmosphere that makes his use of magic ritual a natural and inevitable response. While it might be unusual for an American to react this way, Abram comes very close to identifying with the sensibility of a Balinese, who would share Gedé's view of the way to proceed. He unconsciously adopts this role by making a self-effacing refusal of Gedé's first offer, entering a symbolic vision of the sea universe, and even dressing, Balinese fashion, in a sarong (15). The description of Abram on the boat places him in the physical world of the Balinese fishermen, ready to accept and adapt to their code of behavior (17).

Connections

1.   Abram's situation is, of course, very different from Marguerite's. As a black worker in a white household, Marguerite must cope with the demands and eccentricities of her employer. Their relationship is heavily influenced by racism and classism, and Marguerite's tactics for dealing with Mrs. Cullinan's insistence on calling her "Mary" reflect the complexities of her difficult social and economic position. Marguerite might have coped with the situation as Glory does, by accepting the indignity of being "called out of her name" (para. 30), but instead she begins by using passive resistance. She arrives late, leaves early and makes little effort to do a good job, hoping she will get fired (36). But when this does not work, she tries a more direct strategy, deliberately breaking Mrs. Cullinan's most valued china.

2.   Moody divides life into categories of time for work, family life, and spiritual meditation. His lament that technological innovation has allowed the workplace to invade the home suggests a belief that work should be left at the office. Gedé's story presents a different concept of life, one that integrates all activities. Although his boat and home are separate places, the fishing village he lives in is next to the sea. More important, for Gedé, spiritual belief governs every aspect of his life, including his work. His finding fish or returning home without them depends on his ability to satisfy powerful forces. For the Balinese, success in work depends on propitiation of ancestors, magic talismans, and exorcism of demons (11).

3.   Students will be able to build on their responses to Explorations #3 to help them analyze the contrast Abram sets up between Western and Indonesian culture. His experience in Sri Lanka, where people followed him hoping he would cure them and solve their problems (5) and in Bali, where Gedé demonstrates literal faith in Abram's magic, suggest the contrast between the Western view of magic as illusion and the Indonesian view of magic as a part of everyday reality. Abram suggests, however, that the contrast can be resolved. When he comes down with malaria, Abram suspects he has been cursed by another sorcerer (7). More significantly, Abram's sympathy for Gedé's predicament and his willingness to go along with the ritual exorcism demonstrate that he does not find the Balinese vision entirely foreign. Thus, although Abram draws a contrast between the

West and Indonesian views like the one Bugul draws between Western and African perspectives, he does not present the view that the differences are irreconcilable. Instead, by adapting his behavior to Gedé's need, Abram begins to accept the Balinese vision of the universe.

LE LY HAYSLIP, Rice Farming in Vietnam (p. 432)

Explorations

1. The "snakes' keepers" are French soldiers, as is evident from the children's song following paragraph 6, which begins "French come, French come . . ."

2. Hayslip begins to discuss the specifics of her family's livelihood in paragraph 15, when she mentions the difficulties of a farmer's life during war. When the weather and the war permit, Hayslip's family and the other villagers plant a variety of crops (para. 17), but rice is their staple. The children were often involved in the growing process, acting as scarecrows (19), helping women transplant rice to the field (23), and weeding (24).

3. It should be immediately apparent to students that the war affects every part of the villager's lives. Often they have to flee their village (9, 10) and return to find homes burned and crops destroyed. The war disrupts farming (13, 16, 34). Women and girls are vulnerable to rape by soldiers (37). Hayslip first mentions the war when she describes her earliest memories of learning to walk and playing with other children; the "snake-monsters" that interrupt the children's play become a integral part of her life from that moment and as much a part of her cultural mythology as the legends about how god gave rice to the people (18–20). From the point of view of Hayslip as a child, it is difficult to sort out which effects of the war were intended and which were unintentional. She mentions that sometimes they were warned that the "snake-monster" was coming (9), but it is unclear if they were deliberately given some time to save themselves and a few of their belongings or if villagers were so vigilant that they could predict attacks. She also mentions that when crops were destroyed by soldiers, the farmers assumed that the soldiers had their own "karma" to work out, suggesting that whether or not the destruction was intentional, they held the soldiers responsible for the effects of war.

4. All the forms of recreation Hayslip mentions give the farmers a break from their work and the war, but their "recreations" are productive activities that, in various ways, promote social and familial stability or provide goods for the family. The rituals with which they honor their ancestors are occasions for praying for the family's welfare. Marriage has little to do with romance (39), so making arrangements for marriages is more a matter of doing business than celebrating love. Making clothes and tools are forms of work that seem like recreation because they offer a break from the rice fields. Even the legends they tell and the songs they sing relate to the work of planting and harvesting rice (18–20, 29).

Connections

1. Abram's discussion of the Balinese universe and Hayslip's description of planting rice demonstrate a relationship between people and the land that most Western students will find unfamiliar. Rather than basing the relationship on the idea that land should be dominated by people, the relationship Abram and Hayslip describe is based on cooperation and respect for the land, which possesses significant power to reward or punish people. The Balinese participate in "ceremonies of protection," designed to protect people from nature's destructive powers. Similarly, the ritual exorcism Abram performs for Gedé is not intended to give Gedé control over nature, but to persuade the gods to restore his ability to catch fish. Hayslip's description of planting rice emphasizes the contact between the farmers' hands and feet and the land; they must learn to cope with the mud and the monotony of planting in order to induce the land to feed them. She describes the earth as "receptive," suggesting that it wants to yield a good harvest. In the same way, when Hayslip recounts god's gift of rice, she writes that he wanted to make the work of rice farming easy, but that a mix-up thwarted his plans (paras. 18, 19).

2. Maya Angelou started working outside her home when she was ten years old, but she writes that by that time, African-American girls were already doing basic work such as ironing and washing (2). Angelou writes with irony about how becoming domestic workers in the homes of whites was the "finishing school" for African-American girls. That these jobs were taken very seriously is suggested in her comments about needing to find an excuse for quitting that would satisfy her mother (34). The circumstances for Hayslip were similar in some ways, in that she had to work in order to contribute to the family's welfare and to prepare for the many responsibilities women take on in her culture. However, she does not work for outsiders; instead, all her work takes place within the context of her family's business. Her first jobs were scaring away birds from the crops (17) and pulling weeds in the rice fields (24).

3. Ved Mehta's father emphasizes the idea that women should make sacrifices in order to be good wives and in order to gain the respect and love of their husbands (65–67). Although it is important to find a husband for Pom who is from a cultural, class, and religious background similar to hers, Daddyji says that "it's her life that is joined with his; it is she who will forsake her past to build a new future with him" (75). Similarly, in the Vietnamese farming culture Hayslip grew up in, parents arranging marriages for their children considered compatibility, but they were most concerned with the impact of the marriage on the family's social and economic circumstances. Like Daddyji, the Vietnamese farmers considered it extremely unwise to marry for love. Hayslip recalls that "keeping a husband satisfied" was a wife's most important duty (40), and the necessity of also being a "dutiful daughter-in-law" suggests that Vietnamese peasant women, like many Indian women, are expected to move in with their husbands and serve their parents-in-law.

4. Methods for teaching girls how to take care of the family home and teaching boys how to work for the family are very similar in Hayslip's description of her girlhood and in Menchú's writing about birth ceremonies and childrearing in Quiché society. Menchú writes that the little girl spends so much time with her mother that she learns from her how to take care of the family, while little boys "must begin to live like a man" (18). For all children, education consists of working alongside parents and taking on responsibilities that, in many U.S. communities, would be considered too adult for children to be

able to handle. Similarly, Hayslip recalls working in the rice fields alongside her mother (34) and learning from her everything she would need to know about running a home and raising a family (37,38). Boys, like their counterparts in Quiché culture, were expected to live like men. In both cultures, boys were more likely to be favored and forgiven. The most significant circumstance that contributes to the similarities in teaching methods in the Vietnamese and Quiché communities is that both are based on an agrarian economy in which all family members need to be involved in the work.

EDNA O'BRIEN, Sister Imelda (p. 444)

Explorations

1. Most students will be more aware of the things Sister Imelda has had to give up than of the rewards of her job, since they will be more likely to identify with the point of view of the students in the convent school. The narrator wants to ask Sister Imelda about boys, about the color of her hidden hair, and whether she misses being in the outside world (para. 23) In paragraph 24, O'Brien describes what the girls know about the nuns' daily routine; the litany of privations includes bad food, uncomfortable clothes, waking early for prayers, silence, and self-censorship. Although she admits that these things are difficult to adjust to (64), Sister Imelda most regrets having had to give up visits with her family (71). However, she is devoted to, and excited by, teaching (3). She values the security of convent life and the possibilities for spiritual pursuits, but she has trouble accepting the limited chances for emotional intimacy, a lack that is suggested in her relationship with the narrator. Although O'Brien does not consider it directly, details such as Sister Imelda's gifts to the narrator of religious pictures and spiritual advice (14, 44) suggest that her relationship with God is active and rewarding.

2. O'Brien begins to forecast the development of an enticing but ominous intimacy between the narrator and Sister Imelda in paragraph 8, when the narrator recalls that at first she "had no idea how terribly [Sister Imelda] would infiltrate my life." Later in the same paragraph, she elaborates: "I saw in her some premonition of sacrifice which I would have to emulate." She has begun to identify with the nun, and this initiates two conflicts, one regarding her growing love for Sister Imelda, and the other regarding the question of whether she has a "vocation" to become a nun herself. In fact the two conflicts are inseparable, because it is the narrator's desire to be near to Sister Imelda, and to be like her, that spurs her fruitless decision to enter the convent. Students will feel the effect of these hints differently, depending on their religious background and their interpretations of the narrator's "crush" on Sister Imelda, but most will feel the tension and foreboding inherent in O'Brien's phrasing when she writes that she felt Sister Imelda "invading" her heart (8) and that she became "dreadfully happy" (10). O'Brien provides a future context for these hints when she has the narrator say that at the time she "had no idea" of the effect Sister Imelda would have on her life. Thus the narrator is reflecting back on her own ignorance and naïveté from a position of greater maturity and wisdom. In that sense, the hints she provides forecast the process of maturation she will undergo as a result of her relationship with Sister Imelda.

3. The power that Sister Imelda is able to wield over her students is apparent throughout the piece. The girls are fascinated by the differences between Sister Imelda and the other nuns, as is suggested in the effect she has on her cooking students, all of whom, from the narrator's perspective, seem to be in love with her (16), and in their sense of freedom about asking her questions about her life (65–70). She has differentiated herself from the other nuns by seeming to be a human being, with problems and desires, as well as being a nun. This comprises a large part of her power, since she seems to her students an oasis of humanity in an otherwise dreary and impersonal school. However, she has a passionate temper, a trait that gives her even greater power, but that also makes her seem dangerous. The possibility of violence is suggested in the rumor that circulates among the girls of Sister Imelda's having beaten a student (7) and the narrator's prayer that Sister Imelda would not ever have to punish her (8). The violence of Sister Imelda's temper is shown directly in her anger at the narrator when the latter does poorly in geometry class (11), an incident that makes the sense of danger that she exudes seem all the more real. However, Sister Imelda is perhaps most dangerous because of her ability to manipulate the narrator's emotions, not only in her moments of anger, but when she apologizes by giving presents (13, 14) and when she takes risks in order to be more intimate with her (20, 44, 52, 87). Because she embodies both earthly authority as a teacher and spiritual authority as a nun, Sister Imelda's acts carry more weight than an ordinary person's. Moreover, her sacrifices for her faith make her seem heroic. Had Sister Imelda been an ambitious, competitive character rather than humble and self-sacrificing, she would have been much less sympathetic. She wouldn't have been as accessible, nor as romantic, and her connection with the students, especially the narrator, would never have developed, leaving us essentially without a story.

4. Students will find Baba's wry comments sprinkled throughout "Sister Imelda." Wherever she enters the narrative, Baba serves as a foil for the narrator's romanticism and spiritual longings. When the narrator comments on Sister Imelda's beautiful eyes, Baba replies that Sister Imelda has "Something wrong in her upstairs department" (5). When the narrator receives gifts from Sister Imelda, Baba says it's "foul to be a nun's pet," a comment that demonstrates not only her antagonism toward the narrator's involvement with Sister Imelda, but also her jealousy of their relationship (14). Baba sees clearly the line that separates the nuns from the students, and her comments suggest she sometimes views the narrator as a traitor to her own peer group and to Baba personally. While Sister Imelda kisses and praises the narrator for her performance in the Christmas play, Baba tells her she "bawled like a bloody bull" (35). As the narrator begins to become obsessed with Sister Imelda, Baba's comments become increasingly acerbic. However, Baba also serves to help keep the narrative grounded in the realities of convent-school life; since the narrator views events through the lens of her love for Sister Imelda, her narrative needs Baba's barbed words to help the reader realize how impossible are the obstacles of age, sex, and religious devotion that divide the narrator from the object of her affections.

Connections

1. The most important difference in the asceticism of convent life in "Sister Imelda" and the farmers' lives in "Rice Farming in Vietnam" is that the nuns have chosen to live without luxuries, while the farmers often do without even the necessities of living, such as an adequate diet (para. 13), because of a war over which they have no control. The nuns,

on the other hand, accept an austere and reclusive life as a way of developing their spirituality. The narrator, noticing a sty on Sister Imelda's eye, wonders if she has "overmortified herself" by refusing to eat (8). Their periods of silence outside the classroom, inadequate diet, interrupted sleep, and seclusion from friends and family are all privations that the nuns believe better prepare them to serve god. In "Rice Farming in Vietnam," on the other hand, the farmers and their families struggle to stay alive, to feed and house themselves and their families. The war continually brings destruction to their village, and they are unable to prepare for it or completely stave off its effects. When the "snake-monsters" arrive, they flee, often without a change of clothes or any food (10), and later arrive back in the village to find their homes burned to the ground (12). However, the farmers, like the nuns, show their strength by enduring hardships and by placing no importance on the luxuries they lack. They keep their families together, continue to farm, and keep their culture alive in the form of myths and prayers (26, 39).

2. Students will better appreciate Sister Imelda's unique values when they compare her attitude toward work with those represented in *Looking at Ourselves*. For instance, Elliot Liebow's piece on the plight of the unskilled African-American laborer, who never has a chance at a job worth persevering for, highlights the difference between Sister Imelda and other workers. She is not alienated from work; instead, she is entirely devoted to her work, in the sense that the convent and its school comprises almost her entire life. She has no private life; even when she goes home for her brother's funeral, another nun goes with her. Sister Imelda's work ethic validates some of the values represented negatively in Fred Moody's piece, "When Work Becomes an Obsession." Although she is seeking what Moody calls "spiritual and philosophical truths," she also seems to take her devotion to her calling so seriously that she deprives herself of rest and food. She does not seem to achieve the "balanced life" Moody advocates. Students may be able to see an analogy between Sister Imelda and the labor organizer who speaks in Studs Terkel's piece from *Working*. His job involves creating a community, a "brotherhood," of workers who will be better able to have a good life and fair working conditions if they band together. Although the purposes of convent life are different, the need to belong wholeheartedly to a group of people with the same interests is represented in "Sister Imelda" as well as the Terkel piece. Another analogy is possible between "Sister Imelda" and Linda Hasselstrom's piece about ranching in South Dakota. Hasselstrom's friends wonder why she would want the simple and hard life of a rancher when she has a college degree that could help her get a well-paying job. In "Sister Imelda," Baba wonders why Sister Imelda spent four years at a university only to come back to "poverty, chastity, and obedience" (7). Hasseltrom lives the life she does because she wants to achieve variety and balance between simple physical labor and intellectual effort, a goal that Sister Imelda might be sympathetic with, although her own goals involve devoting herself to the narrow life of the convent.

3. Students may have some difficulty in discussing "Sister Imelda" as a love story because it describes a relationship between a grown woman and a young girl, but the full impact of the story can only be appreciated when the romantic nature of the narrator's feelings for the nun is acknowledged. The narrator finds in Sister Imelda a woman she wants to emulate, as indicated in her fleeting desire to become a nun (6, 62), and she values her as a mother figure as well (17), but mixed in with these desires and wishes is a new sense

of how special she is in Sister Imelda's eyes. Sister Imelda enjoys the narrator's adoration, but she also makes the narrator feel that she is a valued person. The narrator wants to take her "place in a new and hallowed" world, and her relationship with Sister Imelda seems to offer her a way to enter that world. In "Yellow Woman," the narrator seeks through Silva a similar validation of herself as a special person separate from her life in her own family and community. Silva seems to embody the Native American myths the narrator feels herself to be a part of. But both women ultimately reject the people they fall in love with in order to choose the more ordinary route; Yellow Woman returns home to her family and leaves the mythic world behind, and the narrator in "Sister Imelda" does not return to the convent to be a nun. Instead, she chooses the more conventional route Baba urges her to take. She reports that "life was geared to work and to meeting men" even though she realized that marriage and motherhood had little to offer her (92).

PRIMO LEVI, Uranium (p. 463)

Explorations

1. Bonino wants Primo Levi to write down the story of Bonino's "escape," and sends him the "uranium" to convince him that the story is credible. Most students will find it easy to see the difference between the way Bonino wanted Levi to write the story and the story as Levi tells it in this piece. Bonino hoped to be taken seriously; the story as he wanted it told would have centered on his own heroism and would have been full of unlikely adventures. The frame that Levi sets up for Bonino's story makes it clear that the story is not credible and that Levi only listened to it because his job requires him to behave diplomatically with customers. The story as Levi conveys it is a sad example of self-aggrandizement and simple-mindedness, but Bonino is so naïve that Levi's ironic retelling might not have made any impression. If so, then he might consider himself well repaid by Levi's story.

2. Levi describes his job in the opening paragraphs. At the time the story took place, he was working as a customer service representative for a chemical company. His primary duties involved arranging for customers to order products from the company. In his "real job," Levi is a storyteller. Students will be able to pick up from Bonino's comments on Levi's novel that Levi is a popular writer of novels, and the fact that Levi used an incident from his customer service job in his writing suggests that Levi's "real job" is that of writer.

3. Both the manner in which Bonino tells his story and some of the events he relates suggest that he has invented it. Levi is wary as soon as he hears Bonino mention the Badogliano (para. 9). He knows that someone who had actually been with the Badogliano would not have used that label. From that moment, Levi assumes that Bonino has nothing to offer but a long-winded story. Bonino's story-telling style, which is full of digressions and vague references, also causes doubts (10). At one point, Bonino describes himself walking behind a guard and then quickly corrects himself (11), suggesting that he is unable to get his own story straight. Bonino's references to Levi's experience in the Holocaust, when he says that Levi's book might be too disturbing for children (7) and

then says that he (Bonino) "risked finishing up like you did" (8), imply that Levi has reason to know if Bonino's account of his own adventures had no truth. Levi's testing of the "uranium" at the end of story confirms that his assumption was correct, that the "little man's paranoic tale" was entirely invented (21).

4. In spite of his skepticism and his ironic approach to Bonino's story, Levi writes early on in the piece that his job in customer service had forced him to pretend to "esteem and like" others for so long that he had actually begun to do so. His irritation with Bonino's story is mingled with tolerance and even interest, since as a writer he is curious about how and why Bonino created his fictional history. The biblical quotation indicates that, although Bonino is alien to Levi, Levi will put up with the story patiently because he recalls that he too has sometimes told stories to people who didn't want to hear them. Bonino and Levi continue to be "strangers," however, in the sense that Levi doesn't want to hear Bonino's story because it is badly told and untrue, whereas people sometimes didn't want to hear Levi's stories because they are compellingly told and disturbingly realistic.

Connections

1. Both Sister Imelda and Primo Levi are as much (or more) interested in people and personal relationships than in their official duties. This has advantages for both. Sister Imelda inspires respect and, in the case of the narrator, a kind of love that makes students more attentive to her teaching and more open to her religious views. That Sister Imelda has an unusually positive effect on her students is evident when she enters the classroom to teach cooking and, the narrator reports, "It was as if every girl was in love with her . . . as she entered, their faces broke into smiles" (para. 16). However, on occasion Sister Imelda's passionate nature prevents her from doing well, as when she becomes angry and storms out of the classroom (11). In addition, her close involvement with the narrator suggests that she has trouble keeping a professional distance, a fault that could have a detrimental effect on her students. Primo Levi, like Sister Imelda, is interested in people. This in itself makes him good at his job, but Levi also demonstrates that he understands the hierarchical "game" that he must play with customers (2). However, when Levi assesses his own abilities as a customer service representative, he reports that he performs the job with "compunction and little human warmth" (3), attitudes that make it difficult for him to play the game of winning over the customers.

2. Like "Making Magic," "Uranium" begins with the narrator's assessment of his own abilities. Abram sees himself as a "sleight-of-hand magician" (4) who can use his limited abilities to gain access to people who would otherwise have little to do with him. Similarly, Levi tries to convey an illusion of competence and enthusiasm in order to sell his company's products. At the center of each writer's piece is a visit to someone who is a stranger, whose views are in many ways foreign to the narrator. Gedé and Bonino both expect the writers to do them an unusual service: Gedé wants Abram to make real magic and help him catch fish again, and Bonino expects Levi to believe in and, he hopes, publish his incredible story. Both writers come away from these experiences feeling simultaneously disillusioned and satisfied with their encounters. Students will be able to locate several places in "Making Magic" where Abram might have cited the same biblical quotation as Levi: when he is being followed in Sri Lanka by sick and troubled people who want him to perform curative magic; when he visits the Balinese sorcerers who "felt

their status threatened by a stranger" (7); and when Gedé comes to his hut to insist he perform magic (15), Abram might well have considered the wisdom of respecting people even when they and their customs seem particularly alien.

3.   Levi writes that a good customer service representative is able to "infuse faith in the customer" and give the impression of being "superior" without being condescending (1, 2). The ability to create a context of trust and inattention on the part of the customer is similar to Abram's approach to performing magic. He recalls that when he sees the eyes of people in the audience "slowly widening with astonishment" he almost begins to believe in his own magic. In the same way, Levi writes that creating an atmosphere of trust with a customer has the effect of giving the representative faith in himself (1).

TOMOYUKI IWASHITA (Toe-moe-yoo-ki Ee-wuh-SHEE-tuh), Why I Quit the Company (p. 471)

Explorations

1.   Tomoyuki Iwashita gives little information about the company he worked for and virtually no information about what he did for the company. In the second paragraph, he identifies the company as "a big, well-known trading company," but having made this brief comment, Iwashita turns to the issue that is important to his essay: the effect of company indoctrination on the lives of employees. Initially, many students may be at a loss about how to respond to the last part of the question, but once they understand that Iwashita is more interested in portraying the social and psychological effects of company life than in discussing Japanese business, they will find it easier to analyze the effects of Iwashita's omissions. One effect of giving little specific information about the company is that it seems to take on some of the qualities of Big Brother in George Orwell's *1984*, in that the company seems to be able to take over many aspects of employee's lives and command their complete devotion, without having to justify its own existence or explain the reasons for the demands it places on employees.

2.   It should be immediately apparent to many students that "Japanese yuppies" share with their Western counterparts a strong drive to succeed in corporate life — even to the point of being willing to give up their social and family lives out of loyalty to the company's interests (paras. 5, 8, 9). They tend to try to live a luxurious lifestyle, even to the point of going into debt to achieve it (11). However, unlike the stereotype of the American yuppie, Japanese corporate employees focus on the needs and interests of the company and the Japanese economy, rather than on individual achievement and satisfaction (10). They fear failing to justify the financial investment the company claims it has made on their behalf (5), and tend to overwork in an effort to keep up with the company's expectations. Iwashita has lived the life of a yuppie in corporate Japan. His sources of information for his concept of yuppies are firsthand, drawn from his own experiences and observations on the life-styles of his friends and colleagues in the company.

3.   Japanese companies provide conveniences, and some luxuries, that American employees never receive. The dorm system, with housekeeping and meals taken care of, is completely unknown in the United States (3). However, many students will be quick to

point out that American employees can expect to receive sick leave as a part of their benefits package, but Japanese companies do not offer these benefits. Although many American employees can expect to put in long hours if their goal is to become an executive, they will probably not be expected to give the same level of dedication. Employees of Japanese corporations essentially do all their living within the company, living in company dormitories (3), depending on the company for many goods and services (4), and giving up their leisure time to entertain clients and socialize with other employees (4). Many employees do not marry until the company approves of it (8), and Iwashita writes that even the quality of family life is determined by the needs of the company (9).

Connections

1. In paragraph 5, Iwashita discusses the isolation that the company tries to impose on its employees. The effect of this isolation is to create a relationship between employer and employee that is based on control and obedience. Iwashita discusses how the company needs only three months to train its new employees. They arrive as individuals who are "active, clever, and tough," but they will not be really useful to the company until they are "brainwashed" to be devoted to the company. Employees who have gone through this process often express the fear that they are not contributing enough; they have lost some of the self-confidence they arrived with and have adopted the attitude that the company's interests are more important than "their own mental and physical wellbeing." The employer-employee relationship suggested in Primo Levi's "Uranium" is very different. The company Levi works for does not seem to expect subservience. He describes a working life with a great deal of independence and variety. Levi writes that a customer service representative must have faith in the products he sells; the emphasis is not on unquestioning loyalty to the company, but on knowing the worth of the product. Levi also stresses the benefits for the individual of customer service work. He writes that selling "helps you to know yourself and strengthens your character." The development of the individual is not a goal in Japanese companies, which, according to Iwashita's perspective, prefer obedience and teamwork in their employees.

2. Fred Moody's account of the American work ethic accords strongly with Iwashita's comments about corporate life in Japan. Moody's beginning statement, that work has infiltrated all other aspects of American workers' lives, suggests parallels to Iwashita's description in paragraph 4 of how the working day in Japanese corporations is extended into the evenings and weekend and his comments in paragraph 8 about how the company controls its employee's private lives. After discussing Connections #1 above, however, students may be better able to analyze the differences in the work ethic Moody and Iwashita describe. Like Levi, Moody implies that the individual makes a commitment to his or her own career, not to any particular company. Moody does not say that employees of American companies have been brainwashed, as Iwashita says of Japanese employees (5). Instead, he implies that they are motivated by some of the same qualities that new employees in Japanese companies possess when they are first hired: initiative, intelligence, and strength. While Japanese employees are required to moderate these qualities to become integrated into the company, their American counterparts work on their own behalf. Many students will deduce, however, that although American and Japanese workers are motivated differently, the effect is the same: Overworking is a trait businesspeople in both countries share.

3. Smith makes several generalizations about Japanese business practices and psychology that are supported by Iwashita's account of his life in a Japanese corporation. Perhaps the most significant of Smith's generalizations is that the Japanese do not favor individual choice because it might weaken the sense of obligation "which keeps the Japanese living in a rigidly defined hierarchy of authority" (6). Iwashita notes that employees of the company he worked for worried about their obligations, especially whether they were contributing enough to the company's profits (5). When Iwashita collapsed from overwork, his supervisor put the blame on Iwashita; the idea that the employee alone is responsible for work-related health problems has sometimes led to an employee's death — a phenomenon that underscores employees' commitment to the company's interests (6). Iwashita comments on the company's demand that employees become integrated into the company, committing themselves to it for life (4); in a similar vein, Smith notes that one of the maxims corporate employees offer to each other is *Gambatte*, or "Think long term" (9), suggesting that persistence is considered the key to success. Overall, Smith's perspective on Japanese business seems more positive than Iwashita's, probably because he is a Westerner, an outsider who does not live fully within the system as Iwashita does.

RAYMOND BONNER, A Woman's Place (p. 475)

Explorations

1. The title of Bonner's essay comes from the expression "A woman's place is in the home." Students' expectations about "A Woman's Place" will vary according to their backgrounds and their ideas about women's roles, but few will identify with the Kuwaiti perspective on domestic labor. Only a few American students will have grown up in homes where maids were employed. Those who have had family members or friends employed as domestic workers will recognize that the plight of the Asian maids in Kuwait is in many respects worse than it is for domestic workers in the United States. Bonner includes information about the "liberation" of Kuwaiti women (para. 29), who legally can expect to earn the same wage as men and receive paid maternity leave (27), rights which, as Bonner points out, women in the United States are still struggling to achieve. Many Kuwaiti women are stepping out of their "place" in the home to run businesses (28), but their greater determination to win rights for themselves has not been extended to include women outside their cultural and economic group. Asian maids are still stuck in the home, but ironically they are most out of "place" when they are fulfilling traditional feminine jobs in the homes of privileged Kuwaitis.

2. Because Bonner devotes so much of his essay to examples and narratives that illustrate the predicament of the Asian maid and little to defining the problem directly, students may be able to come up with several differing statements of his thesis. After reading his analysis in paragraph 24, some may say that his thesis is that conflicts between traditional values and modern lifestyles created a society in which abuses like those inflicted on the maids can occur. Others may identify gender, class, or cultural conflicts as the basic

problems that underlie the exploitation of poor, foreign, female workers (24, 32). In fact, however, Bonner's essay demonstrates how these conflicts have worked together to create a social system with a built-in potential for the exploitation of these workers, who lack legal rights and protections because they are foreigners (32), because they are women (28), and because they are poor. One of the most succinct statements of the Kuwaiti perspective on Asian maids comes from an agency representative who tells Bonner that he can have his housemaids work any number of hours because "they belong to you" (18). Their system of domestic employment amounts to slavery.

3. Bonner relies primarily on anecdotal evidence to support his argument about the exploitation of Asian maids in Kuwait. His essay begins with the example of a maid who fled the house where she was employed after she was beaten by her employer. To a Western reader, unacquainted with human rights issues in Arab countries, this example might seem extreme, but Bonner piles example on example, some even more extreme than the case with which he opens the essay. He creates an image of a nation of wealthy households marred by violence and abuse of domestic workers. Bonner did firsthand research (he went to the embassies (1) and police stations (11) where maids had taken refuge, and he posed as a potential employer when he visited agencies (19)), used testimony taken directly from the women who had fled the houses where they were employed, and talked with Kuwaiti women about their social and professional status. He also cites a few statistics about the numbers of foreign workers and domestic workers in Kuwait (22) and how many Asian maids have taken refuge at embassies (23), but the lack of interest among Kuwaitis about the fate of foreign workers suggests that no one has taken the trouble to document abuses. For this reason, and because his technique helps to put a human face on the problem, Bonner chose to rely heavily on anecdotal evidence gleaned during interviews.

Connections

1. Students will be able to discuss the differences and the similarities between the situation of the Asian maids in Kuwait and the corporate employees in Japan by considering the social and economic context in which each group is attempting to deal with its labor problems. The Japanese workers are in their own country, near their friends and family. They still have civil rights and are making a relatively good living. They have some employment options open to them if they decide to leave the company. The Asian maids in Kuwait have none of these advantages. Most have no friends in Kuwait, do not speak the language, and have virtually no opportunities to improve their lot either by staying in a particular job or by attempting to leave it. In spite of these clear differences, there are some significant similarities in their situations. Both groups of workers have limited freedom of movement and little free time. Bonner, for instance, cites the case of Jenny Casanova, who worked eighteen-hour days and received no day off (para. 4). Similarly, Iwashita recalls that his life in the company "rapidly became reduced to a shuttle between the dorm and the office" (2) and that many employees became exhausted from overwork (6). The dorm system imposed by many companies on unmarried employees is somewhat similar to the situation of the maids, who also have no choice about where they reside, and whose personal lives are rigidly controlled by their employers (4–6).

2. Aside from the similarity in the kind of work, a comparison between Mary's job and the situation of Asian maids in Kuwait can best be made by considering the moment when Mrs. Cullinan decides to call Marguerite "Mary". Mrs. Cullinan believes it is her privilege to call black domestic workers by any name she likes. In the act of naming her, Mrs. Cullinan is drawing on a long tradition dating from the slave era. Asian maids in Kuwait have their identities erased as well. Having left their native land and language behind, they are employed by people who regard them as virtual slaves (18). In both Marguerite's situation and that of Jenny Casanova (Bonner, 1), racial, cultural, and economic inequalities produce a situation in which the employer attempts to deprive the worker of dignity, but Marguerite has a somewhat better situation than Casanova, because she is not physically abused, has her family nearby, speaks the same language as her employer, and can end her employment by using her intelligence.

3. Both Kuwaiti and Saudi women have made some progress in employment and entrepreneurship while maintaining their fidelity to traditional values. Cooke mentions the success of Shafiqa Jazzar, who began with a dress shop in her home and now owns a store (8, 9), and describes the women's section of a Riyadh newspaper, where Saudi women accept the veil and physical segregation but refuse to pursue "feminine" stories. Bonner cites similar success for women journalists in Kuwait. He mentions that two editors at the Kuwait News Agency are women (28). In contrast to Saudis, women journalists in Kuwait are not segregated from men. In both Saudi Arabia and Kuwait, there has been a degree of government support for women's employment outside the home. Kuwait adopted a labor code that guaranteed equal pay for equal work (27), and women in Saudi Arabia are receiving business permits (8) and support for their business ventures from the Islamic Bank (9). Bonner compares the status of Saudi and Kuwaiti women in paragraph 26, where he says that Saudis are disadvantaged in that they are not permitted to drive or move about alone in public. Cooke, however, is convinced that wearing the veil and other seemingly restrictive customs are no hindrance to Saudis, who go out unchaperoned (but veiled) and participate freely in religious meetings and educational opportunities (17, 18).

4. Perhaps the first things students will notice about the representations of violence in Sa'edi's story and Bonner's essay is that violence is portrayed as an accepted part of everyday life, passed on through generations and learned through imitation. In the poor Iranian community Sa'edi describes, the narrator and his friend Hasani treat each other in the same way they are treated by their parents. They hit each other as soon as they meet (1), and suggest a beating as the stake in a bet (273, 274). Writing of the abuse of Asian maids in middle-class Kuwaiti households, Bonner quotes Eman al-Bedah, who asserts that Kuwaiti women mistreat their maids as Kuwaiti husbands mistreat their wives. Similarly, the boys in "The Game Is Over" have learned to communicate with each other through violence because their parents, especially their fathers, set the example by beating their children and their wives regularly. The acceptance of violence as a principle of living is so thoroughly rooted in the boys that when Hasani wants a sign that his parents love and value him, he stages a deception that relies on a violent act — his own death. Some Kuwaitis have a similar perspective in that they are so used to certain kinds of domestic violence that they do not see the physical abuse of maids as a problem.

111

YOSHIMI ISHIKAWA (Yoe-SHEE-me Ee-shee-KA-wuh), Strawberry Fields (p. 487)

Explorations

1. Before interpreting Yoshimi Ishikawa's comments about farmers being unable to mold the land, students will need to consider the context. Ishikawa describes how he and his brother learned to drink irrigation water (paras. 6, 7); later, he writes that the land had taught his brother to be a farmer (19). Anchan tastes the soil to find out if it will be good for growing strawberries, but the land is so unpredictable (12) that he can't make any assumptions about it. Ishikawa states the premise behind this comment directly when he writes that the land "transforms and creates" the farmer (7). The fact that they drink, and even enjoy, muddy irrigation water means that they are literally taking the land into themselves, but it also serves as a metaphor for the necessity of the farmer's learning about, and adapting to, the land.

    However, the goal of their adapting to the land is to tame it as much as possible. They "begin by making the land arable" (29). In the process, they adapt the land to their own needs. The success of Frank, who made good money farming, attests to the farmers' ability to mold the land — to some degree at least — to their own purposes (4), but Frank has also been molded by the land, for his hard work over many years has damaged his body and spirit (4).

2. It may be difficult for students to extrapolate from Ishikawa's essay how these characters were before they emigrated, but students will be able to draw inferences from Ishikawa's discussion of the differences in American and Japanese farming. Ishikawa stresses the predictability of farming in Japan. He mentions that farmers there knew how much they could make in a year (3), that the land had always been used before, and that the process of farming varied little (29). His emphasis on predictability may be taken as a cultural, as well as an agricultural, observation; Ishikawa and his brother knew what to expect from Japan, but the United States is much less predictable. Frank is perhaps the most outstanding example of the changes that a Japanese might undergo in the United States. Having his land taken from him, being sent to an internment camp, and rebuilding his farm after his release are all experiences that attest to the unpredictability of life in the West.

    Ishikawa also expresses his concern about change when he writes that he is worried he might become like the nisei, who are too deeply influenced by Western mores. He is troubled by the possibility of becoming acculturated and notes that immigrants change the way they communicate, becoming belligerent and less willing to listen, in an effort to make themselves visible (63). The farmers have also been affected by ethnic and international politics in their area, factors that make their experience in the United States drastically different from what it would be in their own more isolated island nation. Ishikawa has become knowledgeable about border politics and the ways in which ethnic differences among the Mexicans, Anglos, Filipinos, and Japanese affect the agricultural economy. In Japan, where ethnic and national differences are at a minimum, the problems he and his brother have learned to cope with do not exist.

3. Students should find it easy to respond to this question. Ishikawa clearly delineates the process sections of his essay, dividing the process into two parts: 1) preparing the land and 2) planting strawberries. He announces the first part of the process with a question:

"So how did we convert our field?" (21). He describes raking, removing rocks (22), watering and weeding (23), exterminating pests (24), and fertilizing (25). Ishikawa signals the shift to the next part of the process in paragraph 27: "Now, we began to farm." He describes planting, irrigating (28), and the long process of waiting and checking on whether the strawberry plants had taken root (31, 32). Ishikawa completes the process section of the essay while this period of waiting is continuing (32).

Connections

1. Students will be quick to see that the relationships between the Japanese and Mexicans on one hand and Kuwaitis and Asians on the other are similar in that both are based on racial and cultural differences. In Ishikawa's essay, Pete says that the Mexicans don't want to work because it's hot (para. 45), a prejudicial comment that builds on his idea that Japanese are hardworking people and Mexicans are lazy. The Mexican workers are mistreated in that they are often paid below minimum wage — or not at all — and work under poor conditions (44). Similarly, Asian maids in Kuwait are paid little and work extremely hard (6, 19). Raymond Bonner writes that Asian maids in Kuwait "are foreigners in an extemely closed and xenophobic society" (31). Asians in Kuwait "are at the bottom of the heap." In both cases, an economically dominant group abuses its power, and it can do so because the exploited group is composed of foreigners who have virtually no civil rights and no family or friends in the area. Also similar in Bonner's and Ishikawa's essays is the dominant group's willful ignorance of the workers' plight. Ishikawa recalls that he had not been paying attention to media reports of the workers' strike and that even those who had employed Mexicans for years couldn't understand the workers' motives for going on strike. Bonner quotes a Kuwaiti human-rights activist who denies that Asian maids are exploited economically or abused physically (32), and Kuwaiti feminist groups do not recognize the working conditions of maids as a problem (35). The Japanese and Kuwaitis view foreign workers only in light of how they will contribute to their own interests; they are uninterested even in the basic needs of the workers.

   It is important for students to consider some of the differences in the employer-employee relationships Ishikawa and Bonner describe, especially the role that gender plays in both cases. Bonner points out that Asian maids are vulnerable to being exploited and abused not only because they are foreigners, but because they are women (24). Their plight remains hidden because they are scattered and hidden in homes, have no opportunity to form a union, and therefore cannot develop a sense of solidarity. The Mexican workers, however, became visible under the leadership of Cesar Chavez and were able to form a union that helped them work toward achieving better working conditions.

2. Hayslip and Ishikawa write of a sensual relationship between the farmer and the earth. Hayslip recalls "that sensual contact between our hands and feet, the baby rice, and the wet, receptive earth" as a phenomenon that reaffirmed farmers' connection to the land (23). Ishikawa remembers seeing his brother drink muddy irrigation water and pronounce it "delicious" (6). Later on, after he, too, has learned to enjoy irrigation water, he decides that this demonstrates that the land "transforms and creates" the farmer (7). In both "Strawberry Fields" and "Rice Farming in Vietnam," the authors describe a process of preparing the land and then planting the crop. Student will be able to refer to their responses to Explorations #3 in order to compare Ishikawa's description of the process

113

with Hayslip's. Hayslip goes further than Ishikawa in her process description. She relates the steps in preparing the land for planting rice in paragraph 22, and then goes on to describe planting, fertilizing, and weeding (23, 24). Then she goes further, taking the process all the way through harvesting, preparing for the next planting, and preparing rice to be stored for eating (30–33).

3. Among the ideas Ishikawa and Hasselstrom share is the idea that higher education and work on the land go hand in hand. Hasselstrom writes that many people believe "that anyone who enjoys physical labor must be too dumb to get an education." Ishikawa writes that human beings are born with a desire to work (1); his insightful reflections on the intellectual challenges of farming, along with the fact that he was attending school in order to improve his English for college during the time of which he writes, suggest that he and Hasselstrom are in agreement that the hard physical labor of farming contributes to, rather than detracts from, intellectual effort.

4. Ishikawa both fears and hopes that he will become Americanized if he continues to study its language and culture (1). He notices the differences between American competition, which involves the possibility of vast personal losses and gains, and Japanese competition, which is extremely predictable (4). Kimura's editorial also takes note of the extravagance of American competition, where $15 million can easily be spent on a meaningless contest. The Japanese, by contrast, work hard and consistently to build "the best in television sets, Walkman stereos, and cars," but in order to be taken seriously by Americans, they will have to be willing to engage in a kind of extreme financial risk-taking that is foreign to the Japanese.

GABRIEL GARCÍA MÁRQUEZ (Gah-bree-EL Gar-SEE-ah MAR-kez), Dreams for Hire (p. 497)

Explorations

1. "Dreams for Hire" partakes of some elements of the short story and some elements of the essay. Márquez offers little exposition, leaping right into the first scene of his narrative, the tidal wave that smashes into the hotel. Márquez returns to this scene at the conclusion of the piece. Thus the structure of "Dreams for Hire" is similar to a framed story, in which a central narrative is contained within, and contextualized by, another narrative displaced from it in time and space. In addition, Márquez's narrative has elements of suspense ordinarily associated with fiction, especially the mystery. Is it really Frau Frida who died? What is the significance of the serpent-shaped ring? Márquez describes his characters in detail, using their conversation to advance arguments about the association of dreams and poetry, as when Neruda expounds his opinion of dream divination in paragraphs 16 and 17. But he also pays attention to character development; his portrait of Neruda includes the poet's physical appearance (13), his eating habits, his relationship with his wife, and his propensity to dominate others, as in the "inevitable walk along the Ramblas" (18) and the "sacred siesta" (23). These are elements of character development missing in most conventional essays.

The aspects of "Dreams for Hire" that remind us Márquez is writing factually are the writer's physical presence at the real events he describes and his representation of Neruda, a famous poet.

2. Students will quickly be able to identify Márquez's ambivalence about Frau Frida's occupation in his comments to her during their walk along the Ramblas. He tells her that "her dreams were no more than a contrivance," but he still refuses to return to Vienna because he is worried about the unidentified disaster Frau Frida dreamed he would undergo there (17, 22). Frau Frida takes her dreams in a matter-of-fact way, telling Márquez that no danger awaits him in Vienna anymore. She does not create drama around her dreams and doesn't always take them seriously, as when she tells him that not all dreams represent "real life" (33). The irony of her doubting herself — because her dream about Neruda is true — is compounded by her death. Frau Frida foretold disasters for others, but it is possible she was not able to perceive the reality of her dreams when they related to her own life.

3. Márquez describes Frau Frida as "magical," but "fearsome" (3). Neruda, like Frau Frida, dominates his audience with his substantial physical presence and his ability to command attention. He even displays a clairvoyant power like hers when he says to Márquez, "There's someone behind me who keeps staring at me" (14). The elements of character they share suggest the possibility of competition between them — a possibility expressed directly by Neruda when he says, "Only poetry is clairvoyant" (17). The limits of the poet's "clairvoyance" is suggested in his misinterpretation of his dream as his own new idea (hence his disappointment in paragraph 28 when Márquez points out that the idea has probably already been taken up by another Latin American literary giant, Jorges Luis Borges). Similarly, the limits of Frau Frida's clairvoyance are established when she believes her dream about Neruda is unrelated to reality.

4. Most students will have little doubt that the ambassador's dead housekeeper was Frau Frida. The unusual ring found on the body is suggestive, but the ambassador's comment that Márquez would have been unable to resist writing a story about her (35) is even more conclusive, because Márquez did go on to write "Dreams for Hire." The ambassador's comment that "she was a dreamer" does not confirm her identity, but it does reinforce Márquez's representation of her as a mysterious, powerful woman whose identity was prone to change. Frau Frida was not her real name, and Márquez apparently never learned what her real name was (4).

Connections

1. Responses to this question will depend on how individual students define "necessity" in relation to job choice. It was a "harsh Viennese winter" that originally drove Frau Frida to sell her skill as a dreamer (para. 8). The practical necessity of obtaining food and housing is also a compelling reason to choose a particular job in Le Ly Hayslip's "Rice Farming in Vietnam," Primo Levi's "Uranium," and Raymond Bonner's "A Woman's Place." In Hayslip's piece, villagers farm because they must feed themselves. They raise their staple diet themselves. In Primo Levi's "Uranium," the author takes a job in private industry as a salesperson in order to supplement his irregular income. And in "A Woman's Place," young Asian women come to Kuwait to be maids because they have so few employment opportunities in their own nations. But practical necessity may be

115

complemented by other kinds of necessity. Some students may view a vocation as a kind of necessity; if so, Frau Frida's vocation is similar to David Abram's in "Making Magic" and Sister Imelda's in Edna O'Brien's piece, in that she is pulled toward her profession as much because of an innate talent as by conscious choice.

2.   Students will be able to build on their responses to Connections #1 when considering the similarities between Frau Frida's and David Abram's work. Both are able to use their unusual talent to give other people a greater sense of control over their own lives. Through the use of illusion, Abram helps a fisherman regain his confidence in his ability to catch enough fish to feed his family. And Frau Frida builds an entire career on her ability to interpret her own dreams as a way of forecasting the future for others. Abram discovers the significance of his talent when he realizes that, in a way, he really does have "powers" he himself can't understand (27). Frau Frida, although she is matter-of-fact about her extraordinary talent and not offended by Márquez's skepticism (19), nevertheless takes her dreams seriously and is charismatic enough to persuade others to take them seriously as well.

3.   Depending on their background, some students may have found disagreeable the image of Neruda wrapped up in a bib, eating a huge amount of rich food, and carelessly sampling from everyone else's plate (14). Octavio Paz describes American cuisine as more concerned with health than pleasure or desire (3, 4), but its primary attribute is the concern with "exclusions" (1). By contrast, Paz suggests that European and Latin American cuisines are endowed with "passion," color, and spices (1, 2), a tolerance for "ambiguity and ambivalence" (3), desire, and pleasure (3, 4). In "Dreams for Hire," Márquez's depiction of Neruda's extravagant relish of his meal illustrates Paz's ideas about the relationship to food enjoyed by Latin Americans. Lunch for Neruda is not a matter of restoring health, but of luxuriating in food because of the pleasure it offers.

ADDITIONAL QUESTIONS AND ASSIGNMENTS

1.   In a journal entry or a collection of informal notes, discuss the role of workers presented in selections representing two or three cultures, with particular reference to oppression. Consider such issues as the employer-employee relationship; the role played by government, ideology, or both; and the existence (or absence) of a clearly defined working class. As you look over your notes, try to discover similarities and differences among the cultures represented. Then consider how you would describe the role of workers in the United States. Can you reach any conclusions about the differences between cultures?

2.   Interview someone whose job you find particularly intriguing. Try to formulate questions that will elicit information about the person's reasons for choosing the job, the training he or she underwent, the person's perception of the importance of the job, his or her self-image with respect to the job, and the particular kind of satisfaction he or she gleans from it. As you write up the interview, try to integrate your own commentary with your subject's words.

3. Write a narrative about a character who makes a living from performing unconventional work, such as faith healing, palm reading, or astrology. Marquez' story or Abram's essay will serve as effective models. The character might be a con man or woman who manages to persuade credulous people to pay his or her way through life. Or he or she might genuinely have a unique and irreplaceable talent. In your characterization, consider what personality traits and what kind of personal history are necessary to this character's work and to what extent the work they do is dependent on the character's belief in his or her own "magic" abilities.

4. Many young women in the United States today are facing difficult decisions regarding balancing a career and family. Explore the issue of working mothers by consulting articles that have appeared in magazines and newspapers over the past several years. Look specifically for pieces that enumerate the problems faced by these women when it comes to running the home, caring for the children, and advancing on the job. Using this material as your evidence, write a classification paper in which you categorize the various problems faced by working mothers. Or write a process analysis in which you inform young women of the methods they might use to deal with the problems inherent in combining motherhood with a career.

5. Conduct further research into one of the cultures represented in this unit, focusing specifically on the country's work force. It would be wise to choose a culture about which information is readily available — the United States, Ireland, Japan, and Italy are likely candidates. If the selection is an excerpt from a larger work, look first at that work. You can find other sources by consulting the headnotes for other selections from that culture and a general encyclopedia, as well as journals devoted to the study of that culture. Narrow your primary focus to something manageable, such as the distribution of wealth in the culture, the economic philosophy, the existence or absence of a class system, or the major employment opportunities for citizens, and write a persuasive paper in which you either applaud or condemn the culture's treatment of workers.

Part Six

WE THE PEOPLE
INDIVIDUALS AND INSTITUTIONS

INTRODUCTION

Although students should find all the selections in this section fascinating, they may exhibit some discomfort with the blurring of ideological lines in many. Accustomed to defining political good versus evil in terms of Western democracy versus communism, some students may resist the negative images of America's contribution to the plight of the poor in other nations, of Israelis as oppressors, and of the South African government; equally disquieting may be the positive attitude toward reconciliation of differences between Western democracies and Communist states expressed in the essays by Havel and Shevardnadze. Precisely because of these unsettling portrayals, however, this section is one of the most important in the text. It provides a marvelous tool for encouraging students to explore political systems before judging them, to resist easy stereotypes, and to recognize similarities among seemingly disparate cultures.

To prepare students for the kind of questioning they'll need to exhibit throughout the section, instructors may want to begin by asking them to articulate their perceptions of how government acts for and against the people. The selections in *Looking at Ourselves* will be a help here: Vine Deloria, Jr., Clifford M. Lytle, and Haunani-Kay Trask all call attention to shortcomings in the U.S. system. Lapham and Berry don't look at the U.S. government per se, but they examine disturbing aspects of life in this country. Lapham traces connections between the official war on drugs and a pervasive racism and classism in U.S. society. Berry indicts our tendency to believe our lives are governed solely by economic laws; Sizer critiques American secondary schools for failing to educate and functioning simply as a way to keep young people off the labor market; and the *New Yorker* piece examines the responsibility of television news anchors for the trivialization of political campaigns. Toni Morrison and Martin Luther King provide commentary on racial issues in the United States; their pieces offer a valuable comparison with stories and essays that deal with racism and ethnocentrism in other nations, such as Nelson Mandela's "Black Man in a White Court," the anonymous writer's "Evicted: A Russian Jew's Story (Again)," and Nadine Gordimer's "Amnesty." The overview offered by these short pieces should provide a relatively easy way to introduce the kind of healthy skepticism students will encounter in the main selections. As they work their way through the section, they may need to be reminded occasionally that the purpose of exploring other cultures is simply to learn about them and to recognize the good and the evil in each government in order to become better able to judge our relationship with our own government.

Among possible subthemes in the section are the individual as victim of a political system (Mandela, Anonymous, Weldon, and Gordimer), views of Communist societies (Havel, Golden, and Shevardnadze), government as its own worst enemy (Golden, Shevardnadze, and Havel),

118

problems resulting from changes in political conditions (Havel, Golden, and Anonymous), and the role of identity politics in the formation of nations (Mandela, Gordimer, Anonymous).

Instructors may wish to consult the following familiar works in preparing related selections from *Ourselves Among Others*:

Essays

Martin Luther King, Jr., "Letter from Birmingham Jail" (*Why We Can't Wait*, Harper, 1963).
Walter Lippmann, "The Indispensable Opposition" (*Atlantic Monthly*, Aug. 1939).
George Orwell, "A Hanging" (*Shooting an Elephant*, Harcourt, 1950).
Jonathan Swift, "A Modest Proposal" (1729).
Henry David Thoreau, "On Resistance to Civil Disobedience" (1849).
Barbara Tuchman, "An Inquiry into the Persistence of Unwisdom in Government" (*Esquire*, May 1980; *The March of Folly*, Ch. 1, Knopf, 1984).

Short Stories

Nadine Gordimer, "Some Monday for Sure" (*Not for Publication*, Viking, 1965).
Shirley Jackson, "The Lottery" (*The Lottery*, Farrar, Straus, 1949).
Ursula K. LeGuin, "The Ones Who Walk Away from Omelas" (*The Winds's Twelve Quarters*, Harper, 1975).
Thomas Mann, "Mario and the Magician" (*Stories of Three Decades*, Knopf, 1964).
Herman Melville, "Billy Budd, Sailor" (1891).

BIOGRAPHICAL NOTES ON *LOOKING AT OURSELVES*

1. Wendell Berry, farmer and college professor at the University of Kentucky, has presented his agrarian, environmental philosophy eloquently in several volumes of essays (*Standing by Words*, 1983; *The Unsettling of America: Culture and Agriculture*, rev. ed. 1986; *The Hidden Wound*, 1989; *What Are People For?*, 1990), novels (*The Memory of Old Jack*, 1975), and poetry (*Collected Poems*, 1985).

2. Haunani-Kay Trask is a professor of Hawaiian Studies and Director of the Center for Hawaiian Studies at the University of Hawaii at Manoa. In 1986 she published *Eros and Power: Promise of Feminist Theory*. She is interested in the political and cultural struggles of native Islanders.

3. Vine Deloria, Jr., a Standing Rock Sioux attorney and professor of political science, has served as executive director of the National Congress of American Indians. Among his

powerfully argued works are *Custer Died for Your Sins: An Indian Manifesto* (1969), *We Talk You Listen* (1970), and *Behind the Trail of Broken Treaties* (1974).

4. Theodore Sizer is on the faculty of the School of Education at Brown University. His incisive analyses of American secondary schools are contained in *Horace's Compromise: The Dilemma of the American High School* (1984) and *Horace's School: Redesigning the American High School* (1992).

5. Winner of the 1993 Nobel Prize for literature, Toni Morrison's widely acclaimed novels include *The Bluest Eye* (1970), *Sula* (1973), *Song of Solomon* (1977), *Tar Baby* (1981), *Beloved* (Pulitzer Prize 1988), and *Jazz* (1992). She also gave a series of lectures at Harvard University published as *Playing in the Dark: Whiteness and the Literary Imagination* (1992). Most recently she edited a collection of essays on the Anita Hill-Clarence Thomas Controversy: *Race-ing Justice, En-gendering Power* (1992).

6. Martin Luther King, Jr., as head of the Southern Christian Leadership Conference, led a series of nonviolent protests and sit-ins against racial discrimination in the 1950s and 1960s that culminated in passage of the Civil Rights Act of 1964. Among his most memorable utterances were the "I Have a Dream" speech delivered in Washington, D.C., in 1963 and the "Letter from Birmingham Jail" published in *Why We Can't Wait* (1963). In 1964 he was awarded the Nobel Peace Prize. He was assassinated in 1968.

7. Shelby Steele teaches English at San Jose State University. In 1990 he published a much discussed collection of essays, *The Content of Our Character: A New Vision of Race in America.*

8. Editor of *Harper's* magazine, Lewis H. Lapham has written *Money and Class* (1987), *Imperial Masquerade* (1990), and *What's Going On Here?* (1991).

9. Jim Whitewolf, a Kiowa Apache, was born in Oklahoma around 1878. In 1949–50, Whitewolf told his story to ethnographer Charles Brant, whose record is the source for the included selection. Brant notes that Whitewolf "remained the steadfast, devoted member of the Native American Church which he had been throughout his lifetime." Whitewolf died in the mid-1950s.

Reflections

1. This is a question that will allow students to share their general knowledge of world affairs with each other. Responses will vary a great deal depending on how much world history students know and how much international news they have encountered in the media Certainly many will realize that the manipulation of political events by the media discussed in the New Yorker selection is not a phenomenon peculiar to the United States; some will also realize that the struggle for African-American civil rights described by Martin Luther King, Jr., takes place within a society deeply influenced by white racist sentiments that also impel events in South Africa. Wendell Berry's concern that Americans are overly devoted to the idea of competition may also be familiar to students who have read about the Japanese enthusiasm for economic competition.

2. The *New Yorker* piece mentions many shortcomings of the television news. Many of the most telling criticisms come from the anchors, who said their medium focused on which candidate was ahead in the polls rather than what candidates stood for and that television news tended to privilege gossip and sensationalism over substantive news. They are also guilty of gullibility. Politicians have been able to direct the media's attention away from real news to non-issues, such as empty campaign symbols during the 1988 election campaign. The military as well has been able to mislead the media, deliberately concealing information and allowing reporters to see only carefully chosen battle sites. The *New Yorker* selection has little to say about what contributions the visual media make to American life, but it does contend that, because the media reflect the social system at large, they cannot be held solely responsible for the vacuity of substantive coverage. Further, there is a suggestion at the end of the piece that the public cares enough about the content of news programs to turn to other media in search of better coverage, a tendency that may spur television news to make changes in its practices.

3. According to Haunani-Kay Trask, Hawaiians before the arrival of the *haole* did not see their leaders as owners of the land, but as "stewards" of the land. Everyone, then, had the right to use the land, but no one could sell it. According to Vine Deloria, Jr., and Clifford M. Lytle, a similar concept of people's relationship to the land prevailed among American Indian tribes, in that they "held land in common."

4. Martin Luther King, Jr., sees the impetus for slavery as "primarily economic." Therefore, slavery heavily influenced the development of the unique social, political, and legal systems in the United States. White supremacy was literally founded on the practice of treating other human beings as property and depriving them of all rights, but white supremacy also required that the practice of slavery be rationalized — among whites — as morally just. Toni Morrison uses a similar argument in relation to the study of canonized American literature, which, in her view, has elided the important influence of "the four-hundred-year-old presence" of Africans and African-Americans on the evolution of the nation and its literature. Shelby Steele makes a valuable contribution to the arguments advanced by King and Morrison when he theorizes that white supremacy had to be justified, in the minds of whites, by an assumption of "innocence" that qualified them to subjugate black people. The loss of that sense of "innocence" — a loss brought about by the acknowledgement of the role of slavery in forming American social and legal systems and by the realization that black people have contributed directly and indirectly to American literature — also brings about a loss of power that could lead, under the best circumstances, to the end of white supremacy.

EDUARD SHEVARDNADZE, Life with the Party (p. 521)

Explorations

1. The virgin lands campaign was designed to develop wilderness for agriculture, largely through the labor of young volunteers in the Communist Youth Union. For Shevardnadze, the campaign was a success in that it gave him and other young people a sense that they

could accomplish great things (para. 3), but it was badly planned and badly organized, factors that "canceled out many successes." In particular, they had trouble with equipment and grain storage, which made it extremely difficult to bring the grain in once they had — successfully — grown it in the fields.

2. Shevardnadze recalls being elected Secretary of the Central Committee of Komsomol, an honor that reveals his early commitment to the Communist Party and its ideals. He felt positively about Nikita Khrushchev (4) and identified with the spirit of the Soviet cosmonauts. Later in life — in part, of course, because of his experiences with the virgin lands campaign — Shevardnadze became more skeptical about the ability of communism to create an economic system that would keep people productive. By the 1970s, Shevardnadze was still active and powerful in the Communist Party, serving as First Secretary of the Georgian CP Central Committee. But his attitude had changed; now he would try to get around the party ideologues who insisted on purity of doctrine over economic productivity (12). He currently presides over a non-Communist government.

3. Shevardnadze writes that he and Gorbachev shared "the same peasant roots, had worked on the land at a tender age, and had the same knowledge of folk life" (5). They were peers and compatriots, observing the progress and problems of the Soviet Union throughout their lives. The main risk involved in their friendship was, ironically, the need to be able to trust each other. Gorbachev could have brought Shevardnadze's career to an end after viewing his farm "experiment," which involved a modified capitalist approach to increasing productivity. Instead he recognized the effectiveness of Shevardnadze's ideas.

4. Judging from the virgin lands campaign and Shevardnadze's discussion of socialist farming, Soviet farming involved large-scale operations that were labor intensive, but involved few personal rewards for those who worked hardest. The Soviet workers' saying, "You pretend to pay us, and we pretend to work," suggests the difficulties that go along with expecting people to work for things they will not feel the benefit of in their own lives (11). Shevardnadze recalls that "a corn farmer who worked 400 man-days on a collective farm earned an average of 10-12 rubles a month and 200 kilos of corn a year" (13). This was not enough incentive to keep farmers in the fields. As a result, the Soviet Union suffered economic losses, because it was relying on its workers to produce enough to keep it solvent.

Connections

1. Students will find a number of selections in *Looking at Ourselves* that portray institutions suffering from an obsession with "purity of doctrine." Among them, Martin Luther King, Jr., discusses how the American economy has been taken as an explainer and justifer of any action that seems to support capitalist ideologies. Wendell Berry criticizes the "ideal of competition" on which capitalism is founded, because competition can destroy familial and community relationships. King, analyzing the justifications for slavery in the United States, writes that "the attempt to give moral sanction to a profitable system gave birth to the doctrine of white supremacy." As long as slavery supported the capitalist project — as long as it was profitable — it could be justified as a valid expression of capitalism.

2. Iwashita contends that the company he worked for absorbed the lives of its employees, depriving them of any chance of independent thinking. He writes that the company controls the private, as well as professional, lives of employees (para. 8), and he found

that he could no longer believe that the relative security of life in the company was worth giving up his freedom of thought which was necessary for him if he was to "preserve the quality of [his] life and [his] sanity" (13). Shevardnadze, having lived much of his life devoted to the Communist Party, realizes that most people would think he and Gorbachev were eminently successful. But according to his own standards of success, Shevardnadze had to make "an intense search for a way out" of traditional party expectations.

3. As students discuss the relative advantages and disadvantages of Shevardnadze's work on the land as opposed to Ishikawa's, they may find themselves debating the relative merits of capitalism and communism. There is little doubt, especially in view of Shevardnadze's criticism of his own system, whose work on the land students will feel has the most advantages. Shevardnadze recalls feeling exhilarated by his farm work as a young man in the virgin lands campaign, but the poor management of that project left him skeptical about the efficacy of socialist farming. Ishikawa, by contrast, also has the experience of living very close to the land, but he and his brother — because they are farming on U.S. soil — will reap the benefits of their own labor. Instead of receiving the equivalent of 10 rubles a month, no matter how much they produce, they will take in as much profit as they produce. A few students may note that while Ishikawa's and his brother's initiative benefited only themselves, Shevardnadze's was recognized by the Party bureaucracy as potentially valuable to the larger system, so that from farming he has reaped an illustrious career.

TIM GOLDEN, Cubans Try to Cope with Dying Socialism (p. 528)

Explorations

1. Tim Golden's attitude about Cuba's economic woes is clear from the title of his essay: Cuba's economic system is dying; socialism cannot survive. And in paragraph 14, Golden writes that the achievements of the revolution are eroding. Castro, however, continues to believe that socialism will survive. In paragraph 2, he is quoted as saying that only a socialist revolution could survive the economic attacks on Cuba — a reference to U.S. policies that restrict trade and isolate Cuba economically. At the end of the essay, Golden inserts another Castro quote that suggests Castro will never give up the revolution. Castro says that although many sacrifices will have to be made, "what we will never give up is hope." Golden implies that Castro's insistence on the validity of socialism for Cuba is part of Cuba's problem; he asserts that the people of Cuba doubt they can endure for the "long years that any real economic recovery would take" (para. 7).

2. Students may need to differentiate the various causes of the Cubans' hardships while they discuss the effects of Cuba's policies on the daily lives of its citizens. Golden implies that a large part of the responsibility resides with Castro, although U.S. anti-Cuba policies and the demise of the Soviet Union have contributed much to Cuba's economic woes. Castro rations gasoline at a miniscule five gallons per month and bus service has been cut, making it very difficult for citizens to get across town. Government policies also decree

that food and electricity will be rationed (12, 38), but the rations are so small that citizens are forced into black-market trading (38).

3. "Resolviendo" is an illegal system of bartering in which whoever has access to a certain resource (either through legal ownership or through stealing) can use it to trade for items she or he needs. The system implies that Cubans are betraying the revolution by engaging in private enterprise and that they are therefore in opposition to socialism. However, as one Cuban maintains, "Nobody wants to do it, but everybody does it" (43). He implies that citizens feel guilty about trading illegally, but the dire economic situation drives them to look out for their own interests first. The government, on the other hand, maintains that it distributes all goods equally (31), but special privileges are still available to "members of the Cuban elite" who can shop at stores ordinary citizens don't even know exist (45). Both the government and Cuban citizens, then, are not living up to the ideals they publicly agree on.

4. Golden conveys the grim mood of many Cubans in paragraph 7, where he describes the "gauntlets of blank, sullen stares" of people waiting for buses that rarely arrive. The buses themselves are "dilapidated." When Golden describes a Cuban woman who used to enjoy a middle-class lifestyle and now has almost nothing to eat, he uses words such as "haggard" and — significantly — "disenchanted." The "disenchantment" of some Cubans suggests that their mood is impatient and even angry as well as "grim." Although Golden admits that a "substantial . . . core of support" remains for Castro's government (17), many see two options: endure the sacrifice or leave (18). An unidentified Western diplomat reports that people are afraid of what will happen to them if they speak out (23), but some have become more openly critical (22). A man who says he feels bad about engaging in "resolviendo" also blames the goverment for having "turned us all into thieves," a comment that suggests Cubans' tolerance for sacrifice is growing thin.

Connections

1. Shevardnadze suggests the depth of the Soviet problem with productivity in the first paragraph of his essay, where he writes that all the money and human effort that had gone into cultivating "virgin lands" were wasted when crops rotted in the fields for lack of enough people to bring in the harvest and lack of storage for the grain. The effect of living with immense efforts and immense failures of the kind Shevardnadze describes was similar in the Soviet Union and Cuba; many people became resigned to doing without basic necessities. The Soviet workers' saying, "You pretend to pay us, and we pretend to work," also suggests their resignation about putting up with bad conditions (11). Finally, Shevardnadze states simply, "We . . . were always on short rations," indicating that doing without was as much a "national custom" in the Soviet Union as it is in Cuba.

2. Wendell Berry is writing about the negative personal and communal effects of economic competition under capitalism. However, socialism could also become the target of his attack, because socialism, like capitalism, upholds economic laws as primary shapers of reality. Berry complains that we allow the economic ideal of competition to determine our lives. He would like to believe that other laws guide us, but Golden's essay on Cuba proves that economics really is a kind of "last word" on what people are able to accomplish and how much pleasure they can take in living. Strapped for even the most

basic necessities, Cubans might argue that economic laws are indeed the ultimate laws. Although he never comments directly on socialism, Berry implies that for the losers in the capitalist system, competition will lead to the same probems Cubans are enduring.

3. Havana as Márquez portrays it at the beginning of his story is subject to wild, destructive natural forces. A tidal wave "of monumental size" damages the Hotel Riviera. This is clearly an aberration, however, in what is otherwise depicted as a pleasant, comfortable environment for visitors. While nature is destructive, the Cuban people behave in an orderly and productive way. Volunteers quickly clean up the debris and help the hotel get back to business. Márquez pays no attention to the difficult economic and political issues that plague Cuba; his portrayal is of a modern, attractive seaside city in a well-ordered state.

ANONYMOUS, Evicted: A Russian Jew's Story (Again) (p. 536)

Explorations

1. The shortages are indirectly related to the author's reasons for leaving Russia, since she provides evidence that other Russians are ready to blame Jews for food shortages (para. 14) and the lack of jobs (15). The shortages, she writes, "create bad blood" (3). However, she is correct in saying that she is not leaving because of shortages; it is anti-Semitism, expressed through intimidation, threats of violence, and discrimination, that is driving her out of Russia.

2. The most startling figure the author quotes in paragraph 2 is that almost 40,000 Jews were trying to get out of Russia as of the day the author added her name to the waiting list. The entire passage is full of figures, however. She reports spending six hours waiting out in the cold to enter the American Embassy; she was number 79 on the New Zealand list; she would need to return at 5 PM; and she has lived in Russia for forty years. One effect of using all these figures is to foster a sense of reality and precision, depicting the author as a rational, practical person. This characterization, combined with the weight of the figures as data, helps the reader appreciate her frustration, both with the trauma of leaving her homeland, and with the necessity of waiting in long lines in order to have a chance to leave. Most of all, she conveys the near universality of her recent experience; clearly many other Russian Jews share her concern about rising anti-Semitism.

3. Most students will recall that for many Americans, communism and the Soviet Union served during the Cold War as the ultimate object of hatred and fear. Similarly, Russians were encouraged to identify American capitalists as the enemy. But in a post–Cold War world, the old enemies have largely disappeared. Russians lost the "immediate object" of their hatred when the Soviet Union came to an end but — according to the author's idea — they did not lose their propensity to hate. Russian Jews are different enough from other Russians to be chosen as a new enemy. The author's main point, however, is that the exodus of Jews from Russia will leave other Russians with the same problem: hatred that needs an object. She suggests they will turn it on some other group that can be singled out as different.

4.   The author seems both angry and exasperated with other Russians. She says of one group discussing Jews on the street that they "were genuine intellectuals, people with good faces" (7) but that they use the irrational rhetoric of anti-Semitism to justify their "conviction" that Jews are responsible for all the problems of Russia. Her exasperation takes the form of sarcasm at several points in her essay, as when she refers to the "splendid lads of Pamyat" who want to exterminate Jews. Later she uses the same method to express her anger, when she says that "perhaps peace, happiness, and prosperity will immediately come to Russia" when the Jews are gone (19). This is, of course, precisely the opposite of what she believes will happen. In contrast to her sarcastic response to the irrational convictions of other Russians about Jews, the author's writing is straight-forward and serious when she says that "happiness and prosperity cannot be built on the blood and tears of others" (20).

Connections

1.   The economic conditions the author describes in paragraph 3 are very similar to the conditions of Cubans today. She writes that there is virtually no way to buy basic necessities and that "the reward for any work is unimaginably small." She finds that these privations lead to feelings of humiliation and alienation and may even shorten people's lives. The man that Golden interviews at a party says that he and his fellow Cubans "are weak" and that he finds himself "doing things that are very tough" (para. 43). He compares himself to prostitutes who exchange sex for "a dinner, a dress, some shampoo" (44). The feelings he describes are similar to those the author of "Evicted" notices in Russians: a sense of personal humiliation, of having failed and being alienated from the ideals of the revolution.

2.   Students may refer back to Explorations #1 and #3 to find evidence of Russian non-Jews' attitudes toward Russian Jews. Many non-Jews blame Jews for the economic woes of post–Cold War Russia, and believe that by eradicating the Jewish population — through banishment or by killing Jews — they will become prosperous. Shevardnadze describes a similar attitude among rigid socialists toward "kulaks," peasant landowners who were persecuted and driven off their farms when land was being collectivized (20–24). The systematic process of "de-kulakization" had official support, while efforts to drive Russian Jews from their homeland are not officially sanctioned by the Russian government (16). However, the process is similar in that a group is identified as being a threat to the prosperity of the dominant Russian group and is persecuted and driven away.

3.   Students will be able to come up with several pertinent examples of people in other nations sharing the author's sense of being "evicted" from her own land. Haunani-Kay Trask writes of how the *haole* took land away from Hawaiians by instituting changes in economics — specifically, introducing patterns of private land ownership — that "alienated the people from the land." Vine Deloria, Jr, and Clifford M. Lytle discuss "the decades of erosion" of traditional American Indian cultures and the imposition on tribes of European forms of government — a process that also involved great loss of tribal land. Martin Luther King, Jr.,writes that "Africa had been raped and plundered by Britain and Europe, her native kingdoms disorganized" for hundreds of years before the U.S. slave

trade robbed Africans of their freedom, land, and cultural heritage. And Toni Morrison contends that the Africans who helped to build the United States have been left out of its canonized literature; each of these writers describes a phenomenon of disenfranchisement and exile that the Russian writer of "Evicted" could sympathize with.

VÁCLAV HAVEL (VAHT-slahv HAH-vul), Moral Politics (p. 542)

Explorations

1. Many students will have no trouble identifying communism as the force that caused Czechoslovakia to become "morally unhinged." They will follow Havel's implicit reasoning, which is that people under an authoritarian regime have few opportunities to develop a personal moral sense, since they will not be rewarded and may be severely punished for acting on any principle that runs counter to the regime's goals. When he writes that "the authoritarian regime imposed a certain order" on human vices, he suggests that this repression had the positive effect of limiting people's opportunities to behave badly. However, Havel also implies that these human vices are natural and, therefore, not caused by communism — only encouraged by it. Students may be more divided over the question of whether human beings are naturally full of vices that may be encouraged under an authoritarian regime and discouraged, presumably, under democracy.

2. Havel maintains his focus on morality in Czechoslovakian politics in paragraph 5 and beyond, but in the last sentence of the paragraph he ceases to pile up examples of human greed and corruption and writes that he is convinced that "a huge potential of goodwill" still exists within the Czechoslovakian people. He shifts from decrying his country's present state to considering the nature of politics and the responsibilities of both leaders and citizens. In paragraph 6, he implies again that Czech communism was responsible for people's "selfishness, envy, and hatred," but this time he offers hope that politicians devoted to the principles of democracy will be able to awaken the people's moral sense.

3. Havel's dilemma regarding the passage of a law that would deprive certain groups of people of opportunities for public service on the bases of their associations under the former totalitarian government forced him to reconsider his belief that simply sticking to principles of moral democracy would help him lead his people into "the way of truly moral politics" (23). Some students may agree with Havel that he has to give in when he knows that taking a rigid stance will not benefit anyone materially. Out of respect for the democratically elected parliament and so that he can try to influence the parliament to change the law in the future, Havel signed the bill. Other students will feel that Havel should have set a highly visible example of moral politics; not signing the bill would not have benefited anyone immediately, but his demonstrated devotion to principle might have influenced others to follow his lead.

Connections

1. In "Evicted: A Russian Jew's Story (Again)," the anonymous writer confronts an upsurge in anti-Semitism following the demise of the Soviet Union. It could easily be argued that the release of human vices, such as "selfishness, envy, and hatred," that Havel notices in Czechoslovakia following the end of communism there (para. 6) is also at work in Russia, where people lived under an oppressive regime that influenced their morality in ways that benefited the government. If we follow Havel's reasoning, then, it is up to the contemporary Russian leaders to discourage the envy, fear, and hatred that fuels anti-Semitism and to encourage a respect for basic human rights.

2. Havel's basic point is that a government brought into power by violent overthrow can maintain itself only by oppressive means and will eventually die amid the same kind of violence that brought it into power. If he is correct, then Castro's government in Cuba will follow the pattern he describes. However, there is little evidence in Tim Golden's piece on Cuba that Castro's government is about to go down in a violent overthrow. Golden implies, rather, that economic hardship is killing the socialist government, which can no longer feed its people (37). Golden found that many people still support Castro, and he mentions no evidence that "new revolutionaries" are on the verge of bringing about his downfall.

3. Havel's argument is that pure Marxist philosophy fails to take human values into account. Decency, from that perspective, would be defined as any conduct that promoted production. To Havel, in contrast, decency is a moral choice that is essential to effective political power. Students will find related ideas developed in several selections in *Looking At Ourselves*. The *New Yorker* selection suggests that the mass media during election campaigns in the United States base their choices of what to cover on pressure from advertisers, directly or through consumers, more than on a commitment to honest, responsive reporting. Wendell Berry decries our tendency to devote ourselves to the ideal of economic competition, our willingness "to take another's property or to accept another's ruin as a normal result of economic enterprise. Martin Luther King, Jr., describes the "degradation" of black men when, under slavery, their humanity was ignored so that they could be treated as "commodities for sale at a profit."

FAY WELDON, Down the Clinical Disco (p. 551)

Explorations

1. In paragraph 2, the narrator reveals that she is a former inmate of Broadmoor, a mental institution for the criminally insane, where she was committed after setting fire to her office. Her monologue is directed at a woman named Linda she met at a pub (para. 6), who may be identified with the reader. The story begins with the pronoun "You," suggesting that the reader and Linda are being addressed directly by the narrator.

2. Some students may see the narrator as an obviously paranoid woman who believes people are continuously monitoring her behavior, even during an evening at the pub. In paragraph 1, for instance, she says, "of course there are people watching." Others may

see her as a victim of the mental health system that placed her in the position of being assessed constantly, to the point that she was forced into paranoia as a natural response to having had her smallest gesture watched and judged while she was in the institution. In paragraph 13, the narrator says that "Sister," a nurse, decided who had become "normal" enough to go up for parole and who would remain. Psychiatric professionals and judges seem to have the power to decide what constitutes normal behavior. The criteria the narrator perceives at work are narrow and maddeningly contradictory. For instance, in the first paragraph she says she doesn't drink because she has "to be careful. You never know who's watching." Later in the same paragraph, she says that "it is not absolutely A-okay not to drink alcohol." Many of the criteria she believes are applied in judging who is "normal" have to do with sexual behavior and sexual orientation. She says that women who go into Broadmoor not looking like women do look like women when they leave. Men have to pretend to want to watch heterosexual "blue movies" to prove their manhood, but women can't want to watch because it would suggest a perverted sexuality.

3. The narrator suggests that "abnormal" behavior can more easily be observed in the nurses at Broadmoor than in the inmates. She says of "Sister" that "she's not so sane herself. She's more institutionalized than the patients" (13). The point is made graphically in a scene when she arrives at Broadmoor and is sadistically treated during a bath by a group of men and women who "were sane because they were nurses and good because they could go home after work" (10). A similar madness is evident in a nurse's game in which the narrator is made to be a tea bag for an entire day. The institutional setting, the narrator implies, is itself insane; the medical personnel who run institutions and the lawyers who send people to the institution are just as mad — or more so — than those they commit.

4. Students should be able to come up with several different central points for Weldon's story. Some will focus on the end of the story, where the narrator says that "when you're in love you're just happy so they have to turn you out" (18). The statement implies that happiness and love give people the strength to face up to and to see beyond the efforts of society to oppress them. Others may see in the story's end a central statement regarding the problems with using "normality" as a criteria for sanity. The narrator and Eddie can be more themselves when they go home — but being themselves means they drop the pretense of socially and medically defined sanity, as Eddie gets into drag and the narrator rubs off her lipstick and dons jeans. In spite of their "abnormal" behavior, however, the narrator and Eddie are more sane and certainly more harmless than those who imprisoned them. Some students may see Weldon's story simply as a vivid depiction of a paranoid mind or of the abuses of the criminal justice system and psychiatry.

Connections

1. Václav Havel contends that politicians can, and should, act "decently, reasonably, responsibly, sincerely, civilly, and tolerantly" (para. 11). That, in his estimation is what would allow him, and other politicians, to "live in truth." He means that his actions should be strictly in line with his stated principles, and that any other course leads to corruption and disorder. Students may find it a challenge to apply Havel's statements about the responsibilities of politicians to the experience of the narrator in "Down the Clinical Disco." As an inmate of Broadmoor, she found it impossible to "live in truth" because her eventual release depended on her behaving in ways the medical staff approved of.

Some students may realize that her experience in Broadmoor has something in common with the experience of living under a totalitarian regime, which deprives people of the power to make their own decisions and perhaps live in accordance with their own sense of what is right.

2. Both women face difficult futures, including the possibility of violence against them and the loss of their civil rights. The narrator of "Down the Clinical Disco" says that "They can pop you back inside if you cause any trouble at all, and they're the ones who decide what trouble is" (17). Her sense that she has lost control over her own future is demoralizing and may keep her perpetually in the state she is in now: fearful to the point of paranoia, convinced she is being watched, trying to decide what "normal" behavior is so that she and Eddie will not draw attention to themselves. In effect, she has never left the institution. The anonymous writer of "Evicted: A Russian Jew's Story (Again)" also faces prejudice, a loss of her civil rights, and possibly physical violence. She has not, however, internalized the ideologies that work to oppress her. She is attempting to leave the country where she no longer feels welcome, and there is a chance that she will find a freer existence elsewhere. For these reasons, she probably has a brighter future than the narrator of "Down the Clinical Disco."

3. Weldon has her narrator justify her crime by rationalizing it: The Opera needed to be burned down (7); it was not damaged badly; the office she burned needed redecorating anyway (10). Given what is in her view the minor — even benign — nature of her crime, the narrator conveys the impression that the punishment she receives, beginning with the degrading bath, is far more criminal than the act that brought her into Broadmoor. This sense of her own innocence, and of the culpability of those who imprison her, are all she has. She also recognizes that the staff justify their "superiority" on the basis of their profession and their relative freedom: "They were sane because they were nurses and good because they could go home after work."

4. Weldon's narrator sums up the effect of her initial, traumatic bath in Broadmoor by saying that "even worse than being naked and seen by strangers" is "being naked and unseen, because you don't even count as a woman" (10). Binur makes a similar observation when he recalls being present while a Jewish man and woman, thinking he is Palestinian, almost have sex in front of him. He writes, "For them I simply didn't exist. I was invisible, a nonentity!" (8). For Binur, this moment marked the worst humiliation he experienced while posing as a Palestinian. Weldon's narrator and Binur have something in common that made them likely victims for this kind of humiliation, in that both had been deprived of basic human rights, such as the freedom of self-determination, on the basis of their identities.

NEIL POSTMAN, Future Shlock (p. 559)

Explorations

1. Even students who are not well versed in European history will probably recognize that Postman is referring to the rise of nazism in Germany during the 1920s and 1930s, when art, philosophy, and science were considered worthwhile only when they promoted the

interests of the party and were stamped out whenever they appeared to open the door to dissidence and tolerance of ethnic, political, and religious differences. At the end of paragraph 2, Postman proposes to "worry" the reader with the idea that what happened to culture in Nazi Germany could happen in the United States — though in a different way. Later in the essay, Postman says that although a "decline of intelligent discourse" is taking place in America, intellectuals will not be driven out as they were in Germany (para. 4). Instead, they will simply be ignored. At the end of his essay, Postman returns to the theme of nazism, again differentiating culture under nazism (culture as prison) and in contemporary America (culture as burlesque). Postman's discussion of Mel Brooks's film *The Producers* encourages the reader to believe that the film predicts that Americans will become a "trivial people . . . a people amused into stupidity" (11). Because *The Producers* is built on the theme of nazism, with which Postman opens his essay, his discussion of the film reinforces his point that Americans will accept anything — even *Springtime for Hitler*— as long as it is entertaining. This is a point students may want to debate.

2. Both compound sentences appear toward the end of Postman's essay, where he is attempting to create a sense that the evidence for his view of the death of American culture is overwhelming. His use of *when* suggests a potential condition that sometimes happens in human history and could happen in the United States in the future. However, his repetition of *when* to introduce descriptions he has already applied or implied about American culture builds a sense of accumulating probability that this undesirable condition already exists in the United States, or is in the process of happening.

3. Postman first addresses the reader as "you" in paragraph 2, when he says he wants to "worry you about the rapid erosion of our own intelligence." The effect of speaking directly to his readers is to suggest that his argument is important to them personally. Even before the reader becomes "you," however, Postman has established an "us" in the same paragraph. The effect of creating such a collective is to suggest that we all are affected by, and are responsible for, the death of intelligence. Readers who agree with Postman's position will accept this use of "we," while readers who are waiting to be persuaded may be drawn into agreement by it. Postman's frequent use of "I" suggests his personal commitment and personal sense of responsibility for making "us" aware of the problems he describes. Some students may note that Postman sometimes uses "we" when he is really writing about his own views, as in his assertion "we have also seen 'Sesame Street' and other educational shows in which the demands of entertainment take precedence . . ." (17).

4. Although Postman uses a traditional format for his argument, his language and many of his rhetorical techniques have more in common with the entertainment-dominated media he criticizes than with academic style. His essay appeals fairly openly to readers' emotions along with their reason. Students will identify Postman's use of humor as his most obvious entertainment technique. His tone throughout is ironic; examples include the title "Future Shlock" and comments such as, "There are other ways to achieve stupidity, and it appears that, as in so many other things, there is a distinctly American way" (4). He also relies frequently on humorous exaggeration, as when he says that "the Germans banished intelligence" (2) and that the Empire of Reason has given way to the

Empire of Shlock (3). Postman's informal diction is another technique more common in entertainment than in academic writing. He addresses readers directly, using first and second person as well as the third; his position is openly subjective ("I wish to call to your notice"; "I cannot imagine" (5)) rather than purely objective. His evidence, too, comes from popular sources, such as films (5, 8) and television shows (15–19), as well as from academic sources such as Aristotle (2) and Henry Steele Commager (3). This choice of sources clearly suits Postman's topic, and his argument is logically constructed rather than fragmented like the television news programs he decries; however, students may differ as to whether his efforts to enlighten his audience are weakened or strengthened by his efforts to entertain them.

Connections

1. This question should spark debate among students about what roles entertainment technologies play in the lives of Americans. Postman's main target is television, and because most students will have grown up with television as a continuous presence, they should have strong opinions about whether it is bringing about the death of intelligence and high culture in America. Since many "institutions" in the United States find their way into the electronic media, Postman moves his critique from television to politics, religion (para. 16), education, and business (17).

2. In paragraph 23, Postman describes Orwellian culture as a prison in which, by direct action taken to suppress dissidence, cultural growth is halted and intellect dies. Eduard Shevardnadze argues that the "fundamental principle" of socialism denies "proprietary instincts" in the worker (12). Adhering too closely to "the purity of doctrine" not only destroys the nation economically, but also negates all innovation. It no longer pays to work, and it no longer pays to think. In "Chairman Mao's Good Little Boy," the effects of living according to strict Communist doctrine is demonstrated in the experience of Liang's mother after she is condemned as a Rightist. She is required to assume blame for "thought crimes" she has not committed (30), and even her husband, thoroughly absorbed in Communist doctrine, demands that she "recognize her faults and reform herself" (29).

3. The *New Yorker* selection presents two contrary positions: Economic pressures encourage television newscasts to favor "the superficial and sensational over the important and enlightening," yet the source of these economic pressures — the viewers — "are as unhappy with shallow coverage as the anchors are." Postman's essay suggests a resolution for this apparent contradiction in the nature of television: As a predominantly visual medium, "it conditions our minds to apprehend the world through fragmented pictures" (20). *The New Yorker* reports that journalists who vowed after the 1984 presidential campaign to resist "empty one-liners" found themselves in 1988 emphasizing "Willie Horton, flag factories, and other phony symbols." Their dilemma may owe less to "gullibility" or "voyeurism for the sake of voyeurism" (Tom Brokaw) than to Postman's idea that "on television all subject matter is presented as entertaining" (14). On the other hand, the admissions by Peter Jennings that "politicians and political consultants have learned so well to manipulate us" and by Dan Rather that the networks fear "being serious but dull" may help to explain what Postman describes as "the frightening displacement of serious, intelligent public discourse in American culture by the imagery and triviality of what may be called show business" (3).

MICHAEL DORRIS, House of Stone (p. 569)

Explorations

1. In paragraph 3, Dorris says that Westerners become aware of poverty "from newspaper photographs staged to produce a maximum impact." A shocking image calls people's attention to a problem — at least momentarily — and they are more ready to give. Dorris's opening anecdote works in the same way. Most readers will be shocked and horrified at the mental image of a screaming, skinned baboon, and they may realize that Dorris is correct when he says that the villagers' plan to rid themselves of baboons as competitors is evidence of their desperation. It is, as well, an anecdote that refutes the common perception that people who are desperately poor and hungry cannot act on their own. The villagers' plan is horrifying, but effective. Dorris's impression of the ability and willingness of the poor to work for the improvement of their condition is strongly evident in the example of the secretary near the end of the essay, in which a woman manages to disperse scarce commodities fairly, tries to gain access to tools her people could use to improve their lives, and shows herself to be "absolutely determined to figure something out" (para. 39).

2. In paragraph 31, Dorris is trying to think of new, and more effective, ways to act. He sets himself the goal of finding an original approach to getting help for the poor and hungry people of Zimbabwe. His strategies begin with "empathy," which requires that those who suffer be recognized as human beings with individual lives (32). He says that the fortunate — Westerners — should not use confusion or doubts about where money given to charity actually goes as an excuse for not contributing (33). Anything will help, he writes, and anyway the contributor can have some control if she or he becomes informed.

3. Students will have little trouble identifying the contrasts Dorris sets up between people who share his own position of privilege and people who are starving. In paragraph 25, Dorris posits a "looping line;" at one end is pain and at the other "carefree joy." Dorris's use of the phrase "looping line" suggests a continuum and a connection between those who are economically privileged and those who are not. He continues with a similar strategy, envisioning a starving boy he has met at one end of the continuum and himself — and us — at the other. Although they "stare across the chasm" that separates them, Dorris finds that they are similar, perhaps because they have the same basic needs, although those needs are met on only the privileged end of the continuum. Dorris continues to develop the comparison and contrast he has created, discussing his own daughter, an implicit contrast with the starving boy. Nevertheless, in his daughter's eyes they "have the obvious connection of a brother and sister or potential playmates" (26). And finally, Dorris stages another implicit contrast, this time between his daughter, willing to give her own money to help others, and a group of impoverished children who shot other children who they considered to be too well off. The only difference between his daughter and these children is how much food and security they have.

4. Students may have different ideas about the meaning of Dorris's title, especially considering that he doesn't define it himself. The title might be considered a play on the phrase "heart of stone," suggesting that Westerners who refuse to give so that others can eat are imprisoned in their own unwillingness to perceive and empathize with another's plight.

Connections

1. Postman writes that the weaving together of advertising and news on television "reduces all events to trivialities . . . how serious can a bombing in Lebanon be if it is . . . prefaced by a happy United Airlines commercial . . . ?" (para. 18). According to Postman, when, from the point of view of the television newscaster, the audience has spent long enough thinking about some disaster, the anchor simply moves on to a commercial and the news item is effectively wiped from the consciousness of the viewer. Dorris seems to be in agreement with Postman. He writes that we become aware of "grand-scale poverty" in "sound bites from the network anchors," but that the knowledge fails to make a deep impression (3). Dorris concludes, "If we have the option of looking the other way, usually, eventually, we exercise it."

2. Shelby Steele contends that the privileged usually attempt to justify their dominance through a process of rationalization; they reason that they are wealthy because they have worked hard and behaved responsibly; the poor and oppressed, by contrast, are in distress because of their own shortcomings. Thus the privileged are convinced of their "innocence" of cruelty. Dorris refuses the rationalizations that would permit him to assert his own "innocence;" instead, he goes to Zimbabwe and looks poverty in the face. Having seen for himself, Dorris could not claim ignorance as an excuse for not helping. His essay is designed to take away the reader's sense of his or her own "innocence" or ignorance. Once having listened to Dorris's description of his tour of the famine-ravaged land, the reader cannot claim that she or he has no idea of what is occurring, or has no idea how to help. Steele argues that when the sense of innocence disappears, so does some of the power of the dominant group. Knowledge, in that sense, does not always equate with power, because once the privileged have understood the plight of others, they cannot feel good about turning away.

3. Erdrich, in her introduction to Dorris's book, reveals that Dorris adopted three children before she met him, among them Adam, who suffers the effects of fetal alcohol syndrome. Erdrich writes of Dorris that he "spent months of his life teaching Adam to tie his shoes" (6). He does laundry (8) and writes books. Erdrich characterizes Dorris as a patient, dedicated parent and a social activist. She has more to say about Dorris and their family than Dorris does in "House of Stone," but some of the personal qualities she notices come through in his essay. For instance, in his discussion of the ways in which poverty affect children, Dorris evokes his daughter, "a shining girl whose last act" before Dorris left on his trip was to give him money for the poor. The boundaries between social action and family life are irrelevant for Dorris. Erdrich writes that his book about Adam "was a journey from the world of professional objectivity to a confusing realm where boundaries could no longer be so easily drawn" (7).

NADINE GORDIMER, Amnesty (p. 578)

Explorations

1. The facts Nadine Gordimer offers about the narrator are few, but essential to understanding her situation. The narrator is poor (para. 14) and has always lived on her family's farm (10). She has had almost no chance to see the world outside her community, as is apparent when she says that she has never seen the sea (6). But she has been educated and now teaches children (4). She is a mother (5). Gordimer reveals these facts at the points where they become important to the narrator's relationship with her politically active lover. For instance, her revelations about the limitations of her knowledge of the world occur in the context of trying to imagine his location on the island prison (6), and her mentions of her daughter take place in the context of his trial (5) and his return (19).

2. The narrator is chiefly concerned with maintaining the hope of having a home and family. In that sense, her differences from her lover are drawn along lines of traditional gender differences. As a man, he is concerned with the affairs of the world and she with the home. These differences are apparent throughout, but are especially apparent in her anecdote about the meetings her husband sponsors on her family's farm. Her mother serves beer and then departs before the men's political conversation gets underway (23), but the narrator stays to listen. She does not, however, participate in the discussion; instead, she is treated like a favored student (24). She accepts that the men's discussions are "more important than anything we could ever say to each other" (24), a comment that simultaneously affirms her support of her lover and underlines the unbridgeable gap between them. She says that there is no time to get married (25) and no possibility of having a home (19), but there is some resentment in her comment that "he comes to sleep with me just like he comes here to eat a meal or put on clean clothes" (25). Further, she is strong-minded enough to disagree with his thinking. He says that "the farmer owns" them, and that is why they cannot have a home. She recognizes their oppression under the white Boers, but she also realizes that the farm — and therefore the people — doesn't really belong to the Boer (27), and she clings to the distant possibility that she might be able to "come back home."

3. Gordimer's style in "Amnesty" is primarily conversational. Her narrator, as a teacher, is literate and intellectually adept. This identity makes it possible for Gordimer to sympathize with her narrator, even though the narrator's vocabulary, stylistic repertory, expertise as a writer, and breadth of experience are much more limited than the author's. "Amnesty" reads like an excerpt from the narrator's own journal, as though it is told directly from the narrator's own mind. This close connection between the writer and her narrator's voice makes it easier to accept that Gordimer, a white South African, can represent the point of view of a narrator whose age, race, background, and class are very different from her own.

4. The narrator has so strong an identity in "Amnesty" that students may not even realize that she does not name herself. Like Ralph Ellison's *Invisible Man*, Gordimer's decision not to name her character has several effects. First, the anonymity of the narrator emphasizes that white racism attempts to erase the humanity and identity of black people. Second, although her voice is clearly that of an individual with a personal history and unique opinions, the fact that she is not named suggests that she represents her

people. Although an individual, she speaks for the experience of many. Finally, it is not only the narrator who is not named; no other characters have names, either. Even the leaders (including Nelson Mandela) are designated only as "the Big Man" and "the Old Men." Their namelessness has the effect of suggesting that her lover and his comrades are still in danger from whites, who would track them down and harrass or imprison them if they could identify them.

Connections

1. How students respond to this question depends on whether they recognize Gordimer's story, like Dorris's essay, as a form of activism designed to work against specific injustices the writer perceives. Alternatively, students may read this question as pertaining to the narrator and her lover, both of whom, in their own ways, are "searching for some action . . . some original and efficacious idea" that will help them deal with, and find solutions to, the injustices that deplete their lives. The narrative serves as a record of the development of the narrator's political consciousness, a development she shares with the reader, who may then be moved to act as well. In that sense, the narrator and the writer are closely connected; "Amnesty" is Gordimer's attempt to call her readers to action in opposition to apartheid.

2. When, at the end of her story, the narrator says that she is "waiting to come back home," she expresses a sense of her own homelessness that the anonymous writer of "Evicted: A Russian Jew's Story (Again)" also expresses. It is significant that neither woman identifies herself by name, a strategy that emphasizes their lack of security and lack of identity in their homeland. However, their situations differ in that the writer of "Evicted: A Russian Jew's Story (Again)" is actively trying to leave Russia and has some expectation of finding a better life elsewhere. The narrator of "Amnesty" is poor and lacks the means to leave South Africa; however, she seems committed to staying, expressing the sense that she belongs to the land (para. 27).

3. Martin Luther King, Jr., observes that slavery, a form of racial oppression that has much in common with South African apartheid, "had a profound impact in shaping the social-political-legal structure of the nation." If legal and political structures in the United States were built on slavery and if the economy of the nation was built on the labor of enslaved African-Americans, something similar happened in South Africa, where the government, the justice system, and the system of land allocation were constructed along rigid lines of racial separatism. King writes that in the United States, racist whites rationalized their domination of African-Americans by reasoning that a system that worked to their own economic advantage must also be "morally justifiable." Similarly, the Boer in Gordimer's story who believes he owns the land and the Africans who live on the land could only maintain his position by convincing himself that his domination is morally justified.

NELSON MANDELA, Black Man in a White Court (p. 587)

Explorations

1. Mandela is applying for the recusal of the white magistrate who is presiding over Mandela's case (para. 5). He wants the magistrate to excuse himself from hearing the case because, Mandela argues, an African cannot get a fair trial in a white court (6, 8) and because, as an African, Mandela does not consider himself subject to the laws his people had no part in making (6). It is the white court's racism that is Mandela's main focus; he says that he "fears that this system of justice may enable the guilty to drag the innocent before the courts." Mandela's reasonable manner and eloquence serve another purpose, however. Mandela does not believe that there is a chance he will win his own case, but he is making a larger case for his people. In paragraph 28, he says that the atmosphere of oppression he senses in the courtroom "calls to mind the inhuman injustices caused to my people outside this courtroom by this same white domination." After Mandela's articulate and passionate speech, the judge's only response is to dismiss the application (58) — a move that essentially proves both of Mandela's arguments. If Mandela's real purpose had been to win his own case, then he was not successful. But because he had a larger purpose in mind — to speak out against systematic white racism — he was successful.

2. Building on their discussion of Explorations #1, students should realize that neither Mandela nor the court believes that Mandela's application has any chance of being approved. Mandela is elaborating on the starvation and disease his people are experiencing when the magistrate interrupts his speech to say that Mandela is "going beyond the scope" of his application (32). The magistrate goes on to say that he doesn't "want to know about starvation" (34), and he demands that Mandela stick to the "real reasons" for his application (36). The "real reasons," from the magistrate's perspective, are those that stay within the bounds of the immediate proceeding. But his attempts to define the case according to the needs and expectations of the white court are unsuccessful, and Mandela manages to make the case he is most interested in: that his people are without land, the vote, health care, or food (29).

3. From the first words he speaks, Mandela shows that he fully grasps not only the legal but also the social and political implications of the court proceedings. His style and choice of words are similar to — although more eloquent than — the white men who are about to try him. He uses the conventions of legal discourse in paragraphs 4–6, for instance, in stating the purpose of his application and giving the grounds for it. Further, he asserts his equality directly by saying that he has decided to speak for himself rather than depend upon counsel. Only by speaking the language of the court can Mandela hope to speak at all. As a spokesperson for his people, Mandela uses his own educational and professional equality with the white men who accuse him to support his argument that all Africans should have the same rights and privileges as whites.

4. Most students will recognize that "African" is a term that indicates that Mandela's people are the native inhabitants of the land whites now rule. By refusing to call whites "Africans," Mandela suggests that white men are trespassers on land that belongs to Africans. In paragraph 2, Mandela says, "this case is a trial of the aspirations of the African

137

people," and in paragraph 7, he describes the court case as a political one that represents "a clash of the aspirations of the African people and those of whites." In paragraph 45, Mandela describes himself as "a black man in a white man's court." He would like to believe that he was "being tried by a fellow South African," but as his comments on the racism of the court and his choice of the terms "African" and "white" suggest, he knows that the court will not acknowledge his entitlement as a South African to an impartial trial.

Connections

1. Because Gordimer's story focuses on the experience of a woman waiting for the man she loves, rather than on the experience of the political prisoner himself, students may want to consider how gender differences affect their readings of the story and the transcript of Mandela's court case. While her lover's activism takes him away from her, she tries to keep alive the idea, if not the full reality, of home and family. Nevertheless she is politically aware. She suggests that she, too, is a prisoner when she says that she is "also waiting to come back home" (para. 30). Further, when she says that "It's the Boer's farm — but that's not true, it belongs to nobody" (27), the narrator makes a point similar to Mandela's when he designates black people as "Africans." Both imply that black people belong to the African land and that the white man is trespassing on ground that does not belong to him. Throughout "Amnesty," it is apparent that the narrator is as affected by white racism as is her imprisoned lover. Mandela's contention that the "aspirations of the African people" (2) are on trial and that they have been denied "basic human rights" (9) shows that he recognizes his own experience of white racism to be representative of the plight of all other Africans; similarly, the narrator of "Amnesty" recognizes that while white racism rules in South Africa, she will not be able to "come home" any more than will her lover.

2. A law court is by definition an arena for what Shelby Steele calls "a struggle for innocence." In the court where Nelson Mandela presents his case, representatives for both black and white South Africans claim innocence as Steele describes. The judge speaks for his fellow whites, who assert ownership over land and power and therefore claim to be victimized in this case by Mandela's breaking of a law made by whites for their protection. The judge's position matches Steele's statement, "White racism [is] a claim of white innocence and therefore of white entitlement to subjugate blacks." Mandela pleads innocent to the charges and claims innocence on a larger scale, using (as Steele puts it) "the innocence that grew out of . . . long subjugation to seize more power." Verbally Mandela responds to the judge as what Steele describes as a bargainer: *"I already believe you are innocent (good, fair-minded) and have faith that you will prove it."* His tacit position, however, is that of a challenger: *"If you are innocent, then prove it."*

3. Toni Morrison argues that the study of canonized American literature has ignored the important influence of "the four-hundred-year-old presence" of Africans and African-Americans on the evolution of the nation and its literature. Mandela's indictment of the racist system of justice in South Africa, a system in which the civil rights of Africans are universally denied, suggests that he, like Morrison, sees a national history in which the dominant white group attempts to oppress black people and ignores their contributions to the formation of the nation. Nadine Gordimer, a white South African writer, takes up an unusual perspective in "Amnesty" when she attempts to consider the world from the

perspective of a black South African woman. The story is her attempt to recover a form of experience that the literature of her country rarely pays attention to.

4. Several of Václav Havel's statements describe Mandela's position in his courtroom presentation, including: "Politicians have a duty to awaken this slumbering, or bewildered, potential [for goodwill] to life" (6); "The idea that the force of truth, the power of a truthful word, the strength of a free spirit, conscience, and responsibility . . . might actually change something . . . " (7); "Genuine politics . . . is simply serving those close to oneself: serving the community, and serving those who come after us" (10). Mandela's statements focus more specifically on the issues of his case, but some display a similar philosophy to Havel's: "That the will of the people is the basis of the authority of government is a principal universally acknowledged as sacred throughout the civilized world and constitutes the basic foundations of freedom and justice" (39); "We . . . regard the struggle against color discrimination and for the pursuit of freedom and happiness as the highest aspiration of all men" (53).

ADDITIONAL QUESTIONS AND ASSIGNMENTS

1. In a journal entry or a collection of informal notes, discuss governments' responsibilities to citizens as depicted in three or four of these selections, paying particular attention to ideology. Consider such issues as the state's responsibility to protect the rights of individuals, its role in providing economic and social stability, its demands on citizens, and any other issues you find relevant. As you look over your notes, try to discover similarities and differences among the cultures represented. Can you come to any conclusion about the role of ideology in the relationship between the state and the individual?

2. Using Golden and Shevardnadze as models, interview several people who espouse a particular political view and observe their organizations in action. You may use representatives of major parties (especially during an election), but you may also want to consider "special interest" groups (for example, proponents or opponents of U.S. policy toward a particular country, proponents of tax reform, opponents of nuclear power and/or weapons, or members of any organized political group, such as Greenpeace, Amnesty International, or Right to Life). As you gather information, consider the kinds of information you're interested in eliciting. Do you want to know about the group's perception of its role in politics? Its reasons for holding a particular view? Its tactics for accomplishing its goals? Its perception of opponents? As you write your description of the group, try to intersperse your own observation of their activities with members' responses to your questions.

3. Using Weldon as a model, write a narrative about an encounter with a U.S. government agency. Choose something with which you are familiar, for example, the state registry of motor vehicles, the city clerk's office, the county courthouse, or the Internal Revenue Service. In your account emphasize the effect of bureaucratic impersonality on the dignity of the individual as well as on the speed (or lack thereof) with which the system functions.

You might use particular people as illustrations of the government's response to the individual. Let the nature of your subject dictate the tone of your narrative; you need not be serious.

4. The issue of U.S. intervention in Central America has been the subject of heated debate for the past several years. Research the various opinions on American interests in El Salvador, Nicaragua (before and after the 1990 elections), or elsewhere in Central America by consulting magazine and newspaper articles on the subject as well as the opinions of experts found in books and interviews. As you read, try to place the opinions into categories, such as economic, ideological, balance-of-power, and humanitarian arguments. Write a paper in which you classify the arguments according to the categories you've established. Your purpose will not be to advocate any one position but rather to inform your readers of the reasons behind the opinions they encounter.

5. Conduct further research into one of the cultures represented in this section, focusing specifically on the culture's economy. It would be wise to choose a culture about which information is readily available — Cuba, Russia, Great Britain, and South Africa are likely candidates. If the selection is an excerpt from a larger work, look first at that work. You can find other sources by consulting the headnotes for other selections from that culture (if there are any) and a general encyclopedia, as well as journals devoted to the study of that culture. Narrow your topic to something manageable — such as the effect of ideology on the economic system, the culture's financial dependence on the world market, the role played by economics in internal politics, or the effect of economic forces on the individual — and write a cause-and-effect analysis in which you outline the relation between economic forces and some other facet of the culture.

Part Seven

VIOLENCE

INTRODUCTION

This section should provide a rather startling contrast to the currently popular image of war and violence presented in *Rambo* and *Terminator* and their many clones. Having no experience of war on their own soil, most American students will likely find the selections unsettling and provocative. In order to minimize any tendency to focus merely on the sensationalist aspect of the material, instructors may want to begin by exploring the images of war presented on television and in films. Most students will acknowledge the highly unrealistic quality of the *Rambo* image, no matter how they might secretly revel in its potency. In fact, if asked to separate the realistic from the sensational in such portrayals, they should begin to get a sense of what this section is about.

The comments in *Looking at Ourselves* will certainly help — Kovic's disturbing narrative of his battlefield injuries can become a focal point from which to view the remaining perspectives. Kovic's rejection of the warrior mentality belies Broyles's analysis of wartime nostalgia and Sam Keen's smug assumption that the "warrior psyche" is an integral part of the male mind. Together, these pieces should generate a good deal of thoughtful discussion, although it's doubtful that this discussion will result in any firm conclusions, except perhaps the rather facile one that we must end all war. Rudolph and Rudolph problematize the issue of how ethnic differences contribute to war; their more complex analysis should help students rethink their initial opinions about motives for war. The discussion will generate more questions than it answers, preparing students to approach the major selections with the critical eye necessary to sort out opposing views of the causes of war, the conduct of it, its consequences to soldiers and citizenry, and its justification (if there is such a thing).

There are a number of possible subthemes in the section, among them the effects of war and civil violence on domestic life (Milosz, McCafferty, Drakulić, Al-Radi, and Achebe) or specifically on women (McCafferty, Drakulić, Allende, Al-Radi, Walker), the question of a just war (Milosz, McCafferty, Moore, Walker), the uses of torture (Allende, Kelly), and the cost of war to the country that wages it (Moore, Drakulić, Al-Radi, and Achebe).

Students might be particularly affected by Czeslaw Milosz's analysis of American ignorance of war. He is speaking directly to *us*, attempting to jolt us into a realization of the fragility of our comfortable existence. Viewed in relation to the passages in *Looking at Ourselves*, Milosz's selection should ensure that students see themselves in the characters portrayed in this section. A close perspective is essential if this section is to open their minds to the complex realities of civil violence and war. The narratives of those whose lives are touched by violence (Grossman, Drakulić, Allende, Al-Radi, Kelly, Walker) remind us that we are not discussing an abstract theme. In each work we are presented with an ultimatum and forced to confront what is certainly the most pressing reality of our times.

Instructors may wish to consult the following familiar works in preparing related selections from *Ourselves Among Others*:

Essays

Bruce Catton, "Grant and Lee: A Study in Contrasts" (*The American Story*, ed. Earl Miers, Broadcast Music, 1956; Catton, *This Hallowed Ground*, Doubleday, 1956).

Martha Gellhorn, "The Besieged City" (*Face of War*, Atlantic Monthly Press, 1988).

Martha Gellhorn, "Last Words on Vietnam, 1987" (*Face of War*, Atlantic Monthly Press, 1988).

Abraham Lincoln, "The Gettysburg Address" (1863).

William Manchester, "Okinawa: The Bloodiest Battle" (*New York Times*, June 14, 1987; Best *American Essays* 1988, ed. Annie Dillard, Ticknor and Fields, 1988).

Carl Sagan, "The Nuclear Winter" (*Parade*, 1983).

Short Stories

Margaret Drabble, "The Gifts of War" (Winter's Tales 16, St. Martin's; *Women and Fiction*, ed. Susan Cahill, Mentor, 1975).

Ambrose Bierce, "Chickamauga" (*In the Midst of Life*, 1892; rep. Chatto and Windus, 1964).

Ambrose Bierce, "Occurrence at Owl Creek Bridge" (*In the Midst of Life*, 1892; rep. Chatto and Windus, 1964).

Stephen Crane, "An Episode of War" (*Stories and Tales*, Vintage, 1955).

Graham Greene, "The Destructors" (*Collected Stories*, Viking, 1973).

Mark Helprin, "North Light" (*Ellis Island*, Delacorte, 1981).

William Dean Howells, "Editha" (*Between the Dark and the Daylight*, Harpers, 1907).

Tim O'Brien, "The Things They Carried" (*Esquire*, Aug. 1986; *The Things They Carried*, Houghton, 1990).

Frank O'Connor, "Guests of the Nation" (*Collected Stories*, Knopf, 1981).

Luigi Pirandello, "War" (*The Medal*, Dutton, 1939).

William Trevor, "Lost Ground" (*New Yorker*, Feb. 24, 1992).

BIOGRAPHICAL NOTES ON *LOOKING AT OURSELVES*

1. Ron Kovic, born on July 4, 1946, was 19 when he was wounded in action in Vietnam and paralyzed from the chest down. His memoir *Born on the Fourth of July* (1976) was made into a popular movie starring Tom Cruise.

2. William Broyles, Jr., is the founding editor of *Texas Monthly* and a past editor of *Newsweek*.

3. Sam Keen, a professor of religious studies, produced a PBS series with Bill Moyers in 1987 that became the book *Faces of the Enemy: Reflections of the Hostile Imagination* (1988).

His most recent works include *To a Dancing God: Notes of a Spiritual Traveler* (1990) and *Fire in the Belly: On Being a Man* (1991).

4. Susanne Hoeber Rudolph and Lloyd I. Rudolph are both professors of political science at the University of Chicago. They have collaborated on *The Modernity of Tradition* (1984) and *In Pursuit of Lakshmi: The Political Economy of the Indian State* (1987).

5. Colman McCarthy is a *Washington Post* columnist.

6. Rosemary L. Bray lives in Central Harlem and is an editor for the *New York Times Book Review*.

7. George F. Will, a leading neo-conservative spokesman, has taught political science at Michigan State and at the University of Toronto and is a syndicated columnist and political commentator for the *Washington Post, Newsweek,* and ABC television. His columns have been collected in such volumes as *The Pursuit of Virtue and Other Tory Notions* (1982) and *The Pursuit of Happiness and Other Sobering Thoughts* (1979). He has also written on baseball (*Men at Work*, 1990) and in favor of term limits for congressmen (*The Wedge,* 1992). He won a Pulitzer Prize in 1977.

8. Joan Didion, the widely admired prose stylist, has published several volumes of essays and reportage, including *Slouching Towards Bethlehem* (1968), *The White Album* (1979), *Salvador* (1983), *Miami* (1987), and *After Henry* (1992).

Reflections

1. Students may find it most illuminating to compare Ron Kovic's disturbing firsthand account of being wounded in the Vietnam war with William Broyles's and Sam Keen's more distanced reflections on the meaning—and value—of war for men. Kovic's and Broyles's pieces, especially, form an ironic contrast. For many men, Broyles implies, war is a "great" love because it represents the pinnacle of experience. For that reason, "War is not an aberration;" it is an inevitable part of men's lives. Kovic's account, by contrast, is stark and immediate. He writes that "The only thing I can think of, the only thing that crosses my mind, is living." Kovic cannot, at that moment, give reasons for the continuing existence of war. The only comment on war implied in this excerpt is that it is senselessly and brutally violent. Sam Keen asks why men have created "a world where starvation and warfare" are becoming a way of life. He responds to his own question by denying that male biology is at the root of men's predilection for war. Instead, he writes that "men are systematically conditioned . . . to kill, and to die" for their nation. The need to conquer has been built into the male psyche, he says, and that is why we have war. Students may want to take this question further than Keen or Broyles do, by discussing why some men find war a fulfilling experience, and how the desire for it came to be an integral part of the "male psyche." The selections by Susanne Hoeber Rudolph and Lloyd I. Rudolph and by Colman McCarthy identify additional contributing factors to war's continuing existence: the "doctrine of ancient hatred" promulgated by various communications media see (see Reflections #2), and competition among arms producers to sell weapons (McCarthy).

2. Susanne Hoeber Rudolph and Lloyd I. Rudolph point to "identity politics" as they are "crafted . . . in print and electronic media," political campaigns, and education as a contemporary cause of ethnic strife. The Rudolphs contend that political positions based

on gender, race, or religion invite a simplistic treatment by the media, in which there is little or no examination of the complex motives for ethnic conflict. Rosemary Bray writes from a personal perspective, situating herself as a wife worried about her husband's safety. Her rhetorical strategies differ from the Rudolphs', but her piece takes a similar stance. She writes that she knows her husband is at risk on the streets because he is black and therefore a target for fearful and unreasoning whites. Identity politics (the tendency to establish loyalties and a sense of self along lines of racial difference) — again fostered by media oversimplification — contributes to his vulnerability and to racial antagonism in general. Bray cites three specific cases in which racial violence received wide — and biased — media coverage. The anonymous *Mother Jones* writer ascribes racial violence to media-encouraged identity politics when he writes of his initial glee at watching white people on the streets of Los Angeles being beaten on TV during the riots following the first Rodney King verdict. A later television appearance by King was aimed at cooling tempers; however, even King couldn't bring himself to say he loved "everybody." His loyalties, like those of the writer, are determined in part by identity politics: He must side with those who are most like him and who share his perspective. The Associated Press piece addresses identity politics in relation to a related phenomenon, hate crimes. The piece quotes a criminologist who claims that most offenders seek out anyone who is different from them; they attack the "other" as a way of validating themselves. Jack Levin, a sociologist, sees identity politics as contributing to the "resentment" people feel in the contemporary world about not being able to take part in "the American Dream" of economic security.

3. George Will fails to mention the racial aspects of gang warfare and the effects of white racism on the community. Cabrini–Green is a project inhabited largely by African-Americans who are poor (Will does mention that only 9 percent of the residents are gainfully employed). Some students may interpret Will's failure to mention race as an indication of his fair-mindedness. It may appear that, by ignoring race, Will is making an anti-racist gesture. However, such a strategy may in fact promote racism, since it also means Will can ignore the causal relationship between white racism and crime and violence in the African-American community. Will uses Karen—a young and innocent resident of Cabrini–Green—as an advocate for his ideas for what to do about gang violence. He writes that Karen shows "common sense" when she says, "Take the gangbangers out and take away all the guns . . . . Mow down those buildings." Neither Will nor Karen is prepared to say how to go about "taking the gangbangers out" or what the 7,000 residents of Cabrini–Green would do for housing if the high-rises were "mown down."

4. Students will be able to use their discussion of George Will's recommendations regarding Cabrini–Green as a springboard for considering how other writers approach the problem of how to decrease violence. Ron Kovic implies that teaching people to consider life as an ultimate and inviolable value is one way of decreasing the violence associated with war. William Broyles, in his last paragraph, states that "progress has simply given man the means to make war even more horrible" and that there is nothing anyone can do to change this. Sam Keen, without addressing the issue explicitly, implies that violence is an inevitable part of our lives when he writes that, for men, "violence has been central to our self-definition." The Rudolphs, by contrast, suggest that the media encourage ethnic violence by refusing to analyze the complex motives associated with it. By implication, greater attention to these matters by the media could have a positive effect

on ethnic violence. Neither the Associated Press piece nor Rosemary Bray's essay offers solutions to the problem of white-on-black violence, but the anonymous writer of "Nobody Listens" suggests that violence could decrease if whites would wake up and begin to listen to black people, who have been "screaming for a long time."

NELL McCAFFERTY, Peggy Deery of Derry (p. 615)

Explorations

1. The impression created in McCafferty's prologue is that the Deery family is a closely knit Catholic family. Woven into McCafferty's depiction of Peggy Deery and her family, however, is the impression that the family is threatened by civil strife. In the first paragraph, McCafferty mentions that family members have a hard time sleeping and that the wedding video shows Peggy the last time she was with all her children when all were "looking glad to be alive." Her son Paddy is on the run (para. 2) and Peggy herself cannot dance well because of a problem with her left leg (5). A guest sings a song for an IRA hunger-striker. Although everyone ignores the singer, Peggy's bad leg, and the possibility of police arresting Paddy, McCafferty's inclusion of these unhappy reminders of the Irish Troubles foreshadows the events that threaten the Deery family and others like them: the wounding of Peggy on Bloody Sunday, the imprisonment of those who belong to the IRA (31), and the ambiguous position of the Catholic Church in relation to the civil-rights movement (33, 37).

2. The Deery family's political position apparently arises from their religious loyalties and (by implication) their socioeconomic status. In Northern Ireland, to be Roman Catholic is almost inevitably to side with the Republicans against the Protestant Loyalists. The Deerys' activism undoubtedly was encouraged as well by their limited resources and their observations of the hard lives of others. Peggy Deery, a widow, had fourteen children, which would put a financial strain even on a middle-class family. But the Deerys live in a "prefabricated one-story aluminum bungalow" (17) in a poor housing development. Peggy's best clothes include a mock-leather coat trimmed with "fun fur" (16). Father O'Gara, who knew the Deerys and other families like them, speculated that being unable to meet basic practical needs made people insecure and might cause them to "cheat, draw false dole, drink, and even kill" (38).

3. McCafferty first mentions Protestantism in paragraph 10, where she describes how the "strict and doleful grip of a Protestant Sabbath" restricted Catholic women who would have liked to be able to shop or go to the pub on their only free day. With this depiction of Protestantism as a grim and oppressive institution, McCafferty sets up a contrast with the enthusiastic celebration of the Catholic wedding, where dancing and drinking are not only permitted but expected. Even the Sunday trips to the Catholic cemetery are full of play and socializing. From the cemetery, they can see "the mountains marching toward the Republic of Ireland beyond," which represents to them "beauty, freedom, and reward" (11). In the next paragraph, McCafferty carries on the image of "marching" she first associates with the Republic. She writes that the civil-rights movement brought people out of the cemetery and into the streets to march. Thus, while the Protestant

Church represents everything that oppresses the poor Catholic community, the Republic of Ireland is an inspiration to them to fight for their civil rights.

4. McCafferty says relatively little about the goals of either side in Northern Ireland's civil-rights movement. She notes that the movement brought women as well as men and children out to march "demanding freedom" and joining "the chant for votes, houses, and jobs" (12). Their victories, as of 1972, included better housing and the defeat of a Unionist politician who supported the Protestant police. The ostensible goal of the police appears to be to keep order — to control rioters in order to prevent property damage and bodily injury. However, their unnecessarily violent tactics on Bloody Sunday suggest that their real goal was to obliterate or severely damage the civil-rights movement. Because McCafferty wrote this narrative for an Irish audience familiar with the goals of both sides, her purpose here is more to win sympathy than to inform.

Connections

1. Rosemary Bray, in her selection in *Looking At Ourselves*, writes about waiting for her husband to come home and worrying that he would become the victim of white violence. She and Peggy Deery have something in common, in that Peggy Deery had similar worries about her son Paddy. In the prologue to McCafferty's essay, she mentions that Paddy is pursued by police for his involvement in the civil-rights movement. Neither Bray's husband nor Peggy's son is safe on the streets; they are both vulnerable to attack because of their backgrounds—Bray because he is black, and Paddy Deery because he is Catholic. The Associated Press piece describes the biased thinking of those who identify an Other and strike out as a way of affirming their own superiority. In the United States, for many whites, African-Americans are in the position of the Other. Peggy Deery, as a victim of police violence that could be described as a hate crime, is also in a position of being an Other in relation to the mostly Protestant police and British army. Similarly, the child in George Will's piece who comments that he hopes "that next time it won't be somebody I know" who dies from gang violence, has much in common with the Irish Catholics, whose relatives and friends are daily harrassed, arrested, and killed in conflicts with the army and with police.

2. The Rudolphs focus on the contemporary rise of "politics of identity" to explain civil violence. They write that religion and ethnicity are among the aspects of identity that have become politicized in Eastern European conflicts. The politics of identity are also important to the Irish Troubles because they are based on religious differences between Catholics and Protestants and on cultural and nationalist differences between the British and Irish. The Rudolphs also point out that there is no need to identify these conflicts as "ancient hatreds" for which no resolution is possible; rather, they are the result of contemporary events and injustices — encouraged by simplistic and sensational media coverage — that could be resolved if everyone involved would realize the limitations of identity politics.

3. In both "Peggy Deery of Derry" and "Amnesty," the authors look at social and political conflicts from the point of view of women whose lives have been blighted by a government's injustices. Peggy Deery took a much more activist role than does the anonymous narrator of "Amnesty," in that she marches for her own civil-rights, but both women are politically conscious and aware of the sacrifices they have had to make. In addition, both women worry about the men in their lives who place their own lives in

jeopardy because of their political activism; a conflict between their political convictions and personal lives is apparent in both. Gordimer and McCafferty both use their narrator's love and fear for those close to them to dramatize the anguish of living with poverty and oppression.

4.   In both "Peggy Deery of Derry" and "Sister Imelda," representatives of the Catholic Church are deeply involved in the lives of parishioners. Father Tom cares for the Deery family personally. He delivers not only spiritual comfort and guidance, but also practical help, as when he brings food to Deery's children and helps put them to bed (32). Sister Imelda, as a nun, is not permitted to have an involvement with her students as close as that of Tom with his parishioners, but she is expected to keep close watch over their intellectual and spiritual growth. Her passion for her vocation, like Father Tom's, suggests that the Catholic Church does not function as an abstract religious entity, but as an organization deeply integrated into the lives of Catholics.

CHARLES MOORE, Ireland Must Fight the IRA Too (p. 624)

Explorations

1.   Moore's initial anecdote makes the point that British citizens have been exposed to IRA terrorism for so many years that it has become an integral, and almost familiar, part of life. The anecdote lends a more human face to the statistic Moore offers in the second paragraph: Ninety-seven British people died as a result of terrorism in Britain in 1991.

2.   According to Moore, a fair assessment of the view of the IRA in Northern Ireland can be derived from the fact that only one of the seventeen Ulster seats in the House of Commons is held by a supporter of the IRA (para. 5). The "dominant view" implied by this, and by the fact that a majority of people in Northern Ireland vote for Unionists, is a lack of support for the IRA in Northern Ireland. Moore contends that the IRA has far more support outside of Ireland (in the United States, for instance) than within Ireland (8). Moore does not identify nor discuss IRA supporters within Northern Ireland.

3.   In paragraph 7, Moore asserts that in the Republic of Ireland, most people are glad the British are occupying the North and there is virtually no support for the IRA. They fear that without the British in place, there would be civil war in the north and that IRA terrorism would reach the south. By never stating a British view of the IRA beyond "weary resignation" (4), Moore implies the British offer little or no support to the IRA; but his references to IRA terrorism in Britain suggest a more active opposition.

4.   The thesis of Moore's essay is that with present conditions and policies there is no chance of resolution—there can be neither a united Ireland, nor a final acceptance that Northern Ireland is a part of Britain (13). Since Moore is not in favor of a united Ireland, he recommends that Britain integrate "Ulster politics into those of the rest of the kingdom" (16). And Dublin should cooperate fully in order to bring about the resolution Moore promotes.

Connections

1. Moore and McCafferty agree only on the definition of internment and that it happened in the 1960s. Moore describes it as "the detention of named individuals for extended periods without trial" (para. 9). He says that both the United Kingdom and the Republic of Ireland thought internment for IRA terrorists was justified to "prevent intimidation of juries" — a view he apparently shares. McCafferty, in contrast, refers to internment as a "ploy" against which "international opinion was ranged" (19). She says that "hundreds of Catholic males" were held, that most of them shared a "commitment to civil rights," and that few fo them were associated witht the IRA.

2. Students' discussion of Connections #1 should lead effectively to a consideration of the differences in McCafferty's and Moore's treatment of the role of religion in the violent acts of the IRA and the response of Britain. Moore, in fact, ignores the role of religion and writes as though there are no pertinent religious differences among the combatants. For McCafferty, the conflict between Catholics and Protestants is a central issue, as is evident in her opening to the main section of her essay, where she discusses how Catholics have been oppressed by Protestants, and in her continual identification of the civil-rights movement as a Catholic effort.

3. The Rudolphs argue that the increasing tendency to employ "politics of identity" that are "crafted in benign and malignant ways in print and electronic media" promotes violence based on differences in religion and ethnicity. Moore, in his second paragraph, describes how it has become common knowledge that IRA violence has escalated in recent years, a fact he explains in part because of the international response to the IRA, which tends to see the organization as a true representative of the will of the Irish people. Moore attempts to discredit the idea that "identity politics"—pitting the Irish and British against each other—is an accurate way of viewing the situation.

DAVID GROSSMAN, Israeli Arab, Israeli Jew (p. 629)

Explorations

1. The Israeli Palestinian Mohammed Kiwan, looking for a bridge between his country's Palestinians and Jews, believes he can build that bridge with a "common man" like Jojo Abutbul, a Jew who expressed views similar to Kiwan's on television. Both men feel that much of the conflict is fostered at the institutional level, by the government and media, and are hopeful that "if the two of us sit down and talk, we can finish off all the problems in two minutes." Both Kiwan as a Palestinian and Abutbul as a Morocccan have experienced prejudice and view themselves to some degree as outsiders in Israel. Their ability to understand each other's point of view is limited, however, because Abutbul enjoys the civil privileges of being Jewish and wants Israel to be solely a Jewish nation (para. 21).

2. The ladder Abutbul refers to is a hierarchy of influence and power based on "strength." Students may disagree about what constitutes "strength" in Abutbul's mind. He could be referring to military might, or economic resources, or even diplomatic influence. The most important thing in Abutbul's formulation is the idea that power at every level, from local to global, exists as a hierarchy in which "for every strong man there's someone stronger. . . ."

3. Early on in the essay, Grossman refers to Mohammed Kiwan as "Kiwan." Only after Grossman makes a joke in which Kiwan becomes Mohammed going to the mountain that refuses to come to him does Grossman refer to both men by their first names (4). Students may realize immediately that Grossman uses this strategy to emphasize that these are common men (see Explorations #1) meeting as equals. He reinforces this impression by describing them collectively: "Both are solidly built, with black hair and tough faces" (48). He writes that he could "imagine them changing roles and arguing . . . each one making the other's points . . . " (51). If Grossman had referred to each man by his last name or his profession, his effort to establish their common ground would have failed. From the outside, their differences are more obvious than their similarities. The Palestinian Kiwan, a lawyer, is better educated than the Jewish Abutbul, a restauranteur who "manages the entire beach" (49). Using last names, professions, or ethnic designations would have undermined Grossman's attempts to portray them as men with intimate connections and equally intimate conflicts, weakening readers' ability to empathize with them.

4. Students will be able to come up with many examples of Abutbul's use of metaphors and analogies. Some seem apt, others seem misdirected or confusing. In general, the technique makes abstract ideas more concrete and vivid, but it also distorts them, as the parallel between substance and symbol is never exact. Abutbul first uses "allegory"—and calls attention to it—in paragraph 6, where he compares his life when he was a sleeping child to a "box" that was "deposited" with the Arab housemaid who cared for him. This "allegory," in his estimation, describes the "trust" between Arabs and Jews, but significantly, the Arab in his "allegory" is a housemaid in an inferior social and economic position. In paragraph 15, Abutbul implies that since he didn't buy his Jewish identity at a store—did not, in other words, choose to be Jewish—he deserves a nation. Kiwan, of course, could have made the same point about being born Palestinian, but Abutbul thinks that Palestinians would feel at home in any other Arab nation. Perhaps the most uncomfortable analogy Abutbul draws appears in paragraph 25, where he describes his relationship to Kiwan—and the relationship of Jewish Israelis and Palestinians—as a marriage: "I love you, you're my soul, everything. I don't want to live with you!" He offers a "dowry" if the Palestinian will leave. This analogy, with its implications of a gender hierarchy in which the Palestinian is the unwanted wife of the Jew, seems particularly inflammatory between two men who consider wives as private possessions who symbolize their masculine honor (61). However, the expression of intimacy that slips out ("you're my soul") suggests that Abutbul realizes that the fate of the Jews and Palestinians are closely linked.

Connections

1. The most basic comparison that students might make between the Troubles in Ireland and the conflicts between Palestinians and Jews in Israel is that the strife arises from religious and nationalist differences. Like Abutbul, who believes that Palestinians need

149

to accept the sovereignty of the Jewish state, Charles Moore in Britain believes that the citizens of Northern Ireland should (and, for the most part, already do) accept that their proper place is in the British state (paras. 5, 6). McCafferty emphasizes religious differences far more than Moore does; her portrayal of the experiences of Catholics fighting for civil rights in Northern Ireland has much in common with Kiwan's estimation of the plight of Palestinians in Israel. Kiwan says that his people in the intifadah "had no way to remain silent any longer, so they used the stone. . . . It's simply the only tool he has to make the world hear him!" (62). Some Catholics in Northern Ireland, including Peggy Deery, might be able to understand the frustration and sense of having been silenced that would drive Palestinians to "use the stone." One important difference between the Isreali and Irish conflicts is historical: Jews and Arabs have jointly occupied the region known as Palestine for thousands of years, with open conflict erupting when the United Nations created the separate Jewish state of Israel there in 1948. The influx of Scots and Britons into the northern part of Ireland began after England solidified its control of Ireland in the 1600s and was actively opposed from the start, most violently by the IRA in this century and particularly since Great Britain made its partition of Ireland official in 1992.

2. Shelby Steele writes, "To be innocent someone else must be guilty, a natural law that leads the races to forge their innocence on each other's backs." Both Kiwan and Abutbul attempt to do this, Abutbul by claiming he has also been discriminated against (see Explorations #1) and Kiwan by magnanimously saying that he hated seeing Sephardim discriminated against (58–60). Steele says that blacks have reacted to whites' assumption of their own innocence either by bargaining or by challenging. Kiwan uses both strategies with Abutbul, beginning by bargaining. He says that it's all right with him if Abutbul thinks of his nation as Israel as long as it is all right for Kiwan to identify his nation—on the same land—as Palestine (12–14). Later, after Abutbul boasts that Prime Minister Jojo will exile Palestinians who don't accept Israeli sovereignty (29), Kiwan ceases bargaining and challenges Abutbul on the question of who has and will have power, saying that Abutbul is a guest on his land (30).

3. Yoram Binur experienced humiliation when he posed as a Palestinian because of the assumptions Jews made about his competence, worth, and even personhood. He recalls comments from Jews about the idleness of Arabs and their inferiority relative to Jews (7). He remembers a worse humiliation, when a Jewish man and woman almost have sex in front of him because "for them I simply didn't exist" (9). Binur recalls an anecdote about a college student, a Palestinian who was passed over for a job that was later given to an uneducated Jew (15). Another Palestinian tells a story about his Jewish girlfriend, who is ready to believe he is a terrorist (16). The assumption that Arabs are idle, incompetent, violent, and—most significantly—less than human, is also apparent in the exchange between Kiwan and Abutbul. Abutbul feels it necessary to state that he believes "An Arab is a human being. An Arab has a soul" (7). His unsolicited statement suggests that some Jews do not believe that Arabs are human beings. Nevertheless he implies that Arabs tend to be violent, as when he wonders whether Kiwan wants "my plate, my bed, my wife, and my children . . ." (8). He relates the worry of "some Jewish guy" that "some Ahmed [will] come and knife you." Kiwan, sensitive to Abutbul's implications that Jewish people are inherently stronger, says that he has "no feelings of inferiority" about Abutbul; and indeed, Abutbul seems to have feelings of inferiority with regard to Kiwan, in evidence

when he complains about Kiwan's education and when he bursts out that Arab violence insults him: "I'm not his dog, not his snake!" (61).

SLAVENKA DRAKULIĆ, (Druh-kool-itch) Zagreb: A Letter to My Daughter (p. 646)

Explorations

1. Slavenka Drakulić's first paragraph establishes a mood of sad nostalgia and loneliness. She describes her daughter's empty room and the emblems of innocence and youth that once marked it as belonging to a much-loved child. Later in the essay, her attempts to recall her daughter's presence by evoking concrete memories give way to a more powerful realization of loss: "I didn't recognize you because I was losing you" (para. 5). But immediately, she attempts to mitigate the loss with another concrete memory, of a train trip they took together when "R" was two years old. Drakulić continues to feel her loneliness deeply (6), but her mood changes to one of thoughtful reflection, tinged with anger about the chasm war has created between men and women (12), her daughter's generation and hers (10).

2. When Drakulić looks back on her own, and her husband's, focus on their lives (7), she realizes that they should have been paying attention to the world. Instead, they continued to disassociate themselves from the "spiral of hatred descending upon us" (8)—repeating a cycle of denial also apparent in her father's generation, who never "believed that history could repeat itself" (9). Her regret also shows when she writes about her daughter's generation and its unwillingness to look at the past or learn from it (10). As her discussion of the young man who spoke on television of his lack of a future (11, 12) indicates, she realizes that the young want to live their own lives rather than feel they must spend their lives—and perhaps give up their lives—making up for the mistakes of their parents and grandparents. Yet her own generation's having taken a similar attitude is partly responsible for her daughter's now having to grapple with issues of ethnic identity and conflict.

3. Drakulić's second-person address allows the reader to feel the mother-daughter intimacy that, to some degree, connects Drakulić and "R" across the emotional and physical distance between them. She describes the choking loneliness she feels sitting in her daughter's room (6), and reminds her daughter of how well she remembers little details about her, such as her dislike of her mother's tears and her habit of leaving messages in lipstick on the bathroom mirror. She also knows her daughter's limits; she tells her daughter that if she had stayed in her own war-torn country, "your mind would [have] crack[ed] and you would [have] enter[ed] a void where no one could reach you any longer" (5). If Drakulić had used the third-person, addressing the reader rather than her daughter, much of the pathos and sense of intimacy would have been lost. Drakulić seems to want to put a human face on the conflicts between Serbs and Croats—a conflict that traps her daughter in between loyalties to her divorced parents (7). The deep concern of the mother for her daughter is more likely to capture the reader's sympathies than the more distanced approach of a third-person essay. Finally, because the essay is written

in the form of a personal letter, the physical distance between mother and daughter is all the more obvious.

4. Drakulić uses incomplete sentences at several points in her letter. Overall, they are evidence of the informal, personal nature of her writing; she feels no need to attend to the formal rules of grammar in an intimate letter to her daughter. Futhermore, her incomplete sentences have the effect of stream-of-consciousness, in which thought builds upon thought through an associative process. In the second paragraph, Drakulić elaborates the metaphor of a birth to explore connections between her daughter's new maturity and the war; she uses incomplete sentences beginning with "Or" and "And" to build the analogy. Toward the end of paragraph 8, she uses fragments to a similar effect, quickly building a series of connected thoughts regarding the differences among generations. The stream-of-consciousness style is not always apparent in the fragments, however. Drakulić ends paragraph 7 with two concise fragments in response to the idea that her daughter could refuse to take sides in the Croatian/Serbian conflict: "But not now. Not here." Here, her use of fragments seems more decisive and clipped than when she is trying to connect a series of complex thoughts.

Connections

1. In "Israeli Arab, Israeli Jew," Abutbul points to the future when he says to Kiwan, "So I ask you, Mohammed, where do we want to get to?" (para. 8). Their argument throughout is peppered with references to potential actions and consequences, showing that — in contrast to the Yugoslav Communists cited by Drakulić — they are confident of having power over their future. They debate whether the Jews can or should — force the Arabs entirely out of Israel (29). They argue about getting a "divorce" (25, 26) and what that would mean for their future. Abutbul suggests that Kiwan has the option of "getting up tomorrow and moving to Jordan, Egypt, Syria, Lebanon" but he offers to build "another country for you" to end the strife between Arabs and Jews in Israel. Similarly, Kiwan talks about what will happen when Palestine is a nation of its own (30) and questions Abutbul about his idea of the future: "You're saying that this country, this future country of ours, will agree that every man in the world who wants to live in it can?" (34). Perhaps most telling is Jojo's "I'll try to help you as much as I can, so that your son . . . has a future here like my son" (85). Although the two men do not arrive at an agreement, their willingess to argue and their enthusiastic questioning about possible futures suggest that they have a better chance of understanding each other than the Serbs and Croats.

2. The Rudolphs describe the term "ethnic cleansing" as an invention of Serbian nationalists. The term implies that the conflicts between Serbs and Croats are of ancient origin and that only by a process of "cleansing" — complete separation — can their conflicts be managed. The Rudolphs refute the idea that no one has responsibility for resolving the problem; the belief that nothing can be done because the Serbs and Croats are only perpetuating an ancient, irremediable, mutual hatred only has the effect of contributing to its continuation. By focusing on the immediate conflict, the Rudolphs suggest that something can be done now. Drakulić's letter to her daughter supports their views because, in her consideration of the evolution of the conflict over the last three generations, Drakulić cites changes, lulls and squalls, in the Serbian/Croation conflict. Drakulić, a Croat, married a Serb at a time when the difference was considered unimportant (7). Drakulić explains this as an effect of growing up in Communist

Yugoslavia, which she describes as "an artificial nation." Now, "there is no middle position" (7). Her daughter will have to choose between her parents, but there was a time when she didn't have to. The Rudolphs argue that there could be a time in the future when the conflict would be reduced and she wouldn't have to choose.

3. Rosemary Bray writes about her worries for her African-American husband, who is, because of his race, especially vulnerable to violence on the street. While she waits for him to come home, she considers the possibility that he will be the victim of random, fear-inspired violence and that she will be left alone. During the phone conversation between Drakulić and her daughter, Drakulić hears shots and her daughter's terrified response. "[T]hat was the moment when the war began for both of us" (4). It is also the moment when she first realizes her own helplessness (5) to help her daughter deal with the violence that surrounds her and threatens not only her body, but also her mind. Drakulić is separated from her daughter because of the war; she is, in a sense, alone as Bray feared she would be left alone. Drakulić writes that her separation from her daughter is much less terrible than the things that have happened to others, but nevertheless she feels the loss strongly.

ISABEL ALLENDE (Ah-YEN-day), The Los Riscos Mine (p. 656)

Explorations

1. Allende makes it clear near the end of her essay that the public recognizes that the bodies belonged to victims of the government. She writes that when the news finally appeared on television, people heard the official lies and knew the bodies were those of "murdered political prisoners" (para. 54). But the identities of the perpetrators and victims are apparent at several points earlier in the piece. Even in the opening narrative, the posted warnings, barbed wire, and Irene's fear of being discovered by soldiers (5, 9) suggest that the government is trying to hide something in the mine; when the Chief Justice says to himself, "It required no great experience to conclude that the perpetrators of those crimes had acted with the approval of the government," it is apparent that the government has been using him to cover up their crimes against citizens (42). Finally, the continued interest of the General and the readiness of his troops to interfere with the investigation suggest that the government is responsible for the deaths of the people whose bodies are discovered in Los Riscos.

2. Students' responses to this question will vary a great deal depending on their background and political beliefs. Most will agree with the premise of the question, which is that in the United States, political dissidents enjoy the same freedoms as those who agree with the dominant political philosophy. Students will realize that few U.S citizens live with the same kind of fear of the government as the citizens of the country Allende depicts. However, some students may mention the harrassment of communists during the McCarthy era in the United States, the murder of civil-rights workers during the 1960s, or instances of police brutality as evidence that U.S. citizens are not completely free to disagree with their government's policies.

3. The General appears only as a voice. In paragraph 35 he is represented by his "agents," who are spying on the investigative commission. The General gives orders from some safe and unnamed location; by means of high technologies imported from the United States (39) and "the Far East" (40), he monitors the movements of the Cardinal and the Commission. The General orders the Chief Justice to "juggle justice" and has the power to bring about the death of any citizen (42); he appears, in fact, almost as omnipotent as he is ubiquitous. If Allende treated him as she does other characters, rather than as a disembodied but powerful presence, he would seem a less impersonal and amoral force.

4. The Chief Justice clearly feels himself caught between two formidable powers, the Catholic Church and the General. When he receives the Cardinal's letter, the Chief Justice "wished he were on the other side of the world" (41) because his response to the letter will place him in a bad position either with its sender or with the General. The Chief Justice seems to have abdicated his own sense of right and wrong; after years of betraying moral principles in the service of his government, he no longer has a sense of his own responsibility for seeing justice done. If Allende had included this information in the form of exposition rather than as character description, it would have been much harder for her to convey the psychological effects of the Chief Justice's complicity with the corrupt government. Writing in his voice, she follows his distorted thought processes, revealing much more about the personal price of political dishonesty than simple exposition would have.

Connections

1. Allende's use of homely details helps readers understand the events at the Los Riscos mine in a very different way than they would if they read about the discovery of the bodies in the newspaper or heard about it on the news. She conveys the horror of the discovery by showing how people reacted when they encountered the bodies. The details she offers give the story a feeling of reality it would otherwise lack. Drakulić uses homely details in a slightly different way, because in her letter the mention of the contents of her daughter's room in the opening paragraphs is intended to imply her personal involvement in the violence she reports. Allende, although she uses everyday details to emphasize the reality of violence, remains in the background. The events she describes happened not to her, in her own home, but to others.

2. McCafferty portrays a Catholic priest, Father Tom O'Gara, who is in many respects similar to José Leal, the priest who, in Allende's "The Los Riscos Mine," brings representatives of the Catholic Church in to investigate the discovery of the bodies of murdered political prisoners in the mine. Father O'Gara is also deeply concerned for the lives of his parishioners, as is apparent in his close attention to the welfare of Peggy Derry's family (para. 32), and the Catholic Church in both Allende's and McCafferty's pieces becomes involved in conflicts between governments and citizens. The Catholic priests in McCafferty's essay issue a statement following Bloody Sunday in support of the civil-rights marchers (33), and in Allende's account, the commission of Catholic priests initiates the investigation of Los Riscos Mine. In both cases, priests represent the interests of their parishioners rather than abiding by either the law or the interests of the government.

3. The most compelling similarity students may perceive between "The Los Riscos Mine" and Joan Didion's piece is the writers' unusual interest in violent events that most people

would choose to ignore. The woman whose body was, in Didion's words, "put out with the trash" was the victim of violence committed by a man who had enough power to get away with—perhaps—murder; because of his privileged economic class and her uninteresting history, he was not held accountable for his actions. Allende indicts a government for a similarly cavalier disregard for the human rights of its citizens, portraying characters who bring to light an incident that, but for their attention, would probably have gone unnoticed by most people.

CZESLAW MILOSZ (CHESS-law MEE-losh), American Ignorance of War (p. 671)

Explorations

1. This question may meet with some resistance; it's far from pleasant to be reminded that one's comfort and security might be blown to oblivion in an instant. And yet there's very little that can be done to soften the impact, because it's precisely this resistance that breeds the attitudes described as "stupid" by Milosz's questioner. He can't understand why Americans look on their way of life as "natural" and all others as "unnatural." He knows that the social order can be destroyed in an instant, that what was once considered natural and ordinary can suddenly become meaningless. Milosz's answer to the question is no, Americans are not stupid, just ignorant, and his reason is that Americans have never experienced war on their own soil. Even those Americans who have served in wars have always enjoyed the knowledge that a safe, sane home still existed for them to return to.

2. Milosz gives no specific reasons, but the entire state of affairs he describes may be seen as the ultimate debasement of human beings who finally decide they have little to lose in rebellion. Even under the worst of conditions, a rebellion, which Milosz refers to as the "Underground," existed. Most of the atrocities he describes are based on World War II experiences, but his statement that Central Europeans have learned "to think sociologically and historically" (para. 12) may be interpreted to suggest that they could imagine the repressions of the Soviet state re-creating the situation they had survived earlier. Then resistance might seem a logical course of action. By contrast, his comments indicating how quickly human beings adapt to unfavorable situations would suggest an unwillingness to risk confrontation. Milosz writes that "man is so plastic a being that one can even conceive of the day when a thoroughly self-respecting citizen will . . . [sport] a tail of brightly colored feathers as a sign of conformity to the order he lives in" (11). His fatalism results from having lived under two regimes that made "the fate of twentieth-century man . . . identical with that of a caveman living in the midst of powerful monsters" (7). The repetition of the experience (2) suggests that such conditions are not "unnatural" and could recur ad infinitum.

3. After coming to grips with their emotional responses to the first two questions, students should have no trouble answering this one. If presented with a historical or argumentative essay, we would be able to intellectualize the situation, distancing ourselves from the consequences of the argument. Instead we are forced to come to terms with a "gut" reaction to destruction. It's probably significant that in this case, even though they would normally prefer a personal rather than an intellectual account, most students would

probably feel much more comfortable with an impersonal essay. As students report on the most forceful concepts and comments, they will begin to appreciate the value and impact of the emotional versus the rational appeal.

Connections

1. The desire of many to avoid seeing, and therefore having to deal with, the deaths of citizens at the hands of the government is apparent in both Allende and Milosz. Milosz writes about avoiding a body in the street and refusing to consider the government's culpability (para. 5); similarly, the bodies in the Los Riscos Mine remained there for so long in part because no one wanted to face the consequences of searching for them. The political activists whose bodies turned up in the Los Riscos Mine are similar to the man whom Milosz says is "pushed into a van, and from that moment is lost to his family and friends" (7). Among the differences students may notice in Allende's and Milosz's depiction of countries torn apart by governments that treat their citizens like enemies is the ethnic basis of oppression in Milosz's description of Eastern Europe. He relates how people were divided up and made to live in certain areas according to their ethnic or religious identity (6) and change their names to avoid being identified (8); in Allende's story, by contrast, the people are represented as sharing an ethnic identity that allows them to trust each other.

2. Drakulić writes that when the war broke out between Serbs and Croats, she realized the difference between knowing war can happen and having it become a part of your life: "You no longer watch *Apocalypse Now*, you live it" (10). Milosz describes the isolation of Americans from an immediate experience of war as the difference that makes it impossible for "the man of the East" to "take Americans seriously" (12). The immediacy of war, and its effects on perception, occupy the attention of both Milosz and Drakulić. Milosz writes that the experience of war teaches people that "fluidity and constant change are the characteristics of phenomena" (11). Drakulić's letter illustrates that idea, as she describes how her understanding of the history of the Serbian/Croatian conflict changed over time (7, 8).

3. Students will be able to find an indirect response to Milosz's comments about American ignorance in almost every selection in *Looking At Ourselves*. Ron Kovic's piece about his devastating war wounds points to the limitations of Milosz's contentions: Living American men have known war intimately, in World War II, in Korea, and in Vietnam. Americans have not, however, had a war on their own soil. William Broyles's contention that war is the "great love" of men's lives seems irrational from the perspective of Milosz's essay, although Broyles's statement that we cannot prevent war no matter how hard we try to avoid it seems to support Milosz's statement that "if something exist in one place, it will exist everywhere" (12). The Rudolphs' piece contends that Americans have a very superficial understanding of the problems in Eastern Europe (and at home) based on simplistic treatment of complex issues in the media. Rosemary Bray's piece about her daily fears for her husband also refutes Milosz's contention that Americans are ignorant of the kind of violence war brings to a nation; she describes a race war that is never brought to an end. This impression is deepened in the piece by the anonymous black man in Mother Jones, where he relates his reactions to the riots in Los Angeles following the original Rodney King verdict. Many residents of Los Angeles had firsthand experience of civil violence on their own streets during the riots.

NUHA AL-RADI (Ahl-RAH-dee), Baghdad Diary (p. 677)

Explorations

1.   Many students will be sensitive to Nuha Al-Radi's hostility toward the West. They will notice especially her many disparaging references to George Bush (paras. 28, 37, 49, 61, 89, 90), which suggest that Bush symbolized the "evil" West for Iraqis much as Saddam Hussein symbolized the "barbarous" Middle East for Americans. The fact that the Allies are in the process of bombing Baghdad during the time she is writing is the most immediate and powerful reason for her hostility. Al-Radi is aware that Iraqi radio is more propaganda than real news, but she seems to accept the official version of war, in which the West and especially George Bush figure as a group of immensely powerful bullies beating up on a small nation full of innocent citizens (46). Al-Radi says that "the whole world hates us" (22); the sense of being a cohesive group of underdogs with the world against them helps Al-Radi cope with the magnitude of the country's devastation (60).

2.   Al-Radi makes many references to Western movies that suggest that she enjoys Western popular culture, even if she despises the Allies in general and George Bush in particular. She and her friends have seen *E.T.* (29), *Gone with the Wind* (62), and *The Party* (100); all her comments on the movies imply that she is able to identify with the Western characters they portray. Her dog is named after a Western artist; she prizes seeds for Italian vegetables (1), European radio broadcasts (46), and anemones bought in the United States (92). She clearly values her internationalism, which seems to be a badge of socioeconomic status. However, in paragraph 28, Al-Radi makes an ambiguous comment. Although she had visited the United States recently, she doesn't think she "could set foot in the West again." She thinks she might go to India, where "they have a high tolerance and will not shun us Iraqis." Evidently she did not entirely hate the West before the war; now, however, it is unclear whether she would not visit the West because she would not expect to be welcomed there, or because she would not want to visit it out of loyalty to her own people.

3.   The class discussion of Explorations #2 should lead naturally to a consideration of Al-Radi's definition of culture. Her statement concludes that American jealousy "must be why they have bombed our archealogical sites." Here culture means a long history and its artifacts. Her constant naming of friends, familiy and neighbors reinforces the implication that for Al-Radi, culture means having a well-established place in the world — in her case, as an Iraqi, a place that goes back thousands of years. But her statement is apparently made in anger rather than in earnest. Later, she calls her comment "silly." Throughout her diary, it is clear that she loves food, gardening, celebrations, music, and movies and that her enjoyment of these everyday aspects of culture include Western influences.

4.   The two main effects of writing in diary form are the sense of immediacy — events and emotional responses are recorded as they happened or very soon thereafter — and a high degree of everyday details. Among the advantages of Al-Radi's approach are the probability that readers will experience these events as closer in time and space than they would if Al-Radi had written a reflective essay. Potentially, this could make the emotional impact and sense of suspense greater. The writer, like her reader, does not know what will happen next; she cannot, therefore, anticipate either for herself or for readers how the war will affect her and her friends. Although this method raises the level of suspense

and perhaps the emotional involvement of the reader, it also risks losing the impact of the war in a wealth of relatively inconsequential everyday details. It is clear from her many references to food, for instance, that Al-Radi is very concerned about where meals will come from as the war continues, but readers may be less interested in detailed accounts of what is eaten when than in the writer's overall concern about supplies. In a reflective essay, written after the war and after she had the time to find out more about what happened to others, Al-Radi could have placed her personal experience within a wider context without, perhaps, losing much of the emotional impact of her diary.

Connections

1. Czeslaw Milosz writes that "all the concepts men live by are a product of the historic formation in which they find themselves" (para. 11). The life that felt natural before the war is replaced by a radically different life that can come to feel just as "natural" simply because it is "within the realm of one's experience." Al-Radi notices a similar phenomenon in her friends. M. A. W., for instance, says, "We must have continuous war . . . when we finish this war we must start another" (53). The comment is ironically intended, but it indicates just how "fluid" — in Milosz's term — people are. Al-Radi and her friends quickly grow used to the war. Her record for the twenty-fourth and twenty-fifth days reads, "A sameness. Even war becomes routine" (67). Likewise, behaviors that before the war would have been considered immoral or at least unusual are normalized under wartime conditions. One of her friends reacts to the war by "looking for someone to share her bed today" (13). Milosz writes that people no longer regard "banditry as a crime" (9), and Al-Radi offers several examples of thievery that neither she, nor others, regard as anything to become upset about (109).

2. Al-Radi wonders "Why do they keep bombing the same things again and again?", a question that most Americans would have no better answer to than Al-Radi does. The incomprehension apparent in her comments about how the billions spent on weaponry could be used to feed the hungry is, likewise, something Al-Radi shares with many Westerners. But William Broyles, in *Looking at Ourselves*, offers an indirect explanation when he writes that no matter how much men hate war, they are drawn to it as the most exhilarating experience of their lives. Sam Keen asks a question akin to Al-Radi's: "Why have the best and brightest exercised their intelligence . . . only to create a world where starvation and warfare are more common than they were in neolithic times?" But he answers his own question by simply saying that violence is "central" to men's self-concept. Both these writers would agree with the distinction implicit in Al-Radi's questions and comments that it is particularly Westerners who ignore the real and immediate needs of the world in pursuit of domination; they would say that men as a gender are unable to give much energy to helping the starving of the world because they are too deeply involved in experiencing their manhood through violence.

3. Iraq, like many nations in the Middle East, draws very clear lines of difference in regard to gender roles. Miriam Cooke's "The Veil Does Not Prevent Women from Working" focuses on the lives of women in Saudi Arabia, not Iraq, but it is likely that the same general understanding of gender differences applies to both Islamic cultures. However, Al-Radi is apparently a woman on her own, who maintains her own home and does not live in the shadow of any man. She has a wide circle of friends and seems very capable of caring for herself and for them. Her bicycle ride offended some, but she does not feel

shamed by their response. The man who shouts "We don't like girls that ride bikes" is speaking for the men who agree with traditional notions that women's place is in the home; he may have both religious and social motives in badgering her.

MICHAEL KELLY, Torture in Kuwait (p. 696)

Explorations

1. In his first paragraph, Kelly contrasts the former beauty and "conspicuous civilization" apparent in Kuwait University's School of Music with the barbaric and violent purposes to which Iraq had put the building. This contrast, situated at the opening of the essay, emphasizes the envy and hatred that motivated the Iraqis to torture Kuwaitis and defile and destroy property. The British television producer, epitomizing the civilized British gentleman, seems unaffected by the horror of Jasman's story of his surroundings. He patronizes Jasman, not only by failing to empathize with his trauma, but also calling him "a good chap" and calling him by his first name. The effect of this is that Jasman seems to be in a position of being exploited twice – once by Iraqi torturers, who injured him apparently just because they had the opportunity – and again by British television, which wants to take advantage of the sensational aspects of Jasman's story but has no apparent interest in helping him.

2. Students should be able to locate several different explanations for the extreme and apparently irrational violence of Iraqi soldiers. Perhaps the most telling "explanation" is offered by a torture victim who finds the search for reasons futile. He says simply, "Really, they are all crazy" (para. 39). In the following paragraph, a Kuwaiti with American ties says that Iraqis are "brainwashed" by Saddam Hussein to the point that they are unable to think for themselves. Kelly himself speculates that Iraq found torture and purposeless destruction an effective way "to subjugate a hostile, numerically overwhelming population" (42). Some of these Kelly interviews maintain that the Iraqis are essentially evil (43); in support of the contention that Iraqis enjoy violence, Kelly quotes a speech by an early medieval Iraqi leader and memorized by school children, in which violence and bloodshed are glorified (45, 46). Kelly concludes that the corruption of the Hussein regime inevitably corrupted all those who acted in its interests (48).

3. Kelly first introduces a personal response when he writes that he is used to seeing men cry during war; during this war he has "seen twenty men cry, not counting myself" (2). He hardly needs to offer his own personal responses, however, to stir readers' emotions. His account of Jasman's television appearance vividly portrays the lasting horror of a man's suffering at the hands of Iraqi soldiers. Kelly shows Jasman at the end of his appearance, when the television crew is finished with him, "with one trouser leg hiked up to the knee and tear trails streaking the dust on his face," an image that strongly conveys the disintegration and shock Jasman is feeling. Kelly quotes his interviewees often, letting their own words heighten the emotional impact of his story. Jasman tells of being electrocuted (14); an electrical engineer describes having his fingernails pulled out (28–30); an employee of a petroleum company recalls being hung on a wall and made

to watch the rape of a woman (34–38). By letting his interviewees tell their own stories much of the time, Kelly reduces his role as mediator between the interviewees and the reader.

4. Kelly comes upon the electrical engineer, who is still suffering the physical effects of his torture, by accident when he stops at a gas station. By emphasizing the accidental nature of their encounter, Kelly implies that the experience of torture is widespread. He needn't seek out victims; they are everywhere, and they are eager to talk about what happened to them. The electrical engineer cooperates very willingly, even slowing down his delivery so that Kelly, sitting on a "hard little yellow plastic chair" in the office of the gas station, can record his account word for word. Kelly's representation of his own presence is important because it portrays him as a wide-open listener, ready at a moment's notice to hear and record the words of his interviewees without judgment or interruption. The effects of depicting his own presence is that Kelly sets up a narrative and creates a visual impression, pulling the reader into the scene along with him and making it harder for the reader to remain emotionally detached.

Connections

1. Students will be able to refer back to their discussion of Explorations #2 as they consider the contrast between Kelly's and Al-Radi's portrayal of Iraqis. Kelly does say that the Iraqis he met in Baghdad — Al-Radi's home city — were "generous, likable people," a description that seems to fit Al-Radi herself and that accords with her depiction of her friends and neighbors. He cannot understand the difference between those he met in Baghdad and the savage Iraqis he heard about, and saw evidence of, in Kuwait. In part the contrast can be explained by the national identities of the writers: Al-Radi, as an Iraqi, has a more sympathetic view of her own people than does Kelly. Both write about Iraqi soldiers coming home across the desert. Al-Radi, however, writes empathetically of the soldiers walking "with no food or water" and being gunned down by Allied planes. Kelly writes that "they had fled in the night . . . ashamed to think they would be caught in the place of their sins" (para. 48). But in part the difference can be attributed to the fact that Al-Radi has no way of knowing what Iraqi soldiers did in Kuwait; her information is filtered through the government and has been edited to exclude anything that might suggest the violent excesses of the Iraqi military.

2. Since Kelly is interviewing only people whose entire lives have been turned upside down by the Iraqi invasion of Kuwait, there is little direct evidence of the "privileged ignorance" of war they enjoyed before the invasion. Settings such as the hall at Kuwait University's school of music and drama make it clear that life of comfortable ignorance existed. Kelly quotes other indirect evidence: One witness's idea that the Iraqis cannot be Muslims if they are capable of terrible violence shows that he has little personal acquaintance with the history of war in the Middle East. Similarly, it came as a surprising revelation to another witness that Iraqis "would follow [Saddam Hussein] anywhere, doing whatever" (41).

3. The Associated Press piece contends that those who commit hate crimes in the United States are looking to harm those who are different from them in some way; it actually matters very little what race or religion the victim is, as long as he or she is different.

People who commit such crimes are usually looking for a thrill, rather than having any particular political motive in mind. Kelly asserts that soldiers in Kuwait were mostly young and malleable; they saw their leaders committing terrible violence and learned that no one would stop them or punish them if they, too, beat and tortured Kuwaitis (who fit the description of the "appropriate" victim for a hate crime because they are of a different nationality and culture than Iraqis). Students may be divided on the question of whether Kelly's discussion of Iraqi war crimes will help us understand violence in the United States. Some will be unable to imagine that their own people could be as cruelly inhuman as the Iraqis, but others may be able to cite instances of American cruelties in war or at home that suggest that violence is an international problem rather than a symptom of the "evil" of Iraqis in particular.

4.   An unquestioning acceptance of violence as an integral part of everyday living is apparent in Sa'edi's "The Game Is Over." In paragraph 6, the narrator writes that "Hasani's dad would beat him every night, but my dad would only beat Ahmad and me once or twice a week." There is also a feeling that no one should escape the violence; this attitude seems to perpetuate violence through generations. Hasani says he'll be happy when his father learns "what it feels like to be beaten," not realizing that his father too was probably beaten regularly when he was a child. An Iraqi political scientist quoted in the third section of Kelly's essay observes that the history of Iraq is filled with violence (45) and that the tendency to commit violence cannot be considered a mark of abnormality among Iraqis, because so many engage in it (47). Both writers, then, depict violence as an ordinary and accepted, if negative, aspect of life.

ALICE WALKER, The Concord Demonstration (p. 705)

Explorations

1.   Alice Walker and other demonstrators object to the current use of Concord, California, as a weapons depot. Walker reinforces her objections by citing the history of the site during World War II, when 320 soldiers, most of whom were black, were blown up when the bombs they were loading exploded. Soldiers who thereafter refused to load bombs were imprisoned and dishonorably discharged (para. 18). The goal of the demonstration in which Walker participates is to draw the public's attention to Concord and drum up support for closing it down. The demonstration is peaceful, designed primarily to emphasize the commitment of demonstrators to nonviolence. Their tactics include carrying banners, staging rallies, and blocking the arrival and exit of weapons from the site.

2.   The military and its interests are not damaged in any way by the demonstrations, although its intended image as a protector of the American people may have been damaged when a train carrying weapons ran over demonstrators, seriously wounding Brian Willson (35). The demonstrators, then, are the only ones who suffer real damage as a result of the demonstration.

3.   Walker implies in paragraph 27 the significance of her fame to the cause she is promoting. She wonders if her "statements to the press truly reflected my feelings about weapons

and war." Later, a police officer asks for her autograph (31) and after Walker is released, she addresses a crowd of a thousand demonstrators (33). Walker uses her fame and the media access it gives her to speak out against military weapons; her presence lends credibility to the demonstration, even as it draws more media attention.

4. Walker offers so many vivid images that there should be a great deal of variety in students' responses. Some may focus on Abraham, the old man who sings "Amen" (26), or the Vietnam veterans who offer their angry support to the cause (33), or Brian Willson, the demonstrator who "was willing to give his life to the struggle for peace" and, for all practical purposes, ended up making that sacrifice. The Windela doll that Walker carries may strike some students as an unusual and memorable symbol for the peace demonstration; others may be most affected by the image of the bomb explosion with which Walker opens her journal.

Connections

1. Kelly writes that "Corrupt regimes corrupt those who live under them . . . . The young men who came from Iraq to Kuwait . . . found they had the appetite to do to the Kuwaitis the terrible things that the Mukhabarat did back home" (para. 48). He and Walker would agree that the soldiers' actions in support of an evil cause infects them and destroys their moral principles and individual sense of responsibility.

2. Walker, observing a little girl playing mother to the Windela doll while the demonstration goes on around her, reflects that mothers try to create moments of peace and love for their children, even though the outside world is full of violence. To some degree, McCafferty's portrait of Peggy Deery supports Walker's view of the role of mothers. Deery, a mother many times over, tries to create a sense of unity in hard times by celebrating with her children, and even dancing on her bad leg, during a son's wedding; more importantly, her involvement in the civil-rights movement is an effort to fight for a better and more peaceful future for her children. Slavenka Drakulić poignantly expresses her desire to protect her daughter, both as a child and as a woman (5); she feels it to be her responsibility to create a clear, serene space for her child, and her inability to accomplish that because of the war makes her feel helpless.

3. Walker takes a hat, sunblock, food, and other items that are intended to help her be comfortable during the demonstration and the arrest that will follow. Similarly, Irene and Francisco carry the tools they will need and a thermos of hot coffee. Walker and Irene and Francisco are embarking on risky ventures in which they could be hurt, both emotionally and physically. The small items they take along for comfort remind the reader that they are vulnerable human beings, frightened and having very little to rely on except their own intelligence and courage.

4. Among the writers in *Looking at Ourselves* who deal with issues and ideas similar to Walker's are Ron Kovic and the Rudolphs. Kovic demonstrates, in his graphic account of how he suffered devastating injuries during the Vietnam war, that dealing with war as an abstract principle, and assuming that there is such a thing as a good or just war, cannot lead to peace. From Kovic's perspective, only throwing down weapons and

162

refusing to fight can lead to peace. The Rudolphs also argue against abstractions, though from a different perspective. Their attack on identity politics is based on the idea that identifying certain groups as "natural" enemies actually ignores contemporary causes of ethnic conflict and prevents people from dealing with the concrete, but complex, issues at stake in civil war.

CHINUA ACHEBE (CHIN-oo-ah Ah-CHEE-bee), Civil Peace (p. 716)

Explorations

1. Iwegbu considers himself lucky for a number of reasons: First, he, his wife, and three of their four children survived the war, second, his bicycle is still where he buried it, and third, his house is still standing. It is clear that the death toll in the war was significant; his elation over having a house and a bicycle indicates that material losses were great as well. There is an implication that the Nigerian government came out on top, but more important is the fact that the peasants were certainly the losers.

2. Currency now has become meaningless. Biafran rebel money, while plentiful, is worth little. What people want is Nigerian egg-rasher.

3. The term is a phonetic equivalent for ex gratia, or Nigerian money offered in return for turning in rebel scrip. Iwegbu gets money as he got war, for no apparent reason, and it withdraws just as arbitrarily, leaving him glad that no worse harm was done. Nothing has been gained — economic and political strife continue, but with survival as the object, not victory.

4. The term civil peace, so close to civil war, blurs the distinction between the two.

Connections

1. In "Civil Peace," Jonathan Iwegbu's repeated exclamation that "nothing puzzles God!" (paras. 2, 4, 7) suggests that war is a mystery incomprehensible to humans, but somehow comprehensible to God. Part of that mystery is that the end of the war does not mean the end of violence. It means that a different kind of struggle for survival has begun, a struggle against the poverty brought on by the war. The attitudes expressed in Alice Walker's account of the Concord demonstration are very different. As a peace activist, Walker does not have the idea that war is inevitable. Far from being resigned to the negative effects of war on the postwar society, Walker insists that action can help stop violence.

2. Iwegbu's tendency to understate is most evident in his ability to count himself lucky rather than unfortunate – to shrug off the violence against himself and his family, as well as the loss of the "egg rasher" at the end of the story. "I count it as nothing," he tells his neighbors, because it is no greater a loss than he and many others have suffered during the war (41). Like the torture victim speaking in "Torture in Kuwait," Iwegbu is able to recognize that worse things have happened to others. His sense of perspective amid violence and disorder leads him to understatement.

3. Colonial influence is seen in the use of currency, the entrepreneurship exhibited by Iwegbu, the presence of the shell of the tall building, the coal company, Iwegbu's use of the bicycle, and the reliance on police for order. African influences appear in Iwegbu's refrain, "Nothing puzzles God," implying that supernatural elements are at work in his good fortune, his resilience in the face of disaster, his compromise with the thief, and his philosophical approach to the loss of his money. All suggest traditions that have been rerouted but not fundamentally changed by the materialistic influences of Britain.

ADDITIONAL QUESTIONS AND ASSIGNMENTS

1. In a journal entry or a collection of informal notes, discuss the concept of a noble cause as depicted in three or four of these selections. Consider such issues as the conflict between loyalty to a cause and loyalty to human beings, the individual's understanding of the cause (or lack thereof), the history of the conflict surrounding the cause, and any other issues you find relevant. As you look over your notes, try to discover similarities and differences among the cultures represented. Is it possible for individuals to identify so strongly with a cause that they consider their goals synonymous with the goals of the cause? Is any cause worth dying for? In short, can you come to any conclusion about the role played by a people's commitment to a cause in wartime or in civil conflict?

2. Using ideas about American involvement in international conflict expressed in the Milosz, Al-Radi, or Walker selections as a springboard, investigate U.S. intervention in conflicts around the world. As you do your research, consider the kinds of information you're interested in discovering. You may want to investigate dissident groups, or groups that promote U.S. involvement abroad, and analyze their role in discouraging or advocating U.S. involvement in international conflicts. What tactics do these groups use for accomplishing their goals? How do people on opposing sides of the issue define patriotism? As you write a description of the group, try to intersperse your own observations and analysis of their activities with the group's own perceptions.

3. Write your own version of "Civil Peace," in which you present a fictional view of what life would be like in your community after an event that changed "normal" life forever. It might be easier to imagine a change precipitated by some sort of natural disaster, because so few of us have any experience — of our own or someone close to us — of war on our soil. Describe life without such modern conveniences as the electronic media, currency, motorized transportation, and mass-produced food and clothing. Create a family who, like the Iwegbus, must devise a means for economic survival. You need not include an incident similar to the visit by the thieves, but you should try to emphasize the absolute lack of any recognizable foundation on which to rebuild "normal" society. (If the situation seems too incomprehensible, you may want to start by simply recalling our helplessness when we lose electricity for more than a few hours. Then consider what it would be like if we couldn't expect power to be restored in the foreseeable future.)

4. The issue of nuclear war has been the subject of media attention for the past ten years — two television films in particular, "The Day After" (United States) and "Threads" (Great Britain), have explored the aftermath of a nuclear war. Research various responses to these films in magazines and newspapers, and view them if possible. (Both are available on videocassette.) Considering Milosz's statements about American ignorance of war, write a paper in which you discuss the differences between the two films, focusing specifically on the realism of "Threads," produced in a country that felt the full effect of Hitler's air force in World War II, as opposed to the sentimentality of "The Day After," produced in a country that hasn't experienced battle on its own soil since the Civil War. While your discussion will inevitably compare the two films, it should also analyze the causes of the differences between them, and consider the changes in our attitudes and fears about nuclear war in the aftermath of the demolition of the Berlin Wall and the dissolution of the Soviet Union.

5. Conduct further research into one of the cultures represented in this section, focusing specifically on the experience of war. It would be wise to choose a culture about which information is readily available — Latin America, Israel, Iraq, and Ireland are likely candidates. If the selection is an excerpt from a larger work, look first at that work. You can find other sources by consulting the headnotes for other selections from that culture and a general encyclopedia, as well as journals devoted to the study of that culture. Narrow your topic to something manageable, such as the causes of a particular war or civil conflict, its effects on the populace, the ideologies represented, or the characteristics of the combatants on either side, and write a comparison-contrast paper in which you analyze the perspectives of the two sides involved.

SUGGESTED SYLLABI

This is a basic course description, with options for adaptation to different teaching approaches and thematic considerations. The format of the syllabus is necessarily general, making it more flexible with regard to the needs of individual instructors. Each syllabus includes four short papers and one research paper. The arrangement allows for increasing or decreasing the number of papers to satisfy instructors' wishes or departmental requirements. (It is assumed, however, that each paper will go through several drafts, ensuring a significant amount of student writing.)

BASIC COURSE DESCRIPTION

This syllabus is designed for a lecture-discussion course focusing on reading, writing, and research. In general, the paper assignments move from personal narrative to causal analysis or persuasion involving outside sources. The thematic emphasis is on recognizing how we define ourselves, beginning with an exploration of what it means to belong to one particular culture among others and then moving to more specific roles within a family, to a recognition of ourselves as we come of age and go to work, and finally to an understanding of the conflicts and ideologies shaping us and our culture. This syllabus can be adapted to a collaborative approach simply by charging students with the responsibility for interpreting selections. Individual groups can prepare different selections and present their interpretations to the class for general discussion. Similarly, papers can be worked through a number of drafts by using peer evaluation. Research projects may be conducted individually, using peer evaluation groups for revision advice, or collaboratively, with several students composing one paper.

Weeks 1–4

Readings: "The West and the World"

Writing: Analyses of causes for misunderstandings among different cultures (using Carroll, Paz, Jen, Naipaul, and outside sources), *or* persuasive essay arguing for increased efforts at understanding other cultures (using Reed, Harrison, and Mphahlele).

Discussion: Emphasis in readings on obstacles to dialogue between cultures and overcoming misconceptions about other cultures.

Weeks 5–6

Readings: "The Family": *Looking at Ourselves*, Gyanranjan

Writing: Short essay describing family traditions (using any one of the readings as a model)

Discussion: Different traditions, different types of families, reactions to Gyanranjan.

Weeks 7–9

Readings: "The Family"

Writing: Personal narrative on family memory (see Liang and Shapiro, Mehta, Soyinka).

Discussion: Authors' personal reminiscences; effect of subjective point of view.

Weeks 10–12

Readings: "Landmarks and Turning Points"

Writing: Comparison of initiation rites in diverse cultures (for instance, Orlean, Vargas Llosa, Grass), *or* comparison of male rites (for example, Grass, Vargas Llosa) with female rites (for example, Mehta, Orlean).

Discussion: personal and cultural functions of coming-of-age rituals; differences in initiation experiences for males and females.

Weeks 13–15

Readings: "Work"

Writing: Definition of meaning of work to people in different classes and cultures (for instance, Abram, Angelou, Bonner), *or* classification of workers by identification with particular jobs (for example, García Márquez, Angelou, Ishikawa).

Discussion: Reactions of authors to their jobs, focusing on effects of class, race, and culture on the relationship of workers to their jobs.

VARIATION I

Instructors wishing to alter readings from semester to semester may do so by changing the general theme of the course. For example, the class might explore the relationships between the individual and others, keeping the first, second, and third sections of the basic syllabus and substituting the following for the fourth and fifth sections:

Weeks 10–12

Readings: "Women and Men"

Writing: Comparison of Western or Judeo-Christian images of males and females with those of other cultures (for example, Fuentes, Moravia, Cooke), *or* definition of male or female, based on several selections (for instance, Kazantzakis, Silko, Beauvoir). This might be done as a parody.

Discussion: Focus on how stereotypes and inaccurate perceptions reinforce traditional sex roles; contrast with writers' attempts to represent new and different points of view on meanings of "female" and "male."

Suggested Syllabi

Weeks 13–15

Readings: "We the People: Individuals and Institutions"

Writing: Comparison of benefits and liabilities of a given form of government (using Havel, Golden, Anonymous), *or* definition of oppression (based on Gordimer, Mandela, Weldon).

Discussion: Focus on similarities among different ideologies. With this syllabus, the focus in Sections 1, 2, and 3 would shift from personal identity to relationships between individuals and others, including the state. This syllabus presents a greater challenge to students than the first, because it involves an assessment of the individual's responsibilities to nations and their ideologies and institutions.

VARIATION 2

Instructors may wish to undertake a narrower study of the individual and others, moving from relationships within a family directly to relationships between the individual and the state. Using this arrangement, the first four sections of the syllabus would remain the same, with the following substitution for the fifth section:

Weeks 13–15

Readings: "Violence"

Writing: Comparison or classification of methods of resistance to oppression (for example, McCafferty, Grossman, Allende, Walker).

Discussion: Highlight different approaches to war and violence. With this syllabus, the focus in the first four sections would shift from relatively neutral analysis to assessment of moral responsibility of individuals and governments, clashes between personal and ideological loyalties, and justifications for violence. This is the most challenging syllabus of those offered, because it involves examination of value judgements.

RHETORICAL INDEX

Among the selections listed here are models of specific rhetorical strategies (for example, the essay by Raymonde Carroll uses comparison and contrast and the essay by Ishmael Reed uses example or illustration as primary strategies). Also listed are selections that employ several different strategies.

Analogy

Raymonde Carroll, "Money and Seduction"
Octavio Paz, "Hygiene and Repression"
Salman Rushdie, "The Broken Mirror"
Nikos Kazantzakis, "The Isle of Aphrodite"
Alberto Moravia, "The Chase"

Argument and Persuasion

Ishmael Reed, "What's American About America?"
Paul Harrison, "The Westernization of the World"
Patrick Smith, "Nippon Challenge"
Louise Erdrich, "Adam"
Marguerite Duras, "Home Making"
Günter Grass, "After Auschwitz"
Miriam Cooke, "The Veil Does Not Prevent Women from Working"
Václav Havel, "Moral Politics"
Nelson Mandela, "Black Man in a White Court"
Michael Dorris, "House of Stone"
Charles Moore, "Ireland Must Fight the IRA Too"
Michael Kelly, "Torture in Kuwait"
Alice Walker, "The Concord Demonstration"
Czeslaw Milosz, "American Ignorance of War"

Cause and Effect

Es'kia Mphahlele, "Tradition and the African Writer"
Paul Harrison, "The Westernization of the World"
Yoram Binur, "Palestinian Like Me"
Eduard Shevardnadze, "Life with the Party"
Tim Golden, "Cubans Try to Cope with Dying Socialism"
Anonymous, "Evicted: A Russian Jew's Story (Again)"
Václav Havel, "Moral Politics"
Charles Moore, "Ireland Must Fight the IRA Too"
Slavenka Drakulić, "Zagreb: A Letter to My Daughter"

Rhetorical Index

Classification

Gish Jen, "Helen in America"
Susan Orlean, "Quinceañera"
Amy Tan, "Two Kinds"
Slavenka Drakulić, "Zagreb: A Letter to My Daughter"

Comparison and Contrast

Raymonde Carroll, "Money and Seduction"
Octavio Paz, "Hygiene and Repression"
Gish Jen, "Helen in America"
Margaret Atwood, "A View from Canada"
Patrick Smith, "Nippon Challenge"
John David Morley, "Acquiring a Japanese Family"
Gyanranjan, "Our Side of the Fence and Theirs"
Salman Rushdie, "The Broken Mirror"
Naila Minai, "Women in Early Islam"
David Grossman, "Israeli Arab, Israeli Jew"

Definition

Ishmael Reed, "What's American About America?"
Gish Jen, "Helen in America"
Louise Erdrich, "Adam"
Marguerite Duras, "Home Making"
Susan Orlean, "Quinceañera"
Amy Tan, "Two Kinds"
Carlos Fuentes, "Matador and Madonna"
Alberto Moravia, "The Chase"
Miriam Cooke, "The Veil Does Not Prevent Women from Working"
Tomoyuki Iwashita, "Why I Quit the Company"

Description

Margaret Atwood, "A View from Canada"
Rigoberta Menchú, "Birth Ceremonies"
Wole Soyinka, "Nigerian Childhood"
Gyanranjan, "Our Side of the Fence and Theirs"
Marguerite Duras, "Home Making "
Susan Orlean, "Quinceañera"
Salman Rushdie, "The Broken Mirror"
Tomoyuki Iwashita, "Why I Quit the Company"
Michael Dorris, "House of Stone"
Nuha Al-Radi, "Baghdad Diary"

Example and Illustration

Ishmael Reed, "What's American About America?"
Raymonde Carroll, "Money and Seduction"
Octavio Paz, "Hygiene and Repression"
Rigoberta Menchú, "Birth Ceremonies"
Marguerite Duras, "Home Making"
Salman Rushdie, "The Broken Mirror"
Christopher Reynolds, "Cultural Journey to Africa"
Carlos Fuentes, "Matador and Madonna"
Alice Walker, "The Concord Demonstration"

Exposition

Gish Jen, "Helen in America"
Paul Harrison, "The Westernization of the World"
Louise Erdrich, "Adam"
Salman Rushdie, "The Broken Mirror"
Miriam Cooke, "The Veil Does Not Prevent Women from Working"
Nell McCafferty, "Peggy Deery of Derry"
Slavenka Drakulić, "Zagreb: A Letter to My Daughter"
Isabel Allende, "The Los Riscos Mine"

Interview

V. S. Naipaul, "Entering the New World"
Patrick Smith, "Nippon Challenge"
Rigoberta Menchú, "Birth Ceremonies"
Susan Orlean, "Quinceañera"
Amy Tan, "Two Kinds"
Marjorie Shostak, "Nisa's Marriage"
Miriam Cooke, "The Veil Does Not Prevent Women from Working"
Raymond Bonner, "A Woman's Place"
David Grossman, "Israeli Arab, Israeli Jew"
Michael Kelly, "Torture in Kuwait"
Czeslaw Milosz, "American Ignorance of War"

Irony

Gish Jen, "Helen in America"
Margaret Atwood, "A View from Canada"
V. S. Naipaul, "Entering the New World"
John David Morley, "Acquiring a Japanese Family"
Alberto Moravia, "The Chase"
David Abram, "Making Magic"
Gabriel García Márquez, "Dreams for Hire"
Fay Weldon, "Down the Clinical Disco"
Václav Havel, "Moral Politics"
Nuha Al-Radi, "Baghdad Diary"

Rhetorical Index

Narration

V. S. Naipaul, "Entering the New World"
Louise Erdrich, "Adam"
Liang Heng and Judith Shapiro, "Chairman Mao's Good Little Boy"
Wole Soyinka, "Nigerian Childhood"
John David Morley, "Acquiring a Japanese Family"
Gyanranjan, "Our Side of the Fence and Theirs"
Ved Mehta, "Pom's Engagement"
Gholam-Hossein Sa'edi, "The Game Is Over"
Liliana Heker, "The Stolen Party"
Mario Vargas Llosa, "On Sunday"
Salman Rushdie, "The Broken Mirror"
Amy Tan, "Two Kinds"
Yoram Binur, "Palestinian Like Me"
Leslie Marmon Silko, "Yellow Woman"
Alberto Moravia, "The Chase"
Ken Bugul, "The Artist's Life in Brussels"
Yashar Kemal, "A Dirty Story"
Maya Angelou, "Mary"
Edna O'Brien, "Sister Imelda"
Gabriel García Márquez, "Dreams for Hire"
Primo Levi, "Uranium"
Anonymous, "Evicted: A Russian Jew's Story (Again)"
Nadine Gordimer, "Amnesty"
Fay Weldon, "Down the Clinical Disco"
Isabel Allende, "The Los Riscos Mine"
Chinua Achebe, "Civil Peace"
Nuha Al-Radi, "Baghdad Diary"

Process Analysis

Rigoberta Menchú, "Birth Ceremonies"
Ved Mehta, "Pom's Engagement"
Marguerite Duras, "Home Making"
Susan Orlean, "Quinceañera"
Marjorie Shostak, "Nisa's Marriage"
Le Ly Hayslip, "Rice Farming in Vietnam"
Yoshimi Ishikawa, "Strawberry Fields"

CHART OF RHETORICAL WRITING ASSIGNMENTS

NOTE: "Elaborations" or writing assignments asking students to write an essay in a particular rhetorical form or using resources are listed below. The number following the author's name refers to the corresponding "Elaborations" question for the selection.

(For the Index of Authors and Titles, see text pp. 735–738.)

Analogy	Argument and Persuasion	Cause and Effect
Vargas Llosa 2	Achebe 2	Achebe 2
	Abram 1	Al-Radi 2
	Bonner 1	Beauvoir 1
	Cooke 1	Binur 1
	Dorris 2	Bugul 2
	Golden 1	Drakulić 2
	Grass 2	Gordimer 1
	Grossman 1	Grass 1
	Harrison 2	Harrison 1
	Havel 2	Heker 2
	Heker 2	Kelly 2
	Iwashita 2	Kemal 3
	Liu 1	Levi 2
	Mehta 1	Mandela 2
	Moore 2	Milosz 1
	Moravia 1	Mphahlele 1
	Postman 2	Reynolds 1
	Sa'edi 1	Sa'edi 1
	Smith 1	Shevardnadze 1
		Silko 2
		Tan 1

Rhetorical Chart

Classification	Comparison and Contrast	Definition
Abram 1	Abram 2	Abram 2
Allende 2	Atwood 1	Achebe 1
Al-Radi 1	Binur 2	Allende 2
Binur 3	Dorris 1	Atwood 2
Carroll 1	Drakulić 2	Beauvoir 2
Duras 2	Fuentes 1, 2	Carroll 1
Erdrich 2	Grossman 1, 2	Erdrich 2
Heker 1	Hayslip 1, 2	García Márquez 1, 2
Jen 2	Jen 2	Gordimer 2
Kelly 1	Kazantzakis 1	Grass 2
Liu 2	Kelly 1	Gyanranjan 1
Mandela 1	Liang/Shapiro 2	Havel 1
Menchú 1	McCafferty 2	Minai 2
Minai 2	Mandela 1	Naipaul 2
Mphahlele 2	Mehta 2	Paz 1
Paz 1	Minai 1	Reed 2
Reed 2	Moore 1	Silko 1
Shostak 2	Orlean 2	
Silko 1	Paz 2	
	Reed 1	
	Rushdie 2	
	Shevardnadze 2	
	Shostak 1	
	Soyinka 1	
	Vargas Llosa 1, 2	
	Walker 1, 2	
	Weldon 1	

Description	Division/Analysis	Example and Illustration
Angelou 2	Achebe 1	Bonner 2
Duras 1	Bonner 2	Havel 1
García Márquez 1	Bugul 1	Morley 2
Golden 2	Carroll 1, 2	Naipaul 2
Gyanranjan 1	Dorris 1	
Havel 2	García Márquez 1, 2	
Heker 1	Havel 1	
Ishikawa 2	Kazantzakis 2	
Iwashita 1	McCafferty 1	

Description	Division/Analysis	Narration
Jen 1	Naipaul 1	Achebe 2
Kemal 1	Orlean 2	Angelou 1
Liang/Shapiro 1	Reynolds 2	Erdrich 1
Liu 2	Shevardnadze 1	"Evicted" 2
Menchú 2	Smith 2	Gordimer 2
Milosz 2	Silko 1	Gyanranjan 2
Minai 1	Tan 2	Kemal 2
Morley 1	Vargas Llosa 2	Levi 1
O'Brien 2		Liu 1, 2
Orlean 1		McCafferty 2
Paz 1, 2		Menchú 2
Rushdie 1		Moravia 2
Shevardnadze 2		Orlean 2
		Silko 2
		Soyinka 2

Process Analysis	Using Sources	Other
Allende 1	Bonner 2	Allende 2 (imaginary debate)
Angelou 2	Bugul 2	Bonner 1 (imaginary dialogue)
Cooke 2	García Márquez 2	Drakulić 1 (letter to a child)
Harrison 2	Havel 1	"Evicted" 1 (letter to the editor)
Ishikawa 1	Kelly 2	Kemal 1 (imaginary travel article)
Levi 2	Mandela 2	Milosz 2 (letter)
		O'Brien 1 (job description)
		Postman 1 (summary)
		Weldon 2 (monologue)

ADDITIONAL RESOURCES

INDEX TO HEADNOTE INFORMATION

The following index is keyed to the headnotes in the third edition of *Ourselves Among Others* and locates specific geographical, historical, and political information about countries found in the headnotes.

ARABIA: geography, distinction between Arab and Islamic countries (p. 361); geography, current monarchy based on Islamic law, general history of the Arabs, discovery of oil, in Gulf War (p. 372)

ARGENTINA: geography, general history, population, twentieth-century governments including Perón's democracy, Falkland Islands War, current President Carlos Menem's economic policies (p. 212)

BALI: see Indonesia

BELGIUM: geography, general history, African empire, political stability (p. 344)

BOTSWANA: racial makeup and description of Zhun/twasi and !Kung San peoples, independence from British rule (p. 354)

CANADA: geography, general history, tension between Canada's English and French heritages (p. 29)

CHILE: geography, Spanish conquest, independence, dictatorship under Pinochet, current seventeen party coalition (p. 656)

CHINA: Chairman Mao's regime, Cultural Revolution, current situation under Deng Xiaoping (p. 22); 1950s government repression, youth movements, Red Guards described, the Great Leap Forward (p. 97)

COLOMBIA: geography, Spanish rule, nineteenth-century independence, population (p. 497)

CZECH REPUBLIC: geography, annexation of Czechoslovakia before World War II, Communist rule, "Prague Spring," uprising and democratic elections, President Václav Havel, division of Czechoslovakia into Slovakia and the Czech Republic (p. 542)

CROATIA: see Yugoslavia

CUBA: geography, general history, struggles for independence, policies of Fidel Castro (p. 528)

FRANCE: French Revolution, nineteenth and twentieth-century political regimes, colonial empire, contemporary history and role in Europe (p. 8)

GERMANY: World War II history, postwar division into East and West, history of Berlin wall including dismantling, problems created by reunification (p. 264)

GEORGIA: independence from the Soviet Union and Russia, recent elections (p. 521)

GREAT BRITAIN: structure of government, geography of empire, history of relationship with Europe and empire, current role in international organizations (p. 551)

GUATEMALA: The Mayan empire, Republic of Guatemala established, ethnic makeup, political struggles between peasant groups and repressive regimes, new government founded by Ramiro de Leon (p. 76)

GREECE: Iraklion, Minos's Palace, Crete, general history, independence, recent governments (p. 322)

HONG KONG: geography, population, contemporary history, British influence, reversion to China in 1997 (p. 219)

INDIA: population, general history including European colonization and trade, twentieth-century, political leadership, Gandhi and 1947 independence, current political climate, clash between Hindus and Muslims and with neighbors especially Pakistan (p. 134); Punjab region, caste system (p. 142)

INDONESIA: geography, European dominance of, independence establishment of Malaysia (p. 422)

IRAN: geography, general history, British and Russian influences on, loss of Afghanistan, dynasty of Shahs, Khomeini's rule, Khomeini's death threats against Salman Rushdie (p. 162)

IRAQ: invasion of Kuwait, events of 1991 Gulf War especially bombing of Baghdad (p. 677)

IRELAND: geography, general history, the Act of Union, nationalist uprisings, Republic of Ireland recognized, first woman president (p. 444), Irish Republican Army, the Troubles (p. 615)

ISRAEL: geography, general history, independence, the Arab minority, discrimination against Arabs (p. 629); Middle East in World War I and II, establishment of by United Nations, Arab-Jewish conflict, Six-Day War, Palestine Liberation Organization, intifada and retaliation (p. 275)

ITALY: geography, general history, nineteenth and twentieth-century political struggles, cultural contribution, involvement in World War II, current political stability, population demographics (p. 337); turbulent history, Benito Mussolini and World War II, short-lived postwar governments (p. 463)

IVORY COAST: geography, French colonization of, independence, economic history, Burkina Faso (formerly Upper Volta) and Benin identified (p. 48)

JAPAN: geography, general history, nineteenth-century arrival of Perry, expansion policy and World War II, current form of government, population (p. 122)

KUWAIT: geography, Al-Sabah dynasty, as British protectorate, independence, oil exports, sided with Iraq in Iraq/Iran war in 1980s, Iraqi invasion of and U.S. involvement (p. 475); geography, oil fields, Iraqi invasion (p. 696)

MEXICO: general history, Cortés and Spanish explorers (1500s), independence, current economy, contemporary art and literature (p. 15)

NIGERIA: geography, population, general history, nineteenth-century British control of and current influence on, changing political climate, women's expanded role, Bishop Crowther (p. 112); British colonization of, independent commonwealth, civil war in Republic of Biafra (p. 716)

NORTHERN IRELAND: general history, founding of IRA, history of Protestant-Catholic conflict, current political climate (p. 615)

PALESTINE: see Israel

PERU: geography, Spanish colonization of, nineteenth-century independence, population, current government, economic and political problems including guerrilla group Sendero Luminosa (p. 224)

POLAND: date of German invasion of, Czeslaw Milosz's break with Communist government, post–World War II domination by Soviet Union, Solidarity Union's fight for independence, Walesa's Nobel Peace Prize, current democratic political system, economic changes (p. 671)

RUSSIA: history of Soviet Union, perestroika, glasnost, Yeltsin, independence (p. 521); history of Jewish persecution, relationship with Israel, effects of Soviet Union's collapse on Russian Jews (p. 536)

SAUDI ARABIA: geography, structure of government, general history, importance of oil, role in Gulf war (p. 372)

SENEGAL: geography, the Wolof and the diverse ethnic makeup, general history, French colonization of, independence, the West African Economic Community (p. 344)

SOUTH AFRICA: geography, racial makeup, apartheid defined, nineteenth-century founding by Dutch, Anglo-Boer War, history of apartheid, 1961 withdrawal from British Commonwealth (p. 35); mission of the African National Congress, worldwide economic and political pressures, current political climate (p. 587)

Additional Resources

SOVIET UNION (former): establishment, perestroika and glasnost, disbanding of Communist Party, dissolution of, independence of Russia and Georgia (p. 521)
SPAIN: geography, general history including Cristobal Colon's (Christopher Columbus's) discovery of America, American colonies, Spanish influence on Latin America (p. 303)
TURKEY: geography, general history of European and Asian Turkey and of Ottoman Empire, history of Istanbul, Young Turk movement, founding of republic, membership in NATO, economic conditions (p. 380)
UNITED KINGDOM: see Great Britain, Northern Ireland
UNITED STATES: ethnic makeup, population trends (p. 3); Pueblo Culture (p. 312); California Gold Rush, Chinese and Japanese immigrants, the Alien Land Act of California, Japanese internment camps during World War II (p. 497)
VIETNAM: forced unification in 1976, general history, French, Japanese, and Chinese control of, North Vietnamese President Ho Chi Minh and Vietcong guerrillas' war for a single Communist nation, U.S. and Western involvement with South Vietnam (p. 432)
YUGOSLAVIA (former): general history, establishment of Tito's Communist government, secession of member republics, disintegration of, current civil war including Serbian policy of "ethnic cleansing" (p. 646)
ZIMBABWE: geography, British colonization of, independence, tensions between black majority and white minority, drought (p. 569)

BIBLIOGRAPHY

The following sources may be useful for further exploration of literary, biographical, and historical topics and for study of particular countries and regions.

Almanacs, Series, Yearbooks

Britannica Book of the Year. Chicago: Encyclopedia Britannica, 1938–.
Contemporary Authors. Detroit: Gale, 1962–. An up-to-date biographical source on international authors in many subject areas.
Contemporary Literary Criticism. Detroit: Gale, 1973.
Current Biography. New York: Wilson, 1940. Biographical sketches of people in the news, published monthly (except December) and annually in a cumulative volume.
Demographic Yearbook 1990. 42nd ed. New York: United Nations, 1989.
Europa World Year Book. 2 vols. Detroit: Gale, 1993. Detailed information on every country in the world.
Facts on File Yearbook. New York: Facts on File, 1941–. Weekly summaries of news events in *Facts on File: A Weekly World News Digest,* indexed every two weeks, are published cumulatively in this annual volume.
Information Please Almanac. Boston: Houghton Mifflin, 1992. Detailed information on countries of the world.
Political Handbook of the World. New York: McGraw Hill, 1975–. Formerly *Political Handbook and Atlas of the World* (1927-1974), contains information on governments, parties, terminology, and so on.
Statesman's Year-Book 1992–1993. 129th rev. and updated ed. Ed. Brian Hunter. New York: St. Martin's, 1992. Detailed economic data on all the world's countries.
Statistical Yearbook, No. 38. New York: United Nations, 1991.
The Universal Almanac 1993. Ed. John W. Wright. New York: Andrews, 1992.
The World Almanac and Book of Facts. New York: Newspaper Enterprise Assoc., 1868–. Factual material on current and historical topics; contains chronology of previous year's events.

Atlases

Hammond Standard World Atlas. Maplewood, NJ: Hammond, 1983.
National Geographic Atlas of the World. 6th ed. Washington, D.C.: Nat. Geographic Soc., 1990.
Oxford Economic Atlas of the World. 4th ed. Oxford: Oxford UP, 1972.
The Prentice-Hall Great International Atlas. Englewood Cliffs, N.J.: Prentice, 1981.
Rand McNally New Cosmopolitan World Atlas. New Census ed. Chicago: Rand, 1984.
Shepherd, William. *Historical Atlas.* New York: Barnes, 1964. Includes maps for world history
   from 1450 B.C. to the 1960s.
The Times Atlas of the World. 9th Comprehensive ed. New York: Random House, 1992.

Dictionaries and Gazetteers

Columbia Dictionary of Modern European Literature. 2nd ed. Gen. eds. Jean-Albert Bede and
   William B. Edgerton. New York: Columbia UP, 1980.
Dictionary of Geography. rev ed. Ed. W. G. Moore. New York: Penguin, 1950.
Dictionary of Islam. 2 vols. Ed. Thomas P. Hughes. New York: Gordon, 1980.
Facts on File Dictionary of Religion. Ed. John R. Hinnells. New York: Facts on File, 1984.
Lacqueur, Walter. *A Dictionary of Politics.* Rev. ed. New York: Macmillan, 1974. Defines terms,
   provides historical, geographical, biographical information.
The Times Index-Gazetteer of the World. London: Times, 1965. Still useful.
Webster's New Geographical Dictionary Rev. ed. Springfield, Ill. Merriam, 1984.
World Facts in Brief. New York: Rand, 1986. A handy inexpensive student reference.

Specialized Encyclopedias

Encyclopedia of Latin American History. rev ed. Ed. Michael R. Martin and Gabriel H. Lovett.
   1968. Westport, Conn: Greenwood, 1981.
Encyclopedia of World Literature in the 20th Century. 2nd ed. 5 vols. New York: Unger, 1981–
   1993.
Harper Encyclopedia of the Modern World. New York: Harper, 1970. Coverage from 1760
   through the 1960s.
The International Geographic Encyclopedia and Atlas. Boston: Houghton, 1979.
McGraw-Hill Encyclopedia of World Biography. 12 vols. New York: McGraw, 1973. Contains
   approximately 5,000 biographical entries on world figures.
The New Illustrated Encyclopedia of World History. Ed. William L. Langer. 2 vols. New York:
   Abrams, 1975. Arranged chronologically, comprehensively covers from prehistory to
   space exploration.
New Nations: A Student Handbook. Ed. David N. Rowe. New York: Shoe String, 1968.
The Penguin Companion to World Literature. 4 vols. New York: McGraw, 1969–1971. Separate
   volumes for American; English, classical, Oriental, and African; and European literature.

Time Line

Grun, Bernard. *The Timetables of History.* 3rd rev. ed. New York: Touchstone, Simon, 1991. This
   edition is based on Werner Stein's *Kulturfahrplan.* The categories are History and
   Politics; Literature and Theater; Religion, Philosophy, and Learning; Science, Technology, and Growth; and Daily Life.

FILM, VIDEO, AND AUDIOCASSETTE RESOURCES

After a section of general resources, the following list is organized according to the units in *Ourselves Among Others*, Third Edition. Within each section, the entries are organized alphabetically by title (or by author in cases where this information provides a more helpful reference.). A number of entries might be useful for more than one unit. For these entries, the full annotation is provided in what seems to be the most appropriate unit. The entry is then listed in other appropriate units with a cross-reference to the listing with complete information.

The Directory of Distributors at the end of the list of resources can help you locate these films, videos, and audiocassettes if you cannot find them in your own library or local video rental store.

General

Americas in Transition. (1982) "Provides a concise, fast-paced introduction to the underlying causes of unrest in Latin America. Examines the roots of this unrest through a close look at Latin America's history of military dictatorships, attempts at democracy, communist influences, and the role of U.S. involvement." Icarus Films. 3/4-inch video. 29 minutes.
The Bear's Embrace. See "We the People."
Be It Remembered. Documentary, hosted by Eli Wallach, about immigrants past and present. 50 minutes.
The Cummington Story. (1945) "The true story of a family of immigrants settling in a small New England town. The participants re-create their own roles. Shows the difficulty of cultural assimilation." United World Films, Inc. 16 mm. 17 minutes.
The Family Krishnappa. See "The Family"
The First 50 Years: Reflections on U.S.-Soviet Relations. See "The West and the World."
Global Village. (1984) "India hurtles into the modern age, but what about its agrarian economy?" PBS: Nova. 3/4-inch video. 50 minutes.
Immigration. (1974) "Traces the influx into this country . . . shows the contributions made by new citizens as well as the resistance of some of the country's original population. . . . The Order of the Star-Spangled Banner (or Know-Nothings), the Immigration Restriction League, and the Ku Klux Klan are examined in their temporal context." McGraw Hill. 16 mm. 25 minutes.
Israel and the Arab States. (1981) "This program from the "Twentieth-Century History" series explores the establishment of the State of Israel and the resulting Arab disputes over the territory which have continued to the present day." Films, Inc. Beta, 1/2-inch video, 3/4-inch video. 20 minutes.
Japan Reaches for the 21st Century. See "The West and the World."
Latin America, An Overview. (1982) "Examines the people, cultures, religions, and geography which bind the peoples of South America, Central America, and the Caribbean into the area known as Latin America." Vladimir Bibic Productions. 16 mm. 25 minutes.
Legacies. See "Violence."
A Legacy of Lifestyles. See "The West and the World."
Mao and the Cultural Revolution. See "The Family."
Mother Theresa. (1987) Profile of the friend of the poor. PBS. 80 minutes.

The Nature of a Continent. (1986) (Africa) "Ali A. Mazrui hosts this overview of Africa, geographically and historically." PBS: The Africans. 1/2-inch video. 50 minutes.
Planting Seeds for Peace. See "Landmarks and Turning Points."
The Rise of Asian-Americans. PBS: Currents. 25 minutes.
The Shadow of the West. (1987) Part of the series "The Arabs, a Living History." Portland State Univ. Continuing Education. 1/2-inch video. 50 minutes.
Tools of Exploitation. See "The West and the World."

The West and The World

Achebe, Chinua, reads *Arrow of God.* See "Violence."
The Asianization of America. PBS: Currents. 25 minutes.
Atwood, Margaret. (1983) "Margaret Atwood talks about a wide variety of issues pertinent to Atwood's Canadian nationalism, feminism, themes of her individual novels and short stories." American Audio Prose Library. Sound cassette. 55 minutes.
Atwood, Margaret. *Once in August.* (1988) "An intimate view of one of Canada's most elusive literary figures." Wombat Productions (NY). 1/2-inch video. 58 minutes.
Atwood, Margaret. *The Author Reads Excerpts from Bodily Harm and Talks About Politics.* (1986) American Audio Prose Library. Sound cassette. 30 minutes.
Atwood, Margaret. *Surfacing.* (1984) "A young woman and her companions set out to look for her lost father in the hostile wilderness of northern Canada." Media Home Entertainment (Los Angeles). 1/2-inch video. 90 minutes.
Bali: The Mask of Rangda. See "Work."
Be It Remembered. See "General."
Bridging the Culture Gap. See "Work."
The Canadian Federation. (1980) "A succinct overview of the people, politics, and government of Canada, combining interviews with documentary footage." National Film Board of Canada. Beta, VHS, 3/4-inch video. 31 minutes.
China: A New Look. (1988) "A look at what life is like in the world's most populous country." International Film Foundation. Beta, VHS, 3/4-inch video. 25 minutes.
City of Refuge. (1980) "Depicts the successful resettlement of refugees in a small midwestern town. Su Thao, the first Hmong refugee to settle in Iowa, is pictured with his family playing, working, and worshipping with the citizens of Pela, Iowa." Beta, 3/4-inch video, 1/2-inch video, 16 mm. 29 minutes.
Crossing Borders: The Story of the Women's International League for Peace and Freedom. (1988) "A fine assemblage of stills, newsreel footage, headlines, and period songs provides a rich historical backdrop for the group's concerns and activities." Film Project for Women's History and Future. 16 mm, 1/2-inch video. 32 minutes.
The Cummington Story. See "General."
Dim Sum: A Little Bit of Heart. See "The Family."
The First 50 Years: Reflections on U.S.-Soviet Relations. (1985) "A comprehensive guide to relations between the two powers since the establishment of diplomatic ties (1933) to the [mid-eighties]. Traces the up-and-down relationship through the eyes of former U.S. Ambassadors. . . . Rare archival footage . . . a concise synopsis of this critical area of international relations." Cafficus Corp. 3/4-inch video. 58 minutes.
Fuentes, Carlos. *Distant Relations.* See "Women and Men."
Global Village. See "General."
The Gods Must Be Crazy. (1980) "Peaceful primitive Bushmen of Botswana caught up in 'civilized' man's violence." Playhouse Video. Beta, VHS. 110 minutes.
Immigration. See "General."

Italian Family. (1975) "On the shores of Lake Bracciano, about thirty miles from Rome, the Giorgetti family carries on the age old traditions of Italian rural life." Britannica Films. Beta, VHS, 3/4-inch video. 30 minutes.

Japan 2000. (1989) "A look at some of the things that the Japanese do to make their products inexpensive and of high quality." Great Plains National Instructional Television Library. Beta, VHS, 3/4-inch video. 2 programs, 30 minutes each.

Japan: The Nation Family. See "The Family."

Japan Reaches for the 21st Century. (1986) "This documentary examines the history and current social structure of Japan, and predicts changes in Japanese society likely to occur as a result of its rapidly growing high technology industries and economy." International Motion Picture Co. 1/2-inch video. 58 minutes.

The Japan They Don't Talk About. See "Work."

Japan at Work. See "Work."

Japanese Women. See "Women and Men."

Latin America, An Overview. See "General."

A Legacy of Lifestyles. (1986) "Modern Africa has been shaped by indigenous, Islamic, and Western influences." PBS: The Africans. 1/2-inch video. 50 minutes.

Mexican Tapes: El Gringo; El Ranch Grande; La Lucha; Winner's Circle. "Four videos explore the lives of Mexicans living as illegal aliens in Southern California." Facets Multimedia. Beta, VHS. 60 minutes each.

The Mexican Way of Life. (1988) "Diversity of Mexican culture is thoroughly explored." AIMS Media, Inc. Beta, VHS, 3/4-inch video. 23 minutes.

Miles from the Border. (1987) "Twenty years after emigration from rural Mexico to southern California, Manuela and Ben Aparico, who arrived in their teens and now work as school counselors with other young newcomers, share their experiences of dislocation . . . and the pressures to succeed in an ethically divided community." New Day Films (New York). 1/2-inch video. 15 minutes.

Mphahlele, Es'kia. *Alex La Guma Discusses the Life and Work of Es'kia Mphahlele.* (1966) Transcription Feature Service (London). Sound cassette, no. 2 on side 2. 19 minutes.

Mphahlele, Es'kia. *Es'kia Mphahlele Chairs a Discussion on West African Writing with African Authors Kofi Awoonor and John Pepper Clark.* (1962) Transcription Feature Service (London). Sound cassette, no. 1 on side 2. 39 minutes.

Mphahlele, Es'kia. *The Author Interviewed by Cosmo Pieterse.* (1968) "The author discusses his writing and the influence of traditional oral literature on modern African writing." Transcription Feature Service (London). Sound cassette, no. 1 on side 2. 44 minutes.

Mphahlele, Es'kia. *Lecture on Black Writing.* (1976) Cornell Univ. Africana Studies and Research Center. Sound cassette. 90 minutes.

The Nature of a Continent. See "General."

Paz, Octavio. *Focus on Octavio Paz: The Great Mexican Poet Talks About His Life and Work.* (1971) The Center for Cassette Studies. Sound cassette. 28 minutes.

Reed, Ishmael. *Big Ego.* (1978) Giorni Poetry Systems Records (New York). 2 sound discs.

Reed, Ishmael. *Flight to Canada.* (1977) New Letters on Air (Kansas City, Mo.). Sound cassette. 29 minutes.

Reed, Ishmael. *Ishmael Reed.* "Reed reads poetry and talks about his battle with some black women writers and his opposition to being labeled a Black writer." American Audio Prose. 1 cassette. 30 minutes.

Reed, Ishmael. *The Poet Reading His Poetry.* (1976) Cornell Univ. Sound cassette. 65 minutes.

The Rise of Asian-Americans. See "General."

The Shadow of the West. See "General."

Tools of Exploitation. (1986) "The history of imperialism — how Africa's natural and human resources were stolen." PBS: The Africans. 1/2-inch video. 50 minutes.

Zimbabwe. See "We the People."

The Family: Cornerstone of Culture

After Solidarity: Three Polish Families in America. (1987) "Depicts the assimilation trials and tribulations of three Polish families in America. . . . Children are the quickest to adjust, followed by the husbands and then the wives." Filmmakers Library. 1/2-inch video. 58 minutes.

Argument About a Marriage. (1966) "Documents a conflict between two groups of Bushmen in the Kalahari Desert over the legitimization of a marriage. The entire conflict is shown with the Bushmen voices and a few subtitles." National Geographic Society. 16 mm. 18 minutes.

Caring. (1984) The urban Chinese family: a case study in the industrial city of Harbin. PBS: The Heart of the Dragon. Beta, 3/4-inch video. 50 minutes.

China: A New Look. See "The West and the World."

China in Revolution. See "We the People."

Dadi's Family. (1979) "Portrait of the women of an extended family in northern India focuses on Dadi, the grandmother, and her ability to maintain a family unit threatened not only by social and economic change but also by internal pressures within the family." PBS Video. 16 mm, 1/2-inch video. 59 minutes.

Dim Sum: A Little Bit of Heart. (1985) "Intergenerational differences in a Chinese-American family." Pacific Arts Video. 80 minutes.

Dorris, Michael. *Born Drunk: Fetal Alcohol Syndrome.* "A series of reports on a defect that's 100 percent preventable." National Public Radio. 1 audiocassette. 45 minutes.

Erdrich, Louise. *Reading and Interview.* (1986) "Erdrich and her husband and collaborator, Michael Dorris, talk about how they work out of a unified vision based on their backgrounds as mixed blood natives. She reads from *Love Medicine* and *Beet Queen.*" American Audio Prose. 2 cassettes.

Families: Will They Survive? (1981) "Examines the importance of the family unit in various cultures. Studies the extended and nuclear families that have existed throughout human history and how each is faring today." Avatar Learning, Inc. 16 mm. 23 minutes.

The Family Krishnappa. (1976) "A realistic documentation of one day in the life of a typical rural family and its village in Southern India. Household tasks . . . farming . . . education . . . religion . . . and social customs are also dealt with." Benchmark Films, Inc. 16 mm. 18 minutes.

The Gods Must Be Crazy. See "The West and the World."

The Good Earth. (edited) (1943) "Pearl S. Buck's story of a Chinese family depicting family life, customs, and the sociological struggle in poverty-ridden China." Films, Inc. 16 mm. 42 minutes.

Guatemala: Roads of Silence. (1988) "This documentary examines Indian life in Guatemala's internal refugee camp where military repression and widescale human rights violations are a daily occurrence." Cinema Guild. Beta, VHS, 3/4-inch video. 59 minutes.

Hong Kong: A Family Portrait. See "Landmarks and Turning Points"

Iran: A Revolution Betrayed (1984) "The events which led up to the Iranian revolution and its aftermath, leaving a trail of political and religious unrest." Films, Inc. Beta, VHS, 3/4-inch video. 60 minutes.

Iran: A Righteous Republic (1989) "The effects of the Gulf War on Iran are considered." Landmark Films, Inc. Beta, VHS, 3/4-inch video. 48 minutes.

Iran: The Other Story (1989) "An examination of the political left in Iran, the fleeting movements which over the years have opposed the government's right fundamentalism." Cinema Guild. VHS. 52 minutes.

Iran and Iraq: Background to the War. See "Violence."

Israel— The Promise of the Jewish People. (1988) "Explores the relationship between the Jewish people and their country, through interviews with Russian refuseniks, Arabs and Jews who live side by side, soldiers, . . . and children." Etz Chaim Fdn. 1/2-inch video. 60 minutes.

Italian Family. See "The West and the World."

Japan 2000. See "The West and the World."

Japan: The Nation Family. (1980) "Examines how the Japanese have developed their technology to an unimagined extent. Part of a PBS series." Wombat Productions. Beta, VHS, 3/4-inch video. 51 minutes.

Japan Reaches for the 21st Century. See "The West and the World."

Japan at Work. See "Work."

Japanese Women. See "Women and Men."

Mao and the Cultural Revolution.: China Scholar John King Fairbank Examines Mao's Cultural Revolution. (1972) Center for Cassette Studies. Sound cassette. 23 minutes.

Marrying. See "Women and Men."

Mehta, Ved. *Chachaji: My Poor Relation*. (1978) "An intense film about the daily struggle for survival in . . . India. Ved Mehta seeks to illuminate an entire people by telling us the story of one man's fierce will to survive." 16 mm. 58 minutes.

Mehta, Ved. *Daddyji*. (1989) Read by David Case. Books on Tape (Newport Beach). 5 sound cassettes.

Middle East Series: Family Matters. (1984) "Shows how the family is central in Middle Eastern society and politics. Details the historical and environmental patterns of extended family development and cultural norms found in the Middle East." Encyclopedia Britannica Educational Corp. 1/2-inch video and teacher's guide. 25 minutes.

Nigeria: Africa in Miniature. (1966) "Describes locations, provinces, topography, cities, and rivers of Nigeria." AIMS Media, Inc. Beta, VHS, 3/4-inch video. 16 minutes.

Nigeria— Problems of Nation Building. (1968) "Survey of Nigeria: its geography, economy, and people, stressing tribalism and nationalism." Atlantis Productions. Beta, VHS, 21 minutes.

Rana. See "Landmarks and Turning Points."

The Three Grandmothers. "A glimpse into the lives of three grandmothers living in widely differing parts of the world: an African village in Nigeria, a hill city in Brazil, and a rural community in Manitoba." National Film Board of Canada. 16 mm. 28 minutes.

Landmarks and Turning Points: The Struggle for Identity

Argentina's Jews: Days of Awe. (1990) "Jews came to Argentina and founded the agricultural community of Moiseville. This video provides a history of Argentine Jews and their current battles with anti-Semitism, assimilation, and loss of Jewish identity." Ergo Media. VHS. 55 minutes.

Hong Kong: A Family Portrait (1979) "Provides a look at Hong Kong, a city concerned with family, luck, gambling, and survival." Live Home Video. 3/4-inch video. 59 minutes.

Hong Kong: Living on Borrowed Time. (1984) "Examines Hong Kong's inhabitants and international markets." Journal Films. Beta, VHS, 3/4-inch video. 28 minutes.

Mexican Tapes. See "The West and the World."

The Mexican Way of Life. See "The West and the World."

Oates, Joyce Carol. *The Author Reads from* Angel of Light *and Discusses Violence, Slavery, Revenge, Grotesques, and the American Novel.* (1980) In Our Time Arts Media (New York). Sound Cassette. 30 minutes.

Peru: Inca Heritage. (1970) "Explores contemporary life of the Peruvian Indians and the remains of the Incan culture." AIMS Media. Beta, VHS, 3/4-inch video. 17 minutes.

Planting Seeds for Peace. (1989) "Focuses on the relationships among four Israeli, Arab, Jewish, and Palestinian teenagers who come together in the U.S. to share their cultures, their personal lives, break down stereotypes, and present their views to U.S. Teens." Educational Film & Video Project. 1/2-inch video. 23 minutes.

Rana. (1977) "Follows the everyday activities of a young Moslem college student in Old Delhi. Points out the restrictions of her religion and includes interviews with her family." Wombat Productions (New York). 16 mm, 1/2-inch video. 19 minutes.

Tan, Amy. *The Joy Luck Club.* (1989) The author reads her novel. Dove Books on Tape. 2 sound cassettes.

Vargas Llosa, Mario, with John King. (1984) "Vargas Llosa discusses his works, including *War of the End of the World.*"Institute of Contemporary Arts: The Roland Collection. 1/2-inch video. 48 minutes.

Vargas Llosa, Mario. *La Ciudad y los Perros.* (1987) In Spanish with English subtitles. Media Home Entertainment. 1/2-inch video.

Women and Men: Images of the Opposite Sex

Argument About a Marriage. See "The Family."

Beauvoir, Simone de. (1960) One of the founders of the women's liberation movement is interviewed by Studs Terkel. "Discusses Beauvoir's book *The Second Sex* and goes deeply into her philosophy of commitment to causes." Center for Cassette Studies. Sound cassette. 29 minutes.

Beauvoir, Simone de. (1982) "The author . . . discusses politics, feminism, aging, and death. . . . Helps bring the written works of the author alive." Interama Video Classics. 1/2-inch video.

Beauvoir, Simone de. *A Sound Portrait of Simone de Beauvoir.* (1980) "Dramatizes Simone de Beauvoir's life and ideas as a pioneer feminist." NPR: A Question of Place: Sound Portraits of Twentieth Century Humanists. NPR, Education Services, Washington, D.C. Sound cassette and summary sheet. 60 minutes.

Beauvoir, Simone de. "Pioneer feminist speaks out." PBS: Vive la France! 52 minutes.

Crossing Borders: The Story of The Women's International League for Peace and Freedom. See "The West and the World."

Faces of Women. (1985) "Feminism, economics, and tradition in modern-day Africa." New Yorker Films Video. 1/2-inch video. 105 minutes.

Fuentes, Carlos. *Distant Relations.* Read by Carlos Fuentes. "Fuentes talks about how the New World corrupts the Old in his novel and reads from *Distant Relations.*" American Audio Prose. 1 audiocassette. 30 minutes.

Germans and Their Men. (1990) "A feminist-oriented look at men in German government and what is being done to improve the lot of women." Women Making Movies. VHS. 96 minutes.

India Cabaret. (1987) "A group of Indian strippers, who meet with difficulty because their stance as single women is not socially acceptable, is followed through daily routine." Filmmakers' Library. 16 mm, 1/2-inch video. 60 minutes.

Islam, The Veil and the Future. (1980) Marriage and divorce, voting and dress for Moslem women. PBS Video. 1/2-inch video. 29 minutes.

Japanese Women. (1987) "The status of women in modern-day Japan is examined in this insightful film." National Film Board of Canada. Beta, VHS, 3/4-inch video. 53 minutes.

Latin America, An Overview. See "General."

Marrying. (1984) "A rural wedding, followed by a look at the changing role of women in Chinese society.: PBS: The Heart of the Dragon. Beta, 3/4-inch video. 50 minutes.

Moravia, Alberto. (1976) "Profile/interview with Moravia about his writing, his social concerns, views on fascism and Italy, accompanied by dramatic readings from his novels." Facets Multimedia. Beta, 1/2-inch video. 55 minutes.

Moravia, Alberto. *The Conformist.* (1986) English version. Paramount Home Video. 1/2-inch video. 108 minutes.

Moravia, Alberto. *Two Women.* (1987) "A shopkeeper and her daughter flee Rome during World War II, and upon their return are brutally attacked by marauding soldiers. They are left traumatized, and must fight to restore dignity and value to their lives." Embassy Home Entertainment. 1/2-inch video. 99 minutes.

Mother Ireland. See "Violence."

No Longer Silent. (1987) "Gives an overview of degrading and cruel treatment of women in India. The women are organizing workshops and resource centers to help them become aware of the help that is available." National Film Board of Canada; International Film Bureau. 16 mm, 1/2-inch video. 57 minutes.

Rape/Crisis. (1983) Docudrama about sexual violence. PBS: Independent Focus Retrospective. Beta, 3/4-inch video. 87 minutes.

Rape Is a Social Disease. (1975) "The interrelationship of women's image and rape is depicted through classical art and modern advertising. Structural sexual roles indirectly indicate how violence against women is accepted in our society." Women in Focus. 3/4-inch video, special order formats. 28 minutes.

Rape: The Savage Crime. (1975) The procedures that follow when a woman reports a rape are examined.... The impersonal and often hostile attitudes displayed by police officers and medical examiners . . . recent police reforms, such as special rape units, that have been created to deal with the problem." The Center for Humanities. 1/2-inch video. 27 minutes.

Saudi Arabia Today. (1987) "Introduces viewers to the people, land, politics, and customs of this Middle-Eastern country." Modern Talking Picture Service. 3/4-inch video. 28 minutes.

The Saudis. (1980) "Politics and business in Saudia Arabia." Phoenix/BFA. Beta, VHS, 3/4-inch video. 49 minutes.

A Sense of Honor. (1984) "Condemns modern stereotypes of Arabic women and offers information on the lifestyle, beliefs, customs, and social situations of fundamentalist Islamic women." BBC Films, Inc. 1/2-inch video. 55 minutes.

The Shadow of the West. See "General."

Silko, Leslie Marmon. *Leslie Marmon Silko.* "Silko reads from her epic novel *Almanac of the Dead* and talks about a return to tribal values in the Americas." New Letters. 1 audiocassette. 29 minutes.

Silko, Leslie Marmon. *Running on the Edge of the Rainbow: Laguna Stories and Poems.* (1981) "Leslie Marmon Silko talks about the nature of Laguna storytelling, its functions, and more of the problems she has faced using Laguna stories in her own work." Univ. of Arizona. 1/2-inch video and transcript. 28 minutes.

Taking Back the Night. (1981) "This program provides a comprehensive look at the problem of violence against women." Washington Univ. in St. Louis. 3/4-inch video. 20 minutes.

A Veiled Revolution. (1982) "In 1932, revolutionary Egyptian women were the first to publicly cast off the veil. Wearing western dress, they demanded rights for women, the vote, and equal education. Yet today, old feminists look on with dismay as their granddaughters reject western dress, putting the veil back on again." Icarus Films NY. 1/2-inch video. 27 minutes.

Women of the Toubou. (1974) "The Toubou of the Sahara are a happy and cheerful people of grace, elegance, and dignity. Toubou women are treated as equals by the men, they share every aspect of life." Phoenix BFA Films & Video, Inc. 16 mm. 25 minutes.

Women Under Siege (1982). "Rashadiyah . . . had become the setting for a camp housing 14,000 Palestinian refugees. . . . Women play a crucial role . . . as mothers, teachers, political organizers, farm laborers, and fighters." Companion film to *A Veiled Revolution.* Icarus Films NY. 1/2-inch video. 26 minutes.

Work: We Are What We Do

Angelou, Maya. (1979) "Angelou reads some of her poetry and talks about herself and her accomplishments as a writer." Tapes for Readers (Washington, D.C.). Sound cassette.

Angelou, Maya. (1986) The author reads *I Know Why the Caged Bird Sings* (abridged). Random House Audio Books. 2 sound cassettes. 179 minutes.

Angelou, Maya. *Black Women in the Women's Movement.* (1980) "Social activist Angela Davis, writer Maya Angelou, and other Black women discuss the role of the Black women in the women's movement." NPR (Washington, D.C.). Sound cassette. 29 minutes.

Angelou, Maya. *Making Magic in the World.* (1988) "Presents a trip from the Deep South to the heart of Africa and back again." New Dimensions Foundation. 1 cassette. 60 minutes.

Angelou, Maya. *Of Life and Poetry.* (1978) Encyclopaedia Americana/CBS News Audio Resource Library. Sound cassette.

Angelou, Maya. *Our Sheroes and Heroes.* (1983) "Angelou talks about her first friendship with a white woman, her sense of religion, . . . and the difference between white and black women." Pacifica Radio Archive (Los Angeles). Sound cassette. 34 minutes.

Angelou, Maya. (1974) "Angelou discusses her life in such places as Arkansas, San Francisco, Ghana, and Israel." Center for Cassette Studies. Sound cassette. 27 minutes.

Bali: The Mask of Rangda. (1974) "Authentic picture of a culture as yet untouched by the West." Hartley Film Foundation. Beta, VHS, 3/4-inch video. 30 minutes.

Brazil. (1985). "Vivid but sobering view of a world where the work ethic has replaced all else." MCA Home Video. 1/2-inch video. 131 minutes.

Bridging the Culture Gap. (1983) "Presents some of the cultural differences Americans must be attuned to and accept, in order to function effectively socially and in business overseas." Copeland Griggs (San Francisco). 1/2-inch video and guide. 28 minutes.

Japan 2000. See "The West and the World."

Japan: The Nation Family. See "The Family."

Japan Reaches for the 21st Century. See "The West and the World."

The Japan They Don't Talk About. (1986) "The lives of Japanese workers are depicted. Contrary to the belief that Japan is thriving and equal opportunities exist in the work force, this film presents the 70 percent of Japanese workers who are paid low wages for long hours under poor conditions." NBC International Films. 1/2-inch video. 52 minutes.

Japan at Work. (1989) "Three case studies illustrate how efficient and hard working the average Japanese worker is." Journal Films. Beta, VHS, 3/4-inch video, 30 minutes.

Japanese Women. See "Women and Men."

Film, Video, and Audiocassette

Kottar: Model for Development. (1979) "In southern India, fishermen, weavers, and other craftspeople have joined in cooperative ventures to increase their incomes and improve their lives. Kottar, the prototype for an entire network of production and marketing cooperation, is documented in several distinct segments." Catholic Relief Services. 16 mm. 18 minutes.

García Márquez, Gabriel. *Magic and Reality.* (1982) "Presents a literary history of García Márquez, through conversations with the author, his friends, and his critics. . . . Explores the history of Colombia." Films for the Humanities (Princeton, N.J.). 16 mm, 1/2-inch video. 60 minutes.

García Márquez, Gabriel. *Magic and Reality.* (1984) "Delves into the world of . . . García Márquez — where historical riots and levitating grandmothers appear to be equally real (or unreal). Shot on the Colombian coast in Aracataca, the Banana Zone, Cienaga, and Barranquilla . . . the film features the author himself and the people of whom he writes." 1/2-inch video. 60 minutes.

García Márquez, Gabriel. "The Solitude of Latin America." In *Faces, Mirrors, Masks: Twentieth-Century Latin American Fiction.* (1984) NPR (Washington, D. C.). Sound cassette. 30 minutes.

No Longer Silent. See "Women and Men."

Two Factories: Japanese and American. (1974) "A documentary comparing and contrasting the environment of two electronic firms: Sylvania in Batavia, New York, and Matsushita in Osaka, Japan. The film examines similarities and differences in needs, employees, and management." Beta, 3/4-inch video. 22 minutes.

Updike, John. *The Author in Conversation with Claire Tomalin.* (1986) "Updike discusses his life and works." The Roland Collection. 1/2-inch video. 52 minutes.

Updike, John. *What Makes Rabbit Run?: A Profile of John Updike.* "Documents the life and work of John Updike. Shows Updike on a promotional tour for his novel *Rabbit Is Rich;* at his childhood home, at the offices of *The New Yorker,* where he was a staff member in the fifties; and at home with his family." Barr Films. 16 mm, 1/2-inch video. 57 minutes.

Vietnam: After the Fire. (1988) "An award-winning, two part documentary which examines the Vietnam conflict." Cinema Guild. Beta, VHS, 3/4-inch video. 53 minutes.

Vietnam Reconsidered. (1988) Thomas Vallely, a state representative from Massachusetts, returned to Vietnam in August 1985, 16 years after he left as a Marine. This film documents his attempt to understand his past and present." Northern Lights Productions. Beta, VHS, 3/4-inch video. 15 minutes.

Vietnam Under Communism. (1989) "Examines what is going on in Vietnam now almost 20 years after the war ended." PBS Video. Beta, VHS, 3/4-inch video. 60 minutes.

Village Man, City Man. (1975) "Shows the life of a young mill worker in an industrial section of Delhi and follows him on a return visit to his village. Changes and continuities in his life are documented through conversations with his friends at the mill . . . and by observing his work. The film suggests that Western models of change and modernization do not necessarily apply to the Indian context." Univ. of Wisconsin. 16 mm. 40 minutes.

We the People: Individuals and Institutions

Americas in Transition. See "General."

The Bear's Embrace. "Shows how the decade of rule by Nikita Khrushchev thrust the Soviet Union into a critical position of international leadership. . . . Covers his movement within the Communist Party in the Ukraine, through the Stalin era, his ascension to Party Secretary, his rise to full leadership, and his final collapse and removal." Learning Corporation of America. 16 mm. 24 minutes.

Brazil: No Time for Tears. See "Violence."

Chile: Hasta Caundo? See "Violence."

China in Revolution. (1989) "Recounts the thirty eight years between 1911 and 1949, during which China was transformed from a centuries-old empire into the world's largest Communist state." Coronet Multimedia. Two 1/2-inch videos. 58 minutes each.

Crossing Borders: The Story of The Women's International League for Peace and Freedom. See "The West and the World."

Cuba: Angry Exiles. (1984) "History of hostility between U.S. and Cuba." Journal Films. Beta, VHS, 3/4-inch video. 14 minutes.

Cuba: In the Shadow of Doubt. (1986) "Examines the origins of Castro's revolution and the current state of Cuban society, including the contrasts between its socialism and the political repression faced by the average person." Filmmakers' Library. VHS, 3/4-inch video. 58 minutes.

Czechoslovakia in Chains. (1983) "Examines 1968 Russian military coup of Czechoslovakia." King Features Entertainment. Beta, VHS, 3/4-inch video. 15 minutes.

Germans and Their Men. See "Women and Men."

Gordimer, Nadine. *City Lovers, Country Lovers: The Gordimer Stories.* (1984) MGM/UA Home Video. 1/2-inch video. 121 minutes.

Gordimer, Nadine. *The Author Reads "A City of the Dead," "A City of the Living," and "The Termitary."* (1986) Spoken Arts. Sound cassette. 58 minutes.

Guns, Drugs, and the CIA. (1988) "Investigates the CIA and its use of drug money to finance covert activities. Concentrates on drug trafficking activities from the Vietnam War to the Contra affair." PBS Video (Alexandria, Va.). 1/2-inch video. 58 minutes.

Mandela, Nelson. *Nelson and Winnie Mandela: South African Leaders Against Apartheid.* "Profiles Nelson and Winnie Mandela. The Mandelas' history since Nelson's imprisonment [but before his release] is revealed through interviews with Winnie, as well as with other friends who have shared the couple's fight against apartheid." NPR (Washington, D.C.). Sound cassette. 29 minutes.

Mandela, Nelson. *Mandela.* (1987) "Traces the life of Nelson Mandela through the founding of the African National Congress, his marriage to Winnie, and his trial and imprisonment for treason." HBO Video (New York). 1/2-inch video. 135 minutes.

Mandela, Nelson. *Mandela in America.* (1990) "An insider's view of the most memorable moments of Nelson Mandela's trip and his message on the continuing struggle against apartheid." Globalvision (New York, NY). VHS, 3/4-inch video. 90 minutes.

Mandela, Nelson. *Part of My Soul Went with Him: Dramatic Readings Based on Journals and Letters of Winnie and Nelson Mandela.* (1985) Norton Publishers (New York). Sound cassette. 60 minutes.

Mao and the Cultural Revolution. See "The Family"

Missing. (1984) "Based on an actual event, the story involves the search by a wife and father for a young American writer and filmmaker who has disappeared during a South American military coup." MCA Video. 1/2-inch video. 122 minutes.

Moravia, Alberto. *The Conformist.* See "Women and Men."

Nigeria — Problems of Nation Building. See "The Family."

Planting Seeds for Peace. See "Landmarks and Turning Points."

Poland. See "Violence."

Poland: A Year of Solidarity. See "Violence."

Return from Silence: China's Revolutionary Writers. (1983) "Interviews with five writers are intercut with old photographs, archival footage, and scenes of performances of the writers' major works. A compelling and enlightening look at recent Chinese history." 1/2-inch video. 58 minutes.

Film, Video, and Audiocassette

Russia: Off the Record. (1988) "American television crews talk to typical Soviet citizens about how their life really is." Journal Films. Beta, VHS, 3/4-inch video. 58 minutes.

South Africa Belongs to Us. (1980) "Interviews with five women living under apartheid. . . . Includes brief interviews with Winnie Mandela and other women involved in the anti-apartheid movement." California Newsreel. 1/2-inch video. 35 minutes.

South Africa: The Solution. (1989) "Historical factors are given to show why South Africa is in the state it is today. A view is also given of how it might look in the future." Journal Films. Beta, VHS, 3/4-inch video. 38 minutes.

South Africa Today: A Question of Power. (1988) "Two South African newspaper editors, one black, one white, talk about the problems their country faces." Journal Films. Beta, VHS, 3/4-inch video. 55 minutes.

Spear of the Nation: The Story of the African National Congress. (1986) California Newsreel (San Francisco). 1/2-inch video. 55 minutes.

Stalin: Man and Image. (1979) "Documents Stalin's rise to supreme power in the Soviet Union from the pre-revolutionary period through the late 1930's. Focuses on Stalin's use of image to expand his power." Learning Corporation of America. 16 mm. 24 minutes.

Stand Your Ground. "The South African group Juluka's response to human rights abuses in that country." Warner Bros. (251551-1).

Tools of Exploitation. See "The West and the World."

Witness to Apartheid. "A look at how racism and police violence affect children." PBS: Intercom. 1/2-inch video. 50 minutes.

Women Under Siege. See "Women and Men."

Zimbabwe. (1988) "Interviews with Robert Mugabe, Joshua Nkomo, Ian Smith, and others trace the history of Zimbabwe through the European search for gold and minerals to the overthrow of white minority rule in the 1970s." Cinema Guild. Beta, VHS, 3/4-inch video. 30 minutes.

Zimbabwe: The New Struggle. (1985) "The current political, social, and economic development of the newly independent nation of Zimbabwe is explored." Icarus Films. 3/4-inch video. 58 minutes.

Violence

48 Hours on Crack Street. (1986) A presentation of CBS News (New York). 1/2-inch video. 120 minutes.

Achebe, Chinua. "Achebe discusses the impact of colonialism on his culture and relates that he began his own writing in reaction to certain stereotypes in western literature." Transcription Feature Service (London). Sound cassette. 30 minutes.

Achebe, Chinua. Interviewed by Jack Ludwis. (1968) "Discussion of the Nigerian-Biafran war, and the involvement of . . . writers in the conflict." Transcription Feature Service (London). Sound cassette, no. 2 on side 2. 34 minutes.

Achebe, Chinua. Interviewed by Robert Serumaga. (1967) "The author discusses his childhood, and the political situation reflected in his novels *Things Fall Apart, A Man of the People, and Arrow of God.* "Transcription Feature Service (London). Sound cassette, no. 1 on side 1. 22 minutes.

Achebe, Chinua, reads *Arrow of God.* (1988) "Achebe reading excerpts from two works: *Arrow of God,* a tale of the colonial and missionary encroachment upon traditional Ibo culture, and *Anthills of the Savannah,* a novel about the making of a dictator in contemporary Africa." American Audio Prose Library. Sound cassette. 88 minutes.

All Our Lives. (1986) "Women who were radicals during the Spanish Civil War discuss their activities and experiences as social reformers. Members of the Confederación Nacional de Trabajo, they had occupations ranging from journalism to nursing and technology." In Spanish with English subtitles. The Media Project, Cinema Guild. 1/2-inch video. 54 minutes.

Americas in Transition. See "General."

Apocalypse Now. (1979) Based on Conrad's *Heart of Darkness,* among the first convincing renderings of the Vietnam experience. Paramount Home Video. Beta, VHS. 150 minutes.

Beyond War: A New Way of Thinking. (1983) "Uses brief statements edited from . . . interviews to explore the reasons why war has become obsolete as a means of resolving conflict. . . . The possibility of new ways to relate to other nations, other cultures, other peoples are expressed by many of those interviewed." 16 mm, 1/2-inch video.

Brazil: No Time for Tears. (1971) "Nine recently released Brazilian political prisoners recount their ordeals under torture." Tricontinental Film Center. 16 mm. 40 minutes.

Chickamauga. (1968) "Adaptation of Ambrose Bierce's story which creates a symbolic world of the horrors of war as a little boy wanders away from home, reaches a battlefield, plays soldier among the dead and dying, and returns to find his house burned and his family slain." Educational Films, Inc. 16 mm.

Chile: By Reason or By Force. (1983) "The ten year anniversary of the military overthrow of Salvador Allende's Popular Unity coaltion government is documented." Cinema Guild. Beta, VHS, 3/4-inch video. 60 minutes.

Chile: Hasta Caundo? (1986) "Oscar nominated, documents the political repression in Chile under General Augusto Pinochet's brutal dictatorship." Filmmakers' Library, Inc. VHS, 3/4-inch video. 57 minutes.

Chile: I Don't Take Your Name in Vain. (1984) "The 'National Days of Protest,' which challenged the military dictatorship in Chile during 1985, are chronicled." Icarus Films. 3/4-inch video. 55 minutes.

China in Revolution. See "We the People."

The Deer Hunter. (1978) "The effect of the Vietnam war on the lives of several Pennsylvania steelworkers." MCA Home Video. Beta, VHS. 183 minutes.

Gaza Ghetto. (1984) "The Gaza Strip's half-million Palestinians live in the Israel-occupied territory most neglected by the outside world. This film investigates Israeli policy toward the area and interviews Israeli officials. The reality of life for the people . . . is brought into focus by the film's portrayal of the daily life of one family." Icarus Films (New York). 1/2-inch video. 82 minutes.

Guernica — Pablo Picasso. (1953) "The horror and ugliness of war and inhumanity are passionately depicted in Picasso's painting *Guernica.* Shows an understanding and empathy necessary to render one of the great artistic achievements of the 20th century." 16 mm. 15 minutes.

The Hooded Men. (1986) "This documentary describes methods of torture used on political prisoners in a number of countries." CBC Enterprises. 1/2-inch video. 56 minutes.

The Hundred Years War. (1983) "Focuses on the lives of individual Palestinians in Israel and on the Gush Emunim movement among Israeli settlers." Icarus Films (New York). Two 1/2-inch videos. 98 minutes each.

Iran: A Righteous Republic. See "The Family."

Irish News, British Stories. (1989) "Examines the way the political situation of Northern Ireland is portrayed on British television." Faction Films. 1/2-inch video.

Israel — The Promise of the Jewish People. See "The Family."

Film, Video, and Audiocassette

Israel and the Arab States. See "General."

Israel: The Golan and Sinai Question. (1984) "Explores the history of Golan and Sinai, their strategic values, and their roles in the Middle East Peace Plan." Journal Films. Beta. VHS, 3/4-inch video. 19 minutes.

Israel: The Other Reality. "Israel's Arabs and Jews try to explain why the hatred between these two races continues after thousands of years." Wombat Productions. Beta, VHS, 3/4-inch video. 58 minutes.

Israel vs. the PLO. (1990) "Examines how the invasion of Lebanon radically changed the character of the country." MPI Home Video. VHS. 60 minutes.

Israel's Shattered Dreams. (1988) "1988 Cable's Best Documentary." MPI Home Video. VHS. 173 minutes.

The Killing Fields. (1984) Adapted from the story "The Death and Life of Dith Pran" by Sydney Schanberg, about "a journalist who covered the war in Cambodia . . . and Dith, the translator and aide, who is exiled to Cambodian labor camps where millions have died." Warner Home Video. 1/2-inch video. 142 minutes.

Latin America, An Overview. See "General"

Legacies. (1983) "Shows the violence and destruction that have asssailed the peopleof Vietnam, Laos, and Cambodia, even since the withdrawal of U.S. troops. Discusses the change in Chinese and American relations and the lack of formal diplomatic relations of the United States with Vietnam." Films Inc. (Chicago). 1/2-inch video.

Miloz, Czeslaw. *Fire.* (1987) "The author reads selections from *Unattainable Earth* and other works. Some selections are in English and Polish." Watershed Fdn. Washington, D.C.). Sound cassette.

Missing. See "We the People."

Moravia, Alberto. *Two Women.* See "Women and Men."

Mother Ireland. (1989) "Examines the centuries-old imagery which has portrayed Ireland as a woman and discusses the social function of these stereotypes of Irish womanhood, and their relationship to the nationalist struggle and Irish women today." Celtic Production (NY). 1/2-inch video. 52 minutes.

Nigeria: Africa in Miniature. See "The Family."

Nigeria — Problems of Nation Building. See "The Family."

No Neutral Ground. (1983) "The fate of two of Vietnam's weaker neighbors was decided as the south disintegrated. The U.S. extension of the war into Laos and Cambodia to stop attacks and supplies from across those borders hurt those countries more that it hurt the object of the attack." Films Inc. (Chicago). 1/2-inch video.

Northern Ireland, Past and Present. (1986) "Giovanni Costigan lectures on the religious and political struggle in Northern Ireland.: Bellingham, Wash. 1/2-inch video. 53 minutes.

Palestinians. (1983) "Palestinian men and women of various ages describe how they feel as refugees in foreign countries. They describe the problems of scattered families and the lack of understanding by outsiders." Martha Stuart Communications. 1/2-inch video. 29 minutes.

"Planting Seeds for Peace." See "Landmarks and Turning Points."

Poland, A European Country. See "We the People."

Poland. (1988) "The story of vigorous people who have struggled a long time to maintain their independence." Journal Films. Beta, VHS, 3/4-inch video. 26 minutes.

Poland: A Year of Solidarity. (1984) "Charts history of the Solidarity movement." Journal Films. Beta, VHS, 3/4-inch video, 25 minutes.

South Africa Belongs to Us. See "We the People."

Street Drugs and Medicine Chests. (1986) "Recovering addicts tell their stories and debunk some commonly held myths about drugs. All the addicts are white and middle-class." PBS Video (Alexandria, Va.). 1/2-inch video. 18 minutes.

The Struggles for Poland. (1988) "Documents the history of Poland in the 20th century through the use of archival films, newsreels, stills, interviews, and readings from novels and poems." Companion book also issued: *The Struggles for Poland* by Neal Ascherson. PBS Video (Alexandria, Va.). 1/2-inch video, 9 cassettes, 58 minutes each.

Tiananmen Square: A Blow by Blow Account. (1989) SUNY Albany Audiovisual Center. 1/2-inch video.

Tiananmen Square Incident. (1989) "Commentary on the Tiananmen Square incident by one of the student leaders." Univ. of Iowa Audiovisual Center. 1/2-inch video. 35 minutes.

To Live for Ireland and *At the Edge of the Union.* "Different strategies in the Irish struggle." PBS: Intercom. 80 minutes.

Torture in the Eighties. (1984) "About Amnesty International's investigations of and campaign to stop torture around the world." Amnesty International. 1/2-inch video. 13 minutes.

Tragedy at Tiananmen: The Untold Story. (1989). "Various news reporters give firsthand accounts of the massacre of student protesters in Tiananmen Square in 1989." Coronet Multimedia. 1/2-inch video. 48 minutes.

Vietnam: After the Fire. See "Work."

Vietnam: Images of War. (1978) "A film montage of scenes which made headline news coverage during the 15 years of the Vietnam War. . . . Contains graphic scenes of war; pre-screening recommended." Journal Films. Beta, 1/2-inch video, 3/4-inch video. 26 minutes.

Vietnam Reconsidered. See "Work."

Vietnam Under Communism. See "Work."

Vietnam: The War at Home. (1978) "Featuring a wide array of news and interview footage, this acclaimed documentary examines the effects of the Vietnam political ambiguities on the home front, concentrating on student activities at the University of Wisconsin. Nominated for Best Documentary Oscar." MPI Home Video. Beta, 1/2-inch video. 100 minutes.

Vietnam War Story II. (1988) Three short, made-for-TV war stories set in Vietnam: "An Old Ghost Walks the Earth," "R & R," and "The Fragging." HBO Home Video. 1/2-inch video. Closed captioned. 90 minutes.

Vietnamese & American Veterans. (1984) "Two American veterans and two South Vietnamese veterans discuss the war from their own points of view." Univ. of California, Santa Barbara. Beta, 1/2-inch video, 3/4-inch video. 30 minutes.

Walker, Alice, *"Nineteen Fifty-Five".* (1981) Read by Alice Walker. "A story about the exploitation of black musicians by the white rock 'n' roll industry." American Audio Prose. 1 cassette. 36 minutes.

DIRECTORY OF AUDIOVISUAL DISTRIBUTORS

AIMS Media
6901 Woodley Ave.
Van Nuys, CA 91406-4878
(818) 785-4111
1-800-367-2467

American Audio Prose Library
P.O. Box 842
1015 E. Broadway
Suite 284
Columbia, MO 65205
1-800-447-2275

Amnesty International
Publications
322 8th Avenue
New York, NY 10001
(212) 807-8400

Atlantis Productions
1252 La Granada Drive
Thousand Oaks, CA 91360
(805) 495-2790

Avatar Learning, Inc.
760 La Cienega Blvd.
Los Angeles, CA 90069

Barr Films, Inc.
P.O. Box 7878
Irwindale, CA 91706
(818) 338-7878
1-800-234-7879

BBC Films, Inc.
Video Distribution Center
P.O. Box 644
Paramus, NJ 07652
(212) 239-0530

Benchmark Films, Inc.
145 Scarborough Rd.
Blaircliff Manor
New York, NY 10510

Books on Tape
729 Farad
Costa Mesa, CA 92627
(714) 548-5525

Britannica Films
310 South Michigan Avenue
Chicago, IL 60604
(312) 347-7958

CBS Video Library
1211 Avenue of the Americas
New York, NY 10036
(212) 975-3454

California Newsreel
149 Ninth St., Rm. 420
San Francisco, CA 94103

Canadian Film-Makers' Distribution
Center
67A Portland St.
Toronto M5V 2M9
CANADA
(416) 593-1808

Catholic Relief Services
1011 First Ave.
New York, NY 10022

Celtic Productions
164 E. 33rd St.
New York, NY
(212) 689-4853

The Center for Humanities
Communications Park
Box 1000
Mount Kisco, NY 10549
1-800-431-1242

Cinema Guild
The Media Project
1697 Broadway, Rm. 802
New York, NY 10019
(212) 246-5522

Copeland Griggs Productions, Inc.
302 23rd Ave., Suite 10
San Francisco, CA 94121
(415) 668-4200

Cornell University
Audio-Visual Resources Center
8 Research Pk.
Ithaca, NY 14850
(607) 255-2091

Coronet, The Multimedia Co.
108 Wilmot Rd.
Deerfield, IL 60015
1-800-621-2131

Dove Books on Tape
12711 Ventura Blvd., Suite 250
Studio City, CA 91604
(818) 762-6662
1-800-345-9945

Educational Film and Video Project
5332 College Ave., Suite 101
Oakland, CA 94618
(415) 655-9050

Educational Films, Inc.
5547 N. Ravenwood
Chicago, IL 60640-1199

Embassy Home Entertainment
1901 Avenue of the Stars
Los Angeles, CA 90067
(213) 460-7200

Encyclopaedia Britannica
Educational Corp.
425 N. Michigan Ave.
Chicago, IL 60611
1-800-558-6968

Ergo Media
P.O. Box 2037
Teaneck, NJ 07666
(201) 692-0404

Facets Multimedia
1517 W. Fullerton Ave.
Chicago, IL 60614
1-800-331-6197

Filmmakers' Library
133 E. 58th St.
New York, NY 10022
(212) 355-6545

Films for the Humanities
P.O. Box 2053
Princeton, NJ 08543
(609) 452-1128
1-800-257-5126

Films, Inc.
5547 N. Ravenswood Ave.
Chicago, IL 60640-1199
(312) 878-2600, ext. 44
1-800-323-4222, ext. 44

Flower Films
10341 San Pablo Avenue
El Cerrito, CA 94530

Giorni Poetry Systems Records
P.O. Box 295
North Greece, NY 14515
(716) 392-2871

Great Plains National Instructional
Television Library
University of Nebraska at Lincoln
P.O. Box 80669
Lincoln, NE 68501-0669
(402) 472-2007
1-800-228-4630

HBO Video
1370 Avenue of the Americas
New York, NY 10019
(212) 977-8990
1-800-648-7650

Hartley Film Foundation
Rock Road
Cos Cob, CT 06807
(203) 869-1818

Icarus Films
153 Waverly Pl., 6th Floor
New York, NY 10014
(212) 727-1711

Audiovisual Distributors

International Film Bureau
332 S. Michigan Ave.
Chicago, IL 60604
(312) 427-4545

International Film Foundation, Inc.
155 West 72nd Street
New York, New York l0023
(212) 580-1111

Journal Films
930 Pitner Ave.
Evanston, IL 60202
1-800-323-5448

King Features Entertainment
235 E. 45th St.
New York, NY 10017
(212) 682-5600
1-800-223-7383

Learning Corporation of America
108 Wilmot Rd.
Deerfield, IL 60015-9990
(312) 940-1260
1-800-621-2131

Live Home Video
15400 Sherman Way
Suite 500
Van Nuys, CA 91406
(818) 908-0303

MCA Home Video
70 Universal City Plaza
Universal City, CA 91608
(818) 777-4300

MGM/UA Home Video
10,000 W. Washington Blvd.
Culver City, CA 90232-2728
(213) 280-6000

MPI Home Video
15825 Rob Roy Dr.
Oak Forest, IL 60452
(312) 687-7881

Martha Stuart Communications, Inc.
147 W. 22nd St.
New York, NY 10011
(212) 255-2718

McGraw Hill
P.O. Box 674
Via De La Valle,
Del Mar, CA 92014

Media Home Entertainment
5730 Buckingham Pkwy.
Culver City, CA 90230
(213) 216-7900
1-800-421-4509

Modern Talking Picture Service
5000 Park Street North
St. Petersburg, FL 33709
(813) 541-7571
1-800-243-6877 (to order)

National Film Board of Canada
1251 Avenue of the Americas, 16th Floor
New York, NY 10020-1173
(212) 586-5131

National Geographic Society
17 and M St. NW.
Washington, D.C. 20036

National Public Radio
Audio Services
2025 M St., NW
Washington, DC 20036
(202) 822-2000

New Day Films
1221 W. 27th St.
Room 902
New York, NY 10001
(212) 645-8210

New Dimensions Foundations
P.O. Box 410510
San Francisco, CA 94141
(415) 563-8899

New Letters on Air
5216 Rockhill
Kansas City, MO 64110

New Yorker Films Video
16 W. 61st St.
New York, NY 10023
(212) 247-6110

Northern Lights Productions
276 Newbury Street
Boston, MA 02116
(617) 267-0391

W. W. Norton Publishers
Trade Sales Department
500 Fifth Avenue
New York, NY 10110
(212) 790-4314

PBS Video
1320 Braddock Pl.
Alexandria, VA 22314
(703) 739-5380

Paramount Home Video
5555 Melrose Ave.
Los Angeles, CA 90038
(213) 956-5000

Phoenix Films/American Film Institute
468 Park Ave. South
New York, NY 10016
(212) 684-5910
1-800-221-1274

Playhouse Video
1211 Avenue of the Americas
New York, NY 10036
(212) 819-3238

Portland State University
Continuing Education Program
P.O. Box 1491
Portland, OR 97207-1491
(503) 725-4891

Random House Audio Books
201 East 50th St.
New York, NY 10022
(212) 872-8235
1-800-638-6460

The Roland Collection
3120 Pawtucket Rd.
Northbrook, IL 60062
(708) 291-2230

Sony Video Communications
Tape Production Department
700 W. Artesia Blvd.
Compton, CA 90220
(213) 537-4300, ext. 331

Spoken Arts
310 North Avenue
New Rochelle, NY 10801
(914) 636-5482
1-800-537-3617

Tapes for Readers
5078 Fulton Street, NW
Washington, DC 20016
(202) 362-4585

United World Films, Inc.
221 Park Avenue S.
New York, NY 10003

University of Arizona Video Campus
Harvill Bldg., No. 76
Box 4
Tuscon, AZ 85721
(602) 621-1735 or -5143

University of California, Santa Barbara
Instructional Department
Santa Barbara, CA 93106
(805) 961-3518

University of Iowa Audiovisual Center
C–215 Seashore Hall
University of Iowa
Iowa City, IA 52242
(319) 335-2539

University of Wisconsin
University Extension
1327 University Ave.
P.O. Box 2093
Madison, WI 53701

Vestron Video
1010 Washington Blvd.
Box 10382
Stamford, CT 06901
(203) 978-5400

Vladimir Bibic Productions
3490 E. Foothill Blvd.
Pasadena, CA 91107

Warner Home Video
4000 Warner Blvd.
Burbank, CA 91522
(818) 954-6000

Washington University
Learning Resources Video Center
George W. Brown School of Social Work
Campus Box 1196
St. Louis, MO 63130
(314) 889-6612 or -6683

Watershed Foundation
6925 Willow St., NW, Suite 201
Washington, DC 20012
(202) 722-9105

Wombat Productions
Division of Cortech, Inc.
250 W. 57th St., Suite 916
New York, NY 10019
(212) 315-2502

Women in Focus
849 Beatty St.
Vancouver, BC V6B 2M6
CANADA
(604) 872-2250

Women Make Movies
225 Lafayette Street
Suite 212
New York, NY 10012
(212) 925-0606

Critically Focused, Critically Priced

**1993/paper
471 pages/$9.50 net
Instructor's Manual**

WRITING WORTH READING
A Practical Guide
Paperback Second Edition

Nancy Huddleston Packer, *Stanford University*
John Timpane, *Lafayette College*

■ paperback edition reprints the highly-praised rhetorical chapters of *Writing Worth Reading*, Second Edition, without the handbook section ■ emphasis on critical thinking and reading ■ in-depth treatment of specific writing assignments across the curriculum ■ extensive coverage of the research process and documenting sources for various disciplines ■ thorough Instructor's Manual

"The best writing text I have found…"
— Patricia L. Skarda, *Smith College*

"Lively, informative, practical and accessible."
— Marci Lingo, *Bakersfield College*

"*Writing Worth Reading* is a splendid book in every way."
— Doree Allen, *Stanford University*

The Most Complete and Accessible Research Guide

**1992/paper
409 pages/$9.50 net
Instructor's Manual**

THE BEDFORD GUIDE
TO THE RESEARCH PROCESS
Second Edition

Jean Johnson, *University of Maryland at College Park*

■ the most comprehensive guide to the process of researching, writing, revising and documenting research papers available ■ more coverage of computers and databases than any other guide ■ a full chapter on non-library sources ■ an annotated bibliography of reference sources expanded to include more than 25 subject areas ■ the only guide to employ the Toulmin model of argument to analyze discourse

"One of the few texts that is really student oriented — full of specific and easily followed guidelines that take the intimidation out of the research process."
— Charles Fisher, *Aims Community College*

Bedford Books *of* St. Martin's Press
For exam copies, call 1-800-446-8923

Once Again — The *Best-Seller*

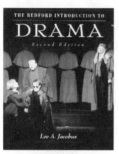
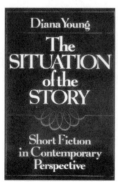